Laosh

— Emergence from Shadow —

by Jan Kauskas

太
極
拳

Printed in the United States of America

The paper in this book meets the guidelines for permanence and durability of the Committee on Production Guidelines for Book Longevity of the Council on Library Resources.

Copyright © 2018
by
Via Media Publishing Company
941 Calle Mejia #822
Santa Fe, NM 87501 USA
E-mail: md@goviamedia.com

Book and cover design by
Via Media Publishing Company.

ISBN-13: 978-1718644885
ISBN-10: 1718644884

Acknowledgments

Once again, I am indebted to Ai-Lien Banks for her eye over the shape and tone of the manuscript. Her own taijiquan practice and interest in Daoist philosophy, as well as her ear for Glaswegian "banter," make her a uniquely-qualified sounding board in bringing *Laoshi's Legacy* to life.

Again, my appreciation goes to James Morrison of Immediate Arts for his continuing encouragement and technical support through the years.

Yet again, I am grateful to Mike DeMarco of Via Media Publishing whose faith in the project helped spur me on: his enthusiasm and commitment have proved invaluable.

Finally, renewed thanks are due to Autumn River Tai Chi students—both past and present— who have supported me over the years and who continue to stimulate my study of taijiquan.

contents

preface

> "Why do you want to teach taijiquan?" asked the master.
> The student enthused, "I really, really want everyone to
> experience the wonderful gifts that taijiquan has given me."
> "You are not ready," replied the master.
> "When will I be ready?"
> "When you really, really want to learn."

For twenty-five years, I have been striving to deepen my understanding of taijiquan, first as novice, then senior student, and finally teacher. A prior "apprenticeship" in the Japanese arts of aikido and iaido, as well as a nodding acquaintance with other fighting systems, no doubt influenced me along the way, but taijiquan is my art.

A few years ago, I sought to record a few memories and observations gleaned on the way from beginner to senior student. The result was *Laoshi: Tai Chi, Teachers, and Pursuit of Principle*—a semi-fictional memoir, using the device of dialogue between student and teacher to examine the agony and elation of sincerely pursuing the art of taijiquan.

The thirty-seven chapters of *Laoshi* shone light on the various aspects of taijiquan and martial arts, which occupied my thinking as I progressed along the Way. *Laoshi*, which translates as "teacher" in Mandarin, was the main character of the book and, though not a real person, represented the best aspects of the many martial artists, whose skills, dedication, and wisdom inspired me in my attempts to match their example. As a wise and compassionate, though sometimes irritable teacher, Laoshi guides his student, the narrator, through many disappointments and false dawns, until the student arrives, if not at mastery, then the fertile ground where mastery grows.

The present volume, *Laoshi's Legacy*, takes up where the previous account left off; the student moves beyond his preoccupation with his own progress to explore the terrain occupied by the teacher. The Way of the teacher, we discover, not only offers insight and reward aplenty, but is every bit as confounding and, often, more treacherous than the path of the student.

With the example of my own teachers once again embodied in the character of Laoshi, *Legacy* describes the challenges encountered in progressing beyond the role of student to survey the art from the viewpoint of teacher. As in the previous volume, Laoshi, the teacher, continues as guide and mentor, advising the novice instructor confronted with the reality of teaching taijiquan in a modern world.

Like its predecessor, *Legacy* relies heavily on allegory, mirroring the paradoxical nature of life, where truth is often hidden in myth, and deception disguises itself as truth. A touch of poetic license may stretch the truth a little to accommodate the narrative, but *Legacy* is a realistic portrayal of dilemmas faced while pursuing the Way of the teacher.

The backdrop for the events depicted in this tale is Glasgow—a city brimming with vitality and passion, combining culture and sophistication with grit and no little edge. It is a city of contrasts: yin and yang writ large.

Glasgow may not be the "mean city" of yesteryear, however, the raw side still exists and comes a-knocking from time to time. In describing such encounters, dialogue in the vernacular (and occasional coarse language) is simply true to life.

Following the Way with integrity asks that we accept the rough with the smooth, the yang with the yin, if you like. This is to truly "embrace tiger and return to mountain."

Author Jan Kauskas.

"Why do you want to teach taiji?" asked the master.

"I don't want to teach, only to learn."

"Ah," said the master, "in that case, you may have to teach."

Laoshi, my teacher, often quoted Wang Lang, his own teacher, as follows: "Taijiquan students don't say, 'You should've seen me twenty years ago.' They say, 'You should see me twenty years from now.'"

This is one of the marvels of studying an art like taijiquan. The gradual physical limitations of age do not prevent progress in the art. Unlike sports such as football, where physicality plays an important role, the taijiquan player can look forward to continual improvement with age. Indeed, the taijiquan player's best years are always ahead, an optimistic attitude, which in itself, I suspect, leads to an improved sense of well-being and positivity about aging. Such an outlook is a vital counter-balance to the commonly held view that aging inevitably leads to weakness and incapacity.

As a corollary to his statement, Wang Lang often added, "A taijiquan teacher should never retire." The logic is clear: if your best years are yet to come, then you will always have more to teach. It came as something of a surprise then, when Laoshi revealed his intention to reduce his teaching obligations. The shock was exacerbated by his expectation that I should take on some of the teaching duties within the school.

By this time, I had been studying with Laoshi for more than ten years, a period in which I had only scratched the surface of the art. I still felt a yearning within myself to grasp the *quan*, the method of taijiquan, and something akin to desperation in my desire to skillfully apply taijiquan principles to the challenges life seemed intent on placing before me. It had taken me some time to find a teacher as competent as Laoshi, and, equally important, a teacher with whom I felt a strong and growing affinity. His announcement provoked in me a fear that the modest gains I had made were in jeopardy. I was gripped by anxiety as I contemplated losing my connection to the vast reservoir of knowledge and experience that was Laoshi.

I have written elsewhere of the effect Laoshi has had on my life, how his guidance had been instrumental in my discovering a sense of balance at a time when I was troubled by insecurity and lack of direction. Although it was always clear to me that there would come a day when Laoshi was no longer part of my life, I pushed that thought to the edge of my mental horizon, savoring his presence all the more for the anticipated loss. While a part of me recognized that the day of last goodbyes would come, today was not the day I had in mind.

"But why?" I demanded, frustration raising the volume of my voice. "Why, when you are still improving? Why would you just give it all up?"

At almost sixty years of age, Laoshi was not an old man, measured by the standard of the day, and even less so in his biological age. He would easily pass for mid-forties and his technique, especially in push-hands and fencing, was a joy to experience: its subtle sophistication seemingly endless.

"I'm not giving up taijiquan," he said reassuring me, "but I feel the need to take a step back in order to sort out a few things."

"What things?" I pressed him, my concern hardly assuaged.

"Well..." he paused, seeking the right words, or perhaps the right excuse, "for one thing, I have to try and get to the bottom of my knee problem."

The problem in question was the increasing pain in Laoshi's left knee over the past eighteen months. Although not incapacitating, it was an uncomfortable accompaniment to his teaching, and his efforts to treat his knee had been hitherto unsuccessful. The root of the problem was long standing: an injury sustained in his late teens during Laoshi's time in the military and aggravated by a subsequent surgical procedure. Occasionally, and ruefully, Laoshi mentioned the circumstances pertaining to the injury with its unwelcome consequence: "In those days, I was perhaps a little too cocky and prideful. And, as they say, pride comes before a fall. In my case this was true: literally and metaphorically. We were on a training exercise traveling in the back of a four-ton truck. It was the start of one of those pointless military exercises, amounting to little more than wandering around a training area for days, getting lost and getting found again.

"Since we were to be out for several days, I had a full pack and webbing. I was also lumbered with the Bren gun. The Bren is an LMG, which means light machine gun, but in fact weighs twenty-two pounds. It was an effective weapon, in its day, but an awkward shape, with folded bipod and a top-mounted magazine. Anyway, the truck shuddered to a halt, simulating a response to attack by our enemy of the day—the 'fantasians.' Ordered to dismount at speed, in my eagerness to show off, I leaped from the vehicle with a negligence that has plagued me since. I should have waited for the tailgate to be dropped, but at the time my blood group was equal parts O-positive and foolhardiness. It was only a drop of about eight feet but encumbered by the pack and the Bren gun, I was unbalanced as I vaulted out and landed on my knee. A piece of hard cartilage under my kneecap broke off. In the ensuing years, what was left of the cartilage has gradually worn away."

"Didn't your study of taijiquan help heal the injury?" I asked when Laoshi first mentioned the incident.

"To a point," he replied with a sigh. "Taijiquan certainly strengthened my weakened left leg. I had been favoring my right leg to avoid the pain in my left knee for some time. While not completely healing my knee, taijiquan restored it considerably, though not completely.

2

"Of course, there was a price to pay for this improvement: at times when studying with Wang Lang, I was expected to hold deep postures for extended periods. At the end of some of these sessions, my bad knee was so severely swollen that my leg would not bend beyond ninety degrees. The swelling would ease overnight, only to be aggravated again the following day by further periods of holding postures. At the time, I considered it the price of admission into the 'courtyard of taijiquan.'"

I sympathized with Laoshi: my own knees suffered as I sought to come to grips with the nuances of taijiquan's postural alignment. Unlike Laoshi, however, my knee problems had occurred from incorrect alignment, not from injury. As an unexpected consequence, however, the periodic ache in my knees taught me a great deal about alignment in the lower body.

Returning to Laoshi's present difficulties with his knee, I asked, "Why do you think you have not been able to heal your knee with your qi? Are there some things the qi cannot heal?"

"I once asked Wang Lang the same question," replied Laoshi, a smile playing on his lips, as he recalled the conversation. "It was during one of those times when my knee was painful and swollen for the entire period of my stay with him. It was a fortnight of intensity, as Wang Lang felt himself on the brink of a break-through and thought he needed one last push to achieve a *satori*. After a tiring morning session in the woodland near his home, we delayed our return to his house by stopping off at a quaint little log cabin, which then operated as a rustic cafe in a midst of the forest. He answered my question by saying, in his opinion, 'The only thing taijiquan cannot heal is decapitation.'"

"But, Laoshi," I asked, "you don't think that is true, do you?"

Laoshi sighed a little before conceding, "Perhaps not. There is no doubt in my mind that, generally speaking, health is considerably improved by practicing taijiquan, and the aging process is slowed down dramatically. But we have only to consider how some of the brightest lights in the taijiquan firmament have died at relatively young ages. Tam Gibbs, for instance, Zheng Manqing's trusted disciple in New York, died well before he fulfilled his potential. Another student, who was one of the most promising of the next generation of Zheng Manqing teachers, died a few years ago of a brain hemorrhage in his early fifties. He was a great loss to the taijiquan community: respected by all, he could have been a unifying figure in a gradually fragmenting 'family.' Consider also the number of well-respected figures in the Zheng Manqing taijiquan family who have suffered from illness and disease, eventually turning to Western medical intervention to save their lives. This is no secret."

"Do you find your faith in taijiquan diminished as a result, Laoshi?"

I asked.

"It is a lesson," replied Laoshi, directing his gaze toward me, "as everything is a lesson, if you want it to be so. In this case, it is a lesson in humility and the perils of expectation."

Having studied with Laoshi for a decade, I was confident I had the gist of his meaning, but, as with taijiquan itself, repetition is no bad thing and often stimulates a deeper insight. I was content, therefore, when Laoshi chose to elaborate further on his reflections: "The promise that cultivating the qi will make us virtually invulnerable to illness is a comforting one; we have the welcome sense that our lives are within our control," observed Laoshi. "But, when that promise is 'broken,' we feel betrayed. However, the qi makes no promises, and neither does the Dao. It is we who make promises to ourselves, and then later, finding them hollow, blame the qi or the Dao. We make these promises to ourselves because we are afraid, and we desperately want to feel secure in the midst of the unpredictability that is life. But, just saying life is secure does not make it so, even if I do a dozen forms a day."

As Laoshi was talking, I recalled the story of Dr. Qi Jiangtao, the renowned taijiquan master and acupuncturist, who lived in London for a few years in the seventies, before settling in Vancouver. Dr. Qi had been one of Zheng Manqing's students in Taiwan, a classmate of Ben Lo and William C.C. Chen. According to one of Dr. Qi's students, his skill in utilizing the martial aspect of taijiquan was formidable, despite his slender build and a severe case of tuberculosis contracted during the Civil War on Mainland China. His abilities were recognized by his peers, and Dr. Qi became vice-president of the Taiwan Taijiquan Association. Encouraged by his success in challenges against other martial artists, he embarked on a mission to prove that taijiquan was the pre-eminent martial art on the planet.

Shortly into his undertaking, Dr. Qi became ill, and, despite his best efforts to heal himself, gradually lapsed into a coma. It was in this helpless state that he reported seeing a vision of Jesus Christ, along with a warning that, should he persist with his mission, he would die. Immediately, Dr. Qi renounced his intention to prove the superiority of taijiquan as a fighting art. He subsequently recovered. Mindful of his experience, he converted to Christianity and abandoned the practice of taijiquan for a number of years, before returning to teach at the request of his students. His view of taijiquan, however, had entirely changed: he concentrated on teaching taijiquan as a vehicle for deepening spiritual consciousness rather than a way of fighting.

"Illness and pain are sometimes devices our bodies use to communicate with us," mused Laoshi, after I had recounted the experiences of Dr. Qi. "How desperate must the heart-mind be to resort to such strong medicine?"

4

"That seems a particularly…" I struggled momentarily searching for the right word, "unique view of pain and illness, Laoshi. You are seldom so blunt about such things in class. Is that because you don't want to scare people off?"

"Not at all," replied Laoshi sharply. "No deception is intended. There is good reason why I keep these ideas to myself. I only tell you because you are so close to me: there is less chance of misunderstanding."

I swallowed a little at his mild rebuke. "I apologize Laoshi, I did not mean to imply any deception on your part."

"I know," he said, his appeasing tone lessening my discomfort, "but we must be careful how we express these matters, so people are not confused."

"So," I proceeded, still a touch warily, "what is the good reason you keep these ideas to yourself?"

He took a moment to consider his reply before answering. "It is one thing for me to say life is communicating with me through illness. It is my prerogative to view life's challenges as I wish and re-establish my life's balance as I see fit. But it is quite another to make such a pronouncement about someone else. To say another person's illness is a lesson from the universe is presumptuous and quite possibly wrong. Therefore, we should be careful with whom we discuss these matters.

"My own understanding," he continued, "stems from a chance conversation I overheard while staying with Wang Lang. At the time both Wang Lang and his wife were particularly concerned that a forthcoming change in their domestic situation should not be the cause of undue concern for their six-year old son, Wendell. They had been discussing those changes openly, but then wondered if the boy might be feeling uneasy about the future. So, when a convenient opportunity arose, Wang Lang sought to offer any reassurances that might be necessary.

"It was a lazy afternoon. The house was quiet with only the three of us at home when Wang Lang judged the time to be right. Wendell was in the kitchen engaged in an important construction project with his Lego when Wang Lang broached the subject. I was reading quietly at the far end of the kitchen and could not help but overhear:

"Is anything worrying you, Wendell?" began Wang Lang.

"Like what?" replied Wendell, still working the Lego.

"Like the changes that will be coming."

"No, Daddy, I'm not worried about anything. Are you worried about anything?"

I suppressed a chuckle at the push-hands-like quality in Wendell's reply, as he returned the energy of Wang Lang's question.

Wang Lang sighed, as he was wont to do, before saying, "Not

really Wendell. Money's always tight, of course, but this cold is really getting me down. I've had it for a while now and can't seem to shift it."

"Dad," asked Wendell, "why do people get sick?"

"Well…" said Wang Lang after a moment's thought, "it's what the body does to make us better."

Laoshi smiled, recalling the incident. "An amazing answer, don't you think?" he asked, turning his gaze toward me.

"Anyway," Laoshi continued with the story before I could reply. "Though my eyes were still on the pages of the book before me, I began to consider Wang Lang's answer. Even when Wang Lang and Wendell went into the garden, I remained in the kitchen considering the subtlety of Wang Lang's reply.

"On a superficial level, the symptoms of a cold are the body's response to an attack from a virus; on a deeper level, becoming 'better' can mean a whole host of things—including becoming more psychologically aware, more spiritually open, or simply more contemplative. As far as I was concerned, Wang Lang had made a simple reply to a simple question, but he had also provoked in me an insight, not only into illness, but about life in general. Life uses all things as mechanisms to facilitate our progress."

Over the next few months, I began to take more responsibility in the running of the school. I had neither expected nor desired the privilege of teaching in Laoshi's stead. There were students of greater seniority, who I would have happily seen privileged ahead of me. Some were prevented from taking a greater role by work or family commitments; others, who felt themselves equal to the task of succeeding Laoshi, were overlooked for reasons never explained. As a result, I felt deeply uncomfortable about my new position and secretly hoped Laoshi would sort out his issues as quickly as possible in order that I could unload the burden, neither sought after nor enjoyed.

Thankfully, those months saw a marked improvement in Laoshi's knee problem, a situation which pleased me on many levels: I genuinely wished the best for my teacher, since fully fit, he would continue to deepen his own skills, but most of all, I thought I could give up teaching.

Occasionally, I raised the subject of desisting from my newfound duties. Laoshi would always say, "Just a little while longer." I was beginning to feel that I had been tricked into assuming the role of teacher, when I was clearly reluctant. I put the point to him.

He replied simply, "Teaching will make you better."

And so I became a taijiquan teacher.

Laoshi's classes lacked the paraphernalia of "achievement" which made explicit the individual's place within the group. Obvious signs of status, such as badges, belts or colored T-shirts were noticeable only by their absence. I was amused, therefore, on occasion to witness the enthusiastic rookie offering advice to the unassuming ten-year-veteran on the performance of a posture. The veteran would nod indulgently, no doubt thinking: Dinae teach yer grannie tae sook eggs (Don't teach your grandmother to suck eggs).

In this status-desert, the one verifiable oasis was the teacher, around whose command the class revolved. In an atmosphere refreshingly free of committee-dom, and not paralyzed by democracy, the teacher was in charge, and I began to enjoy the feeling, as I inhabited the role.

Very quickly, however, I came to see the reality of the matter. There is far more to teaching taijiquan than accurately modeling the position of arms and legs. I had long understood that mastery deceives the eye into presuming ease, and, as far as technique was concerned, I realized quickly enough that my skills and explanations bordered on pedestrian. I had also anticipated that my lesson delivery might have limited impact on the tired faces drawn to taijiquan class after a draining day at the coalface. In addition, I steeled myself for the sufferance of the regular students, accustomed to the magic of the master, but now enduring the organ grinder's monkey. But while these antici-pated difficulties were present in varying degrees, I found myself confronted, at every turn, by the unexpected. Lacking a model to guide my actions at these times, I was often forced into muddling through, relying on instinct to get by.

Laoshi often pointed out, "You only really see the depth of your teacher's gongfu when something unexpected happens." My ten-year associa-tion with Laoshi, coupled with an earlier apprenticeship with other teachers, had instilled in me a misplaced confidence. I was sure that, by this time, I had seen it all.

That confidence was challenged barely two weeks into my teaching career. I had arrived promptly for a Monday evening push-hands class, antici-pating the arrival of a new student, Alan. He had contacted me, asking if he might attend a class, and, in effect, take our measure. Although he had studied form with another taijiquan group, he felt his push-hands had been neglected, and he wanted to see how much our approach might satisfy his needs. For my own part, I was looking forward to seeing a new face at class and relished the chance to assess his strengths and weaknesses.

I had just changed my shoes and set up my administrative base on top of the piano, which served as a desk, when the doorbell rang. As I approached the door, I collected myself into my dantian, as Laoshi had advised countless times.

The front door was, for Laoshi, an often-overlooked training tool. The church hall, which served as venue for class, was a magnet to many poor souls seeking spiritual succor, not to mention the drunk and disorderly, whose ambition was no loftier than food, money, or the church candlesticks on route to the pawnshop. Since we operated a "last in answers the door" policy, any student might find themselves face-to-face with an itinerant pleading for what we could not provide, or a wastrel demanding with menace what we refused to provide. Laoshi felt such basic challenges to be a useful practice in manifesting yang energy for the meeker students, those who would sooner avoid any form of confrontation. "When the meek inherit the earth, they will have to learn to defend it," quipped Laoshi, while explaining the need to challenge those not infrequent "visitors" who assumed that a church hall was there solely to accommodate their needs.

"You can never know," explained Laoshi, "what you are opening the door to. So before you do, center yourself, relax your dantian, fill yourself with qi, and project your energy forward. Anyone who thinks they will simply pass you unchallenged will be forced to stop and reassess. Once they are halted, you will have the initiative."

Suitably centered, I opened the door to be greeted by a thirty something, heavily tattooed fellow, looking at me expectantly. Despite the tattoos, he was not threatening in his energy. At almost six feet tall, we were much the same height, but there the similarity ended. His hair was dark and close-cropped. He sported multiple ear piercings, a cord necklace high on his throat, and hide bracelets at the wrist. His leather biker jacket sat atop dirt-covered leather trousers, tucked into "statement" black boots, decorated with gleaming metal plates. This might have been an unconventional look in some quarters, however, here in Glasgow's West End, "alternative dress" passed without comment.

"Can I help you?" I asked mildly, assuming that it was Alan who stood before me.

"Is this where the push-hands class is?" asked the visitor in turn.

"Yes, come on in," I opened the door fully making space for his entrance. "You must be Alan," I added conversationally.

"No, I'm Johnjo," he replied.

"But you're here for push-hands, right?" I was taken aback.

"Yeah, that's right. Is this the place, then?"

Well, what could I say? I confirmed that this was, indeed, the place and explained that my hesitation was due to another new student's expected arrival.

"So, have you done taijiquan before?" I enquired casually.

"Oh, yeah," he replied confidently, "for about three or four years now."

"Great," I thought to myself, "on the same page at last."

"Who is your teacher?" I pursued.

"Nobody," he pronounced blithely, "I'm self-taught. I bought a video a few years ago, and I've been learning from that."

"A Zheng Manqing video?" I queried optimistically.

"I don't remember which style it is, but it is definitely not the Zheng Manqing one."

By this time, I was on nodding terms with a number of students from various schools, but this was my first experience of a proudly self-taught aficionado. That he could not recall the style he studied, coupled with the bold announcement of his dubious credentials, led me to a less-than-charitable assessment of his ability.

It is wise, when visiting another martial arts school, to adopt an unassuming attitude, even if only as a mask. Any visiting student ought to attempt humility if for no other reason than to avoid alienating a potential teacher and fellow students. Better for the self-taught one to have vaguely hinted at his abilities, saying, "I only did a little bit here and there, nothing serious. You know how it is." A decent teacher can then make an accurate assessment in class and decide where to pitch the newcomer without embarrassment on either side.

Ushering Johnjo into the hall, I felt unsure as to how I should proceed. As other students began to arrive, I suggested Johnjo observe class for a few minutes in order to get a feel for our approach. He complied easily enough, and when I returned to him ten minutes later, I asked if his expectations were in line with what he had witnessed. He wholeheartedly confirmed this was the case, and that he was keen to have a go. I took some time to acquaint him with the basic movements of the *peng-lü-ji-an* push-hands form. Not expecting much in the way of sensitivity, I was pleasantly surprised to find him less tense, less forceful than many students attempting push-hands for the first time. I proceeded to explain the principles of "pushing" and "neutralizing," before demonstrating how these concepts felt in the flow of the form. He seemed impressed, said he was keen to learn, and asked about class fees.

Then it happened. Johnjo asked if he might demonstrate his form, the one he had been perfecting over the past few years with the aid of the video.

"How long will it take?" I sighed.

"Oh, just a few minutes," he reassured me, before launching into a ten-minute sequence of random and bizarre movements, which failed to match any taijiquan of my experience, regardless of style. Since my own expertise was limited to Zheng Manqing's form, push-hands and fencing, I was unsure what to make of the performance just witnessed. On completion of his routine he turned toward me expectantly, clearly awaiting some sort of affirmation.

Feeling that refusing an assessment might lead to Johnjo's disappointment, I tried to look for the positive: he did sink down into his postures fairly well, an observation that he received with obvious satisfaction. But my subsequent comments regarding principle met with less approval: his spine was not straight, he was not single-weighted, he did not turn his waist, his hands looked tense, and, at times, he waved his arms around without any movement in his body.

Although crestfallen, Johnjo took my critique fairly well, I thought, and far better than if our roles had been reversed. Attempting to be conciliatory, I made a suggestion, "Why don't you come to form class as well as push-hands? After all, the principles of our push-hands are intrinsic to the principles of the Zheng Manqing form."

"Hmm…" Johnjo demurred. "I don't want to learn the Zheng Manqing form. I want to learn the Yang long form. Do you teach that at all?"

"Er… Not these days," I replied doubtfully. "Why don't you want to learn the Zheng Manqing form?"

"Well… I don't want to learn a diluted form of taijiquan," he asserted.

"Er… In what way is it 'diluted?'" I asked, feeling the beginning of irritation.

"Well… You know—'simplified,'" he informed me. "Zheng Manqing simplified the form. I want to learn the real stuff, not the easy stuff that he did."

I was dumbfounded for a moment. "Well, then," I drew myself up and indicated the exit with a tilt of my head. "We'd better not keep you from your work."

"Davie, can you show this guy out?"

It was a week or more before I met up with Laoshi, and the events of that evening with Johnjo were still festering. It was not my lack of tact in appraising his form which rankled with me, but his, to my mind, scandalous implication that Zheng Manqing's taijiquan was, at best, an "easy option" and, at worst, some kind of con. His impertinence had angered me. In the interim, I indulged in a fair amount of "should've saids" and hoped for his return so I could deploy a few withering ripostes. At my meeting with Laoshi, then, I was burning to furnish him with a comprehensive account of the Johnjo incident.

When my rant eventually subsided, Laoshi simply looked at me and shrugged. "So, what?" he asked mildly. "The fellow left and you'll never see him again. No problem."

"Yes, but…" I protested. "He went away with the wrong impression. I should have set him straight."

"It would not have made any difference," replied Laoshi softly. "He probably wasn't there to join the class. More likely he was looking to be validated in some way. Let him go and find what he is looking for somewhere else. You did the right thing."

"But what would you have done?" I asked, unwilling to let the matter drop.

"Probably the same as you," Laoshi smiled.

"But," I reminded Laoshi, "he is going around with a pretty low opinion of Zheng Manqing's taijiquan.

"You think he's the only one?" Laoshi laughed. "There are plenty who think the same. Are you going to run around the world setting them all straight? Perhaps your difficulty is that you're not entirely sure that he doesn't have a point."

I was rendered speechless. Part of me felt that Laoshi struck right at the heart of the matter, but I was struggling to acknowledge the point. If my confidence in Zheng Manqing's taijiquan was built on secure foundations, then the red rag of Johnjo's comments ought not to have brought out the bull in me.

"I have to admit, Laoshi," I murmured sheepishly, "I'm not sure how I would adequately explain 'simplified' to a student, but I know it doesn't mean easy."

"Quite so," nodded Laoshi, "so here is an opportunity to learn." He explained: "Some styles of taijiquan display their—shall we say 'difficulty'—for all to see. Those styles with long, deep stances, for instance, look impressive, and take a good deal of stretching to achieve; the sudden stomps and *fajin* strikes of other styles are equally eye-catching. But the Zheng Manqing form possesses its own profound logic and technical difficulties: it is virtually impossible to perform entirely correctly. It is anything but simple.

"If you were to ask long-term students of Zheng Manqing's taijiquan the meaning of the word 'simplified' in this context, some would suggest that this is a reference to the reduced number of overall postures and posture repetitions. The simplification, here, is merely a matter of cutting down the time necessary to learn the complete form. The essence of the form is in no way altered. Others might contend that double-weighted postures, such as 'iron fan penetrates back' have been removed to make the form more consistent. Still others say similarly that the Professor removed 'extraneous' and 'excessive' movements from the form to distill the practice to its essence."

"Okay… yes" I was nodding now. "I have heard you say more or less the same things in class."

"Indeed," concurred Laoshi. "If learning taijiquan was only a matter of remembering a sequence of movements, then it might be true to say that Zheng Manqing's form is 'easier' than the form of Yang Chengfu, his teacher. But, think about this: these differences are only superficial, affecting only the number of postures, the order of the postures, and the transitions. You may argue over which number of postures and which order is better, but this is akin to arguing over the best compilation of your favorite songs. I think you call them 'playlists' these days," added Laoshi, smiling mischievously.

"To my way of thinking," continued Laoshi, "of greater importance than the number and order of postures is the structure of the body as the postures are performed. Now, it is true that I am not a direct student of Yang Chengfu, nor Zheng Manqing for that matter, and my evidence is not first hand, but it strikes me that both their forms appear radically different from one another in terms of the shape of their bodies. This is what we should be looking at: we should not be focusing on the length or make-up of the form, rather we ought to concentrate on the structure of the body while it performs the postures."

Laoshi paused to assess my intake of his reasoning. I could understand his reluctance to discuss these matters openly in class. I also sensed the importance he placed on presenting his thoughts with absolute clarity, since he was, in effect, contradicting the teaching of his own teachers and other first-generation students of the Professor. Ben Lo, for example, has countered suggestions that Zheng Manqing changed the form by saying, "It's not true. What has changed? Which parts of his simplified form aren't the same as the Yang form?" Robert Smith quotes Professor Zheng as saying, "It was not the creation of a new system, but rather a rearrangement not affecting basic principles."

Laoshi continued. "The first and most notable difference is in Zheng Manqing's insistence on a vertical spine. Photos of Yang Chengfu invariably show a forward lean of about twenty-five degrees in front stance. Yang's gaze, however, is level, and he does not look down, which means there is a shortening in the back of the neck."

"But, Laoshi," I interrupted, "was it not the case that Yang Chengfu adopted a more vertical spine in later years? Didn't the Professor say as much when questioned about the discrepancy?"

"I don't know whether Yang Chengfu did or did not adapt his posture," replied Laoshi with a smile, "but for the Professor to suggest that Yang Chengfu did would seem to acknowledge that the discrepancy exists—don't you agree?"

I nodded. Laoshi continued, "Secondly, Yang Chengfu's postures do not have the Professor's softer wrist position, 'the beautiful lady's hand.' I know that this refinement by the Professor is considered crucial in order to remove tension from the hand, and also, the elbow. Furthermore, Zheng Manqing's arms are not as outstretched as Yang Chengfu. The Professor's elbows hang downward in a more pronounced manner, as if draining the tension out of the shoulder by dropping the elbow.

"Similarly," continued Laoshi, "the Professor's rear leg is not straight in front postures, unlike Yang Chengfu."

I was aware of this discrepancy myself, having heard that the straight leg of Yang Chengfu was essential to deliver power into a push. Meanwhile, it seemed that Zheng Manqing could generate quite enough force without straightening the back leg to that extent.

"We must also realize," added Laoshi, "that in postures like single whip, Yang Chengfu's waist is turned off to the right in relation to the direction of his front foot. The Professor, on the other hand, emphasized the idea of the hips, waist and navel pointing in the same direction as the front foot.

"Are you following this?" queried Laoshi.

"I think so," I nodded tentatively.

"Good." He seemed pleased that I was following the thrust of the discussion. "Finally, Yang Chengfu had a markedly long stance, which made single-weightedness all but impossible. Importantly, an excessively long stance militates against the lower spine being dropped, an essential in Zheng Manqing's teaching. As Wang Lang used to say, 'the lower back must be dropped, as if the weight of ten thousand things were hanging from the base of the spine.'"

"Is it possible Laoshi," I ventured, "that Yang Chengfu was... well, concealing the real taijiquan when posing for photographs."

"Hmm, yes, that suggestion has been made before," replied Laoshi. "Robert Smith quotes Zheng Manqing as saying that people were not used to cameras in those days, and so posed accordingly. But once again, the very proposition of an answer to the question of why the Zheng Manqing and Yang Chengfu postures look different indicates that there is, in fact, a difference."

"So why do you think Zheng Manqing's form looks different to Yang Chengfu's?" I asked, still trying to assess whether the differences were fundamental or only stylistic.

"Hmm. Good question," Laoshi mused. He rose from his seat and approached his overstuffed bookshelves. He ran his hand over a number of books before selecting a slim, modest-looking volume. He returned to his seat, spent a minute or two finding the page and said, "Listen to Douglas Wile in his *Uncollected Writings*. Zheng called his new abbreviated taijiquan form 'Simplified Taijiquan' (*jianyi taijiquan*). The significance of simplicity here goes beyond just shortening the form, but has to do with structural changes in the postures that facilitate sinking and relaxation. Relaxation is the precondition for true simplicity. By bringing the spine into plumb, he has done the same for taiji that he did for calligraphy. By reducing the extension of the horizontals (arms and legs), he has emphasized sinking of the elbows and shoulders, dropping the knee, and squaring the hips and shoulders. These, in turn, facilitate sinking qi to the dantian, the starting point of Zheng's teachings on calligraphy."

"So, are you saying," I asked, "it was because of his calligraphy?"

"Not entirely," corrected Laoshi. "You will recall that Zheng Manqing was known as the Master of Five Excellences. You also recall that those 'excellences' were, in addition to taijiquan, Chinese herbal medicine; calligraphy, as we have just mentioned; painting, of which he was a professor at a young age; and last but not least, poetry."

I nodded. From the beginning of my studies, I had been impressed by the Professor's wide-ranging talents. Zheng Manqing was a master in many fields, and highly regarded in other arts, besides, such as Chinese chess and flower arranging.

"All of these arts," continued Laoshi, "were, for Zheng Manqing, an expression of the qi. In a sense, you might say, they were the same art expressed in five different ways: the greatness of the qi expressed in martial arts, medicine, poetry, calligraphy and painting. Here is an example of 'crossing logs' as Wang Lang used to say."

"Crossing logs? What does that mean, Laoshi?" I pursued.

Laoshi nodded. "Well… how do we pile logs on a fire? You appreciate, don't you, that placing them in a neat row in the grate is not effective. The logs have to be crossed over each other in order to allow air to circulate, but, more importantly, in order that they might burn each other. You could say that Zheng Manqing's study was to cross the logs of his various arts in order they might cross fertilize, and so build the fire of his understanding more fiercely."

"Oh… I get that, Laoshi," I nodded in acknowledgement, "and so where does the 'simplicity' come in?"

"Ah! My very next point," continued Laoshi with enthusiasm. "It is not about simplicity in the sense of less complex: simplicity, here, refers to a state of being that emerges from true relaxation. This simplicity is profound, being rooted in sincerity and transparency, guileless but resilient, the very essence of the qi. It is the model for Zheng Manqing's approach to all his arts, and so an apt name for his taijiquan."

To me, this was an interesting appraisal of Zheng Manqing's taijiquan. I reflected upon Johnjo's appearance at class: he had been the catalyst for this,

14

my latest discussion with Laoshi, and I felt rather grateful to him for giving me the opportunity for another fascinating talk with my teacher. Yet, even as I was digesting Laoshi's views on simplified taijiquan, I came to a further realization. My difficulty with Johnjo centered less on a challenge to the integrity of Zheng Manqing's form and more on the challenge I had perceived to my own authority. My faith in Zheng Manqing was total. My faith in Laoshi was equally unassailable. It was my faith in myself, as a teacher, which I lacked.

There are numerous points of contention in the world of taijiquan, not least the question of Zheng Manqing's reasons for changing the form of Yang Chengfu. How does a teacher navigate these differences of opinion, especially when these differences become the subject of bitter debate? Safe in the harbor of Laoshi's school, the question of my own position in such debates was irrelevant. Laoshi was the final arbiter, and I trusted his opinion. But teaching, I soon came to realize, was to bring me face to face with a new and final arbiter—myself. Teaching brings with it the need to step out from the shadow of our own teacher's protection and stand foursquare in our own light.

Reflecting on the situation over the next few days, I recalled a story about my former aikido teacher, Billy Coyle. In those early days, Billy was one of two teachers at the fledgling aikido club he co-founded. A student who attended classes with both teachers drew attention to the fact that Billy and the other teacher performed, and subsequently taught, the same technique in a different manner. The student, perhaps making mischief, wanted to know which approach was correct. Billy, a master of both aikido and aphorism replied, "When I am teaching, I am right. When he is teaching, he is right."

The recollection made me smile. I had forgotten a simple truth about martial arts, and indeed life: there is no one right way. Opinions will differ, and students will follow their preference. My first job as teacher was not to become hostage to opinions and preferences. My first job was to find the "simplicity"—the essence—in myself, that same essence embodied in the form I practiced. As Laoshi said, "Simple yet profound, rooted in sincerity and transparency, guileless but resilient, the very essence of the qi." And, I might add, the very essence of teaching.

I once said, "If I had a pound for every taijiquan class I attended with Laoshi, I would be a rich man." I could easily have added, "And if I had another pound for every cup of tea I drank with Laoshi, I could retire tomorrow." Accompanying Laoshi to a cafe after evening class was, for me, as much a part of the training as form, push-hands, and sword. Sometimes we talked of taijiquan, sometimes not. The topics would range far and wide, and through those meandering conversations, Laoshi continued to broaden his students' education, as well as informally assessing their strengths and weaknesses.

As Laoshi's classes gradually became mine, I continued the ritual without interruption, hoping to impart some of Laoshi's wisdom to a new generation, but also to obtain the measure of my students in a less formal arena.

Initially, we frequented a local bar, but quickly changed venues, responding to the extended opening hours of a favored cafe. (Half a dozen men entering a bar in Glasgow and asking for six cups of tea gives rise to a few quizzical looks.) One of Laoshi's former students, who joined us on occasion, reported a conversation exchanged with the barman, as he sat waiting for us one evening.

The barman was polishing a glass to pass time on a slow night. "Aye," he mused, "there's a right bunch of weirdos come in here on Thursday nights. Must be a pool team or something, but they all come in, looking knackered, and order cups of tea. I mean cups of tea? In a pub in Glasgow? What the fuck is that all about?"

"What makes you think they're a pool team?" Laoshi's student asked.

"Well, they're a' carrying these long skinny bags, like for their pool cues," responded the barman.

"Naw, naw, pal," corrected the student, with deadly serious expression, "I know they lads, and those are no' pool cues. They're all carrying swords. They're a' martial arts guys. The tea thing is a ritual in memory of their dead master: hard bastard he was, but he only drank tea. Strange, eh?"

There was a marked improvement in service that evening in the bar. We were addressed as "gentlemen," and extra milk and sugar were offered.

Despite the recalibration of the bar staff's perspective, we relocated to the late-opening cafe nearby, which served for many years as our after-class haven.

Even without Laoshi's presence, the post-class sessions remained popular with the more committed students, one of whom, Rodrigo, was a long-term student and aficionado of numerous martial disciplines. Rodrigo frequently attended martial arts seminars, regardless of style, to round out his experience.

One evening, he related his experiences at a workshop he had attended the previous weekend. A whole afternoon, Rodrigo recounted, was devoted to the matter of taking blows in a relaxed manner, the course participants exchanging blows to the body in an attempt to discover the skill of "rolling with the punches." Rodrigo's report was positive. He clearly enjoyed the experience and valued the exercise, contrasting it favorably with other arts where protective equipment was deemed a necessity.

I listened without comment, but at a scheduled practice session some days later, I related to Laoshi the gist of Rodrigo's report, soliciting his views on the practice of taking blows.

"I can tell you what Zheng Manqing thought in regard to the practice," said Laoshi. "He was most certainly against it. Wang Lang used to quote the Professor's dictum: 'Don't let anyone put their hand on your body.' It is good advice. I will speak to Rodrigo to set him straight, but, at least, they were not targeting the head. Or were they?"

"I don't think so, Laoshi," I shrugged.

"There is growing evidence," resumed Laoshi, a frown betraying his concern in the matter, "that even slight blows to the head can cause long-term damage. Dementia pugilistica should not be one of the long term 'benefits' of martial arts. Mark my words, brain damage will be the death of MMA, unless they change their ways. Regular full-contact sparring does not make for lucidity in old age."

"I understand that, Laoshi," I countered, "but we are talking about blows to the body. After all, Robert Smith's black and white film of Zheng Manqing shot in the sixties shows one of the students, Mr. Shi, taking blows to the body without ill effect. Isn't the ability to take blows, like Mr. Shi, one of the benefits of taijiquan breathing, as the film claims?"

"Just because it is captured on film, does not mean that the Professor approved of the practice. It is also said that Mr. Shi developed those skills from other arts, not taijiquan. Have you heard of the time the Professor himself tested Mr. Shi's ability to take blows?"

"No, Laoshi," I replied eagerly, "I don't recall hearing that story. Tell me more. It sounds interesting."

"I cannot vouch for its absolute authenticity," cautioned Laoshi, "but I did hear of the incident from two independent sources. The story is that one afternoon in Taiwan, a few of Professor Zheng's students were waiting for him at his home, while he finished some paperwork in an adjoining room. Mr. Shi, it is alleged, was among those in attendance, and, while waiting, took to demonstrating his 'iron shirt' ability. Professor Zheng emerged, apparently irritated by the noise from his students, and advised them against taking blows, due to the danger of injury, or even death. Perhaps to emphasize the point, the Professor took a turn at Mr. Shi. There is some discord in the recollections of the story, but both sources claim that a gentle strike by the Professor, either with fist or sword charm, had Mr. Shi collapsing and holding his stomach in pain."

"Impressive," I nodded, entirely missing the point being made by both Laoshi and Zheng Manqing. "But that suggests that Zheng Manqing had an extraordinary skill in striking. How do you develop that skill, and, more importantly, how do you test that skill if you cannot strike other people?"

Laoshi's sigh was accompanied by a rolling of the eyes. In my early days as his student, the familiar gesture was my constant companion, and I did not welcome its return after so long an absence.

"To be fair," he relented. "It is an understandable question, from a certain point of view."

He gathered himself for a moment. "As I understand Zheng Manqing's approach to the punch, and I claim no great expertise here, it might be likened to a shockwave, which passes into the opponent's body. The Professor instructed his New York students to, 'think of the opponent's body as being a pane of glass. If you were trying to break a pane of glass, in order not to be cut, you would strike it sharply, with a whip-like or snapping motion, producing a shock wave that would break the glass. Hardness in an attacker makes their body brittle. You can learn to strike and shatter them inside as if they were glass. It's terrible.'"

Laoshi's thinking on this topic was not new to me. I knew the theory of striking as outlined by Zheng Manqing, but I remained frustrated by the scarcity of information on the method. Many tales of Zheng Manqing were merely tantalizing, leaving one desperate to know more. One such tale was particularly interesting and, equally, frustrating, due to its lack of detail. It concerned the fabled challenge match, where the Professor defeated another boxer. However, the Professor had been concerned enough to seek out a dianxue master to prepare for the rematch, which the challenger had threatened. Was Zheng Manqing's ability in striking a result of this exotic and mythical *dianxue*, the infamous "death touch?" I waited for Laoshi to put some meat on the bones, hoping that disappointment would not be the dish served.

"The problem with such striking," offered Laoshi, "is that you can only truly prove your ability in shattering someone internally by actually doing it. Such proof would leave a trail of devastated bodies in your wake, and an exodus of sensible students from your school, to be replaced by lunatics with a death wish."

"But wouldn't you then learn how to reverse the effects of shattering the insides?"

Laoshi smiled wryly, "When was the last time you saw a glazier unshatter a pane of glass? Alleged reversing the ill-effects of dianxue may be nothing more than part of an elaborate ruse."

As I struggled to conceal my disappointment, Laoshi sighed, his eyes downcast. A moment or two passed before he quietly added, "As a novice teacher, I too harbored a deep desire to develop this 'shattering' ability. However, it was a desire born out of insecurity, not strength. To this end, I persuaded some of my students to aid me in my experimentation with the method. I began modifying my uprooting technique to deliver a strike designed to leave the energy in the opponent's body. By now you will understand that the uprooting push and the correct punch are only a hair's breadth apart: punching is the yang counterpart to pushing, and pushing is the yin counter-point to striking.

"At regular intervals I would practice punching the arms of some of my students, who were willing guinea pigs, convinced, as they were, that we were on the cusp of discovering something profound. Needless to say, it was my own enthusiasm and certainty, which persuaded them of the enormity of the rewards to be gained. As I continued with my experiments, my former teacher, Wang Lang, earnestly implored me to desist saying, 'If you don't know what you are doing with that stuff, don't play about with it.' Secretly, I defied him, as I was desperate to have the ability, and I knew of no other way to proceed. The potential costs seemed to me worth the endeavor, and so I carried on whenever an opportunity presented itself.

"In mitigation, my actions were a little less reckless than might be supposed, as a former teacher had assured me that punching the upper arm was a safe way to practice: the energy imparted into the arm by a punch was unable to penetrate all the way into the chest cavity. I felt compelled to carry on. Then at class one evening, when I was teaching the punch posture, I demon-strated the punch, using the upper arm of one of my senior students. At the time, the student reported no ill effects, which was simultaneously welcome and disappointing. However, that was the last class that this particular student ever attended. Initially, his absence from class surprised me, as he had been studying with me for over five years. Then, just as my surprise slipped into disappointment, he phoned to inform me he had quit taijiquan."

"Why, Laoshi?" I pursued uneasily.

"Apparently on the day after his last class, when I had punched his arm, he suffered a heart attack. His words hit me harder than any physical blow. A cold tingle spread throughout my body, my nerves reacting to my distress: I had punched his arm a few times one evening, and then he was telling me of his heart attack the following day. In my mind, one was linked to the other."

"Wow," I interrupted uncertainly, not sure whether to be impressed or appalled. "You mean you think you gave him a heart attack just by punching him in the arm?"

"At the time I feared the worst," admitted Laoshi, "I listened numbly to the details of the student's life-saving surgery which followed. I did not mention to him my fear that I was in some way culpable. I only mumbled occasionally as he continued with his account. It was only toward the end of this phone call that he related his doctor's categorical opinion: it was his eating habits and sedentary work that left his arteries in a poor condition, and a more aerobic exercise routine would be essential if he was to avoid a repetition of heart trouble. The upshot of the phone call was to inform me that, as much as he enjoyed taijiquan, he had taken up running.

"I was relieved," sighed Laoshi, as if reliving the incident, "but I also decided, in that instant, to take Wang Lang's advice. Imagine the all-around distress if my inept experimentation resulted in a student with shattered internal organs? My aim in embarking on my study, and subsequent teaching, of taijiquan has never been to severely injure my students, or, worse still, end up like Yang Banhou, who reputedly killed one of his daughters in a training accident. From that day, my study of the punching technique has taken a back seat, while I still grapple with the subtleties of form and push-hands."

Perhaps due to my own expectations, my initial reaction to Laoshi's tale was one of disappointment. I could understand Laoshi's distressed reaction, but a part of me felt he had stopped short in his efforts. However, disappointment or no, after hearing Laoshi's story about his student's heart attack, I was not inclined to risk such an incident myself. Quite apart from the distress of injuring a student, I was concerned about the legal implications of such a practice, living as we do in an increasingly litigious society.

As a result, I followed the example of Laoshi. I restricted my activities to improving my uprooting skills in push-hands, and, in form, I contented myself with a purely theoretical demonstration of the differences between the taijiquan punch and those practiced in the arts of karate, Shaolin, or boxing. Thus far, no one has ever been injured in my teaching of the punch posture.

Further, in line with Laoshi's example, I explained to students (and reminded myself) that the bizarre-looking punch we execute in the form arises from the preferred fighting distance a taijiquan player employs.

I often quoted Laoshi word for word: "As a fighting system taijiquan is of the close-range variety. We seek to close with an opponent and get inside their preferred fighting distance."

With the assistance of the senior students Laoshi would demonstrate the preferred fighting distance, explaining that, "When we are this close, our opponents' most powerful weapons become less dangerous. On the other hand, we too are limited: we cannot mount an offense by winding up to deliver a blow with the fist, or make distance to kick. If we were to open the space for our own strike, we would only provide our opponent with an opportunity to fill the hole in our defense, which a competent fighter will fill with his own fist or elbow. Therefore, we must be able to strike with no wind up and generate power from our own style of 'one-inch-punch.' Unlike Bruce Lee's method, however, our short-range punch generates its power by connecting into the root and into the ground. In effect, we hit the opponent with the floor."

To dissuade students from becoming too excited, Laoshi would point out the downside of this style of punching: "Of course, this style of punching is extremely difficult to learn. As a prerequisite, we must have an exceptional grounding and an ability to push correctly. We then require the ability to convert the push into a strike."

Returning to a note of levity, Laoshi would quip, "For the time being, wet paper bags up and down the land may continue to exist in safety, unfazed by the power of the taijiquan punch. Meanwhile, should the need ever arise, confine yourself to attacking the more sensitive parts of the body, like the eyes and the throat. No internal power is needed for these soft targets."

Shortly after talking to Laoshi about punching, I was leafing through some old taijiquan magazines, which he had given me. I cherished these old periodicals, some dating back to Zheng Manqing's time in New York. Although short-lived as publications, they documented the Professor's activities and recorded the impression made by the Professor on the youthful New Yorkers of the time. I guarded these magazines jealously, feeling them to be part remuneration from Laoshi for my teaching efforts in his school. Contributions to the pages of these periodicals covered various aspects of Zheng Manqing's taijiquan. One article, in particular, was germane to the topic of taijiquan punching. It was the text of an interview with Tam Gibbs, the Professor's clos-est student in New York, conducted shortly after the death of the Professor.

In the article, Tam relates how he asked Professor Zheng to teach him dianxue: "One time I asked him, saying: 'Hey, Lao Shr, teach me that deadly killing art—the acu-punch.' He looked at me, said, 'Why?' I said, 'Well, because I think I'd like to learn that.' 'Why? Tam, you want ghosts? You wanna kill somebody? You want ghosts following you around? I have ghosts following me around. You want them?'"

The answer given Tam by Professor Zheng is remarkable in a number of ways, not the least being the notion that Zheng Manqing was followed around by ghosts. Was it possible that his Spartan sleeping regime, of only four hours nightly, was the price he paid to escape their ghoulish presence?

Leaving aside the intriguing, possibly disturbing, implications surrounding that question, it seems clear that Zheng Manqing thought the ability that Tam was seeking, like me and Laoshi before me, was more trouble than it was worth.

Reflecting on the whole issue of the punch, I asked myself the same question that the Professor asked Tam. Why should I want to develop that kind of ability, and, more importantly, why would I wish to teach it? My life was not in danger: crossing a road was as much peril as I found myself in these days. It occurred to me that the lure of the acu-punch (or something similar) is, at its root, a response to fear. As a solution to the problems of fear, however, the acu-punch is likely singularly inappropriate. Far from being a comfort, the nagging desire to develop such an ability might, ironically, reinforce the fearful thinking from which such desire springs.

I speculated that the reason that Zheng Manqing was reluctant to impart his knowledge of the acu-punch, was his assessment that it is not only unnecessary, but also potentially harmful to those seeking its power. Perhaps, he felt it was like putting a loaded gun in the hands of a child, which suggests there is a need for the gun, in the first place, and inevitably increases the risk of misadventure. I have no doubt that Zheng Manqing wanted the best for both his children and his students: turning them into potential killers is simply unfitting. As the saying goes: "Who gives their children a snake when they ask for bread?"

As I pondered Zheng Manqing's words, I perceived that in searching for the essence of taijiquan, we must make a choice between a Way that is life affirming, and one that is life threatening. For me, only the former held appeal. Moreover, in following that Way, I have felt increasingly less inclined to venture far into the realm of its more destructive twin. The mythical skills of the dianxue master will never be mine, but then neither will my sleep be disturbed by the ghosts of men who proved those skills real.

Laoshi once concluded one of his regular classes with the following observation: "As we delve deeper into martial arts training, we realize that everything in life is part of the training, and every moment is bursting with instruction, if we only had the eyes to see."

Laoshi lived his philosophy and guarded against his own practice becoming stale. He sought to remind himself that the Dao is all encompassing by encouraging his students to remain alive to its workings in the apparently trivial. Laoshi sometimes referred to the long hours spent with Wang Lang, his teacher. This was instrumental in opening up his appreciation of the Way as being "vast as the universe." Thus, Laoshi found significance even in the mundane: "Just watching Wang Lang drink his coffee was a lesson," he once commented.

Laoshi also watched us, his students, and measured our progress without recourse to "ambushing" us with tricks or tests—the perverse pleasure of some other teachers. He simply observed and knew us, sometimes better than we knew ourselves. There was no "off-duty" with Laoshi: he seemed always to be "on."

"It is a remnant of my time with Wang Lang," he explained, when I once pressed him on the subject. Spending time with Wang Lang on long road trips had felt, for Laoshi, invaluable. He would encourage his teacher to talk about taijiquan, Zheng Manqing, his time at the Shr Jung School, and life in general. "At times it was as if liquid gold poured from the man, and I feverishly absorbed every drop. It is not difficult to be completely 'in the moment' at times like these.

"Once," continued Laoshi, "as the miles drifted by, I took a turn at the wheel to give Wang Lang some time to rest. His schedule was particularly heavy that week, and he fell asleep, only to awaken abruptly and ask if he had missed his turn to drive. I reassured him that twenty miles remained before the rest stop and the scheduled changeover. Wang Lang was surprised by my assertion, since this was but the second time I had been on this particular road.

"How do you know there are twenty miles left?" queried Wang Lang. "You do not know this road."

"Well," I replied, "the last time I noted the distance, and I've had my eye on the odometer while you have been sleeping."

"Ah," chuckled Wang Lang. "You truly understand the Way of the Warrior."

"How so?" I asked him.

"The Way of the Warrior has as much to do with logistics as it has with fighting," smiled Wang Lang.

"Wang Lang was right," mused Laoshi. "The Way we follow is about… everything."

I have also come to realize that the "Way of the Teacher" is more complex than giving instructions to students in the intricacies of form or push-hands. Logistics are certainly involved: without a venue, there would be no class; without students, there would be no teacher. Yet during all the years I attended classes in the role of student, I paid little attention to the logistical realities of venue and students, until I became the custodian of hall keys, payment books, class registers, and the assorted paraphernalia that attaches itself, barnacle-like, to the butt of the teacher.

In addition, came the demanding, and sometimes deflating, need to advertise for new students. Having inherited the lion's share of teaching responsibility, I was now tasked with the laborious and thankless effort of balancing the gradual decline in enrollment by encouraging a periodic swelling of the ranks. It was not something I enjoyed and found myself unsure as how best to market my classes.

Some time back, a school website had come into being, almost in opposition to Laoshi's wishes. He reluctantly allowed one of his very keen IT-literate students to service the school website, but that was the limit of Laoshi's engagement with the online world in this new cyber age.

"I don't do anti-social media," retorted Laoshi one day to a student. The student had earnestly recommended that he review his "outmoded" point of view and *get with the trend*. "I prefer to keep my distance from fake-book and trotter," added Laoshi, with a low growl, which suggested a change of subject might be prudent.

"It's *Facebook* and *Twitter*," corrected the student unfortunately, entirely failing to register the warning edge in Laoshi's tone.

"I know what it is," intoned Laoshi with ice. "It is you who do not."

In the end, while permitting his student to update the website and field email enquiries, Laoshi persisted with his own tried and true, though possibly antiquated, method of publicizing new beginner's classes. Each spring, summer, autumn, and winter, Laoshi would spend several days trudging around the local neighborhoods, seeking out shop windows in which to display leaflets announcing the start of a new class. The student who updated the website took his cue from the leaflets and presented the information online without bothering Laoshi.

As a novice teacher, I soon came to appreciate the vital importance of replenishing classes with new beginners. The school hemorrhaged students at a steady rate, many feeling that the commitment was too great for the anticipated rewards. Prior to becoming teacher, my interest in "new blood" had extended little beyond assessing who might, in time, graduate to push-hands and fencing. Now, as the embodiment of marketing and advertising for the school, I sought to examine Laoshi's reluctance to engage with the methods of modern mass media, methods I felt sure would yield a greater crop of new students.

On posing the question, I was greeted by Laoshi's customary diversion into the beginning of a tale, which would, I knew from experience, eventually answer the energy of the question: "Have you ever heard Zhuangzi's story of Zi Gong and the farmer drawing water from a well?"

In truth, the story was not new to me, the source possibly being Laoshi himself, but the twinkle in his eye betrayed his wish to relate it once more.

"Er… I'm not sure, Laoshi." I played along, knitting my brows, as if in search of a fading memory.

"Ah, in that case, I will tell you!" offered Laoshi delightedly. "Zi Gong was on his way to… well it doesn't matter to where… but he was on his way, when he saw a farmer using a bucket to draw water from a well. Zi Gong paused on his journey to helpfully inform the farmer that there now existed a machine made of wood, known as a well sweep, which could efficiently draw water from the ground without effort. The farmer replied, 'I have heard from my teacher that those who have cunning implements are cunning in their dealings, and those who are cunning in their dealings, have cunning in their hearts, and those who have cunning in their hearts, cannot be pure and incorrupt. Those who are not pure and incorrupt are restless in spirit, and those who are restless in spirit are not vehicles for Dao. It is not that I do not know of these things. I should be ashamed to use them.'"

A mischievous smile crossed my lips as I felt the inclination to engage in some verbal fencing with Laoshi. "Very true, Laoshi," I replied, "but isn't a car or a television a cunning implement? And don't you own both?"

Laoshi burst out laughing—a laugh that was infectious. I could not help but mirror his mirth.

"Don't you just love those passages from Zhuangzi," he said when his laughter allowed. "I also like this one from Confucius; 'I investigate things to complete my knowledge. My complete knowledge makes my thoughts sincere. My thoughts being sincere, my heart is pure.' Have you seen that TV series about the cop who is a student of Zen? He uses that line in one of the episodes."

Perhaps it was the laughter, or maybe the mention of a television program touching on Zen, but my attention was easily sidetracked, and the original thrust of my question became lost to me. It was only while returning home at the wheel of my car, that I felt my question remained unanswered.

Then it struck me. Laoshi had simply distracted me. I had lost focus and been neutralized as easily as a child. And yet, Laoshi's answer had been perfect as an illustration: a child of the modern era, I was ripe for distraction with a ludicrously short attention span, eroded still further by an irresistible urge to check texts and emails every few minutes. A hostage to technology, my awareness had been drawn ever further away from my true self, my heart-mind. In that instant, I knew why Laoshi instinctively recoiled from dependence on "cunning" devices: unless we are careful, our reliance on technology tends to separate us from our true selves and from the Dao.

Caught in traffic, I mused on the reality I had created for myself: here I was sitting in a tin can, on a tarmac surface, struggling to reach home, where I would lose myself in images beamed into a plastic box, as I lounged on a settee, which was crushing my internal organs and straining my spine. As I looked around me, I saw the next generation, oblivious to the traffic, headphones on, hoods up, a glazed look in their eyes, wandering around in a manufactured world of constant stimulus. Where was the time to feel the Dao? Where was the time to be inspired by the trees, or marvel at the sky, or appreciate birdsong? We pay a price for every piece of "cunning" that ensnares our attention. Laoshi knew himself enslaved, like the rest of us, but was resisting the pressure to add to his chains.

On reaching home, I slumped onto my organ-crushing, spine-wrecking sofa and pondered the dilemma that Laoshi had been dealing with for years: the inherent contradiction of "advertising" a Daoist-orientated art like taijiquan. A Daoist, purely speaking, eschews the limelight, avoids the public gaze, and escapes from society's attempts to fashion him into something usable, and yet here was I attempting to devise efficient ways of advertising my taijiquan classes. I was attempting to combine the, arguably, mutually exclusive worlds of teaching classes for money, with the spiritually orientated tradition of martial arts and qi development. To make a living, it becomes necessary to try to fuse together the provision of a "service" with a rigorous training, a notion that is generally rejected by the modern-day consumer. The doors of our art are thus thrust open, so that anyone can come in, sneer at our traditions, and leave in search of some "buy-one-get-one-free" spirituality in the shopping mall or cinema.

Just as I was confronting that image in my mind, the phone rang.

"Er... Are you that taijiquan teacher guy?" A nasally-challenged voice with a super-strength Glaswegian accent, "the wan what put up they leaflets in the shoaps?"

"Yes, that would be me," I tried to sound upbeat. "Are you interested in coming to class?"

26

"Aye," replied the voice with vigor, "Ah'll tell you whit it is. Ah'm pure fuckin hard, see. I done it all, man. Ah've done the boxing, an' the K'rate, an' everythin'. Ah've battered loads of guys, by the way, some o' them wur even hard men, know whit Ah mean?"

The voice paused for effect. Then, almost conspiratorially added, "Whit it is," I could almost feel the neck-twitch that accompanies this type of delivery—"Whit it is, ah want tae learn tae kill guys wi' ma bare hauns wi' just a touch. Dae you teach that?"

I could not believe it. Was this gentleman genuinely requesting instruction in some form of dianxue? As I considered the possibility that I was the victim of a radio prank call, the would-be killer grew impatient for my answer and demanded, "Well, dae ye, or dae ye no?"

"Erm… D' you know the Maryhill Road?" I growled, deploying my hardest Glaswegian accent—the one that says—"Ah'm hard as fuck myself man, know what Ah mean."

"Aye," replied the voice.

"D'you know the community center up near the Barracks?" I continued in growl mode. "Well, see in there, right. There's guys that can teach you that stuff. Top men they are. Hard, know whit Ah mean? Go up there, man. They'll sort you oot."

Then, before he could debate the matter further, I ended the conversation saying, "Oh, there's the police at ma door. Got tae go, pal. Good luck wi they guys up in the Barracks." I put the phone down with relief, feeling only mildly guilty about the possibility of the Barracks class receiving a visit from a maniac looking for a type of exotica beyond their scope.

The experience of trudging around my neighborhood pestering local shopkeepers into displaying leaflets tested my patience. Finding the process tedious beyond measure, I began to feel that my students should not escape a share of this particular "punishment." For a short time, I succeeded in persuading a clearly skeptical student to plague the local shopkeepers with my requests for window space by offering a reduction in class fees.

However, I was soon to learn that even this strategy was not to be totally incident-free. Having arranged for a round of leaflet advertising, I was getting some enquiries and, with high hopes, I answered the phone to another would-be student. His tone was clipped, as if strangling down some annoyance. He asked, "Are you the guy who's teaching the taijiquan?"

"Yes, that right," I answered, politely but cautiously, not too remote, but with just the right hint of gravitas to suggest that I was the keeper of esoteric knowledge, which could be revealed for the appropriate fee.

"Is that your leaflet that's in the Rio Café in Partick?"

"It probably is, yes," I replied tentatively, recalling my conversation with the would-be killer lunatic.

"Well," he growled, having identified me as the source of his angst, "I teach the xingyi class in Partick, and you just put your leaflet right on top of mine."

"Er… Look," I sighed. I needed not to inflame the situation. "I'm sorry that happened, but I didn't put the leaflets up personally, and the guy who did would not deliberately cover up somebody else's. Perhaps my leaflet fell off the wall, and the café owners just put it up anywhere."

He did not seem convinced by my explanation and informed me that my attempt to interfere with his classes was not "the done thing."

"Covering up people's leaflets is serious: people have been killed for less," he hissed. Wound tight or what?

I tried to subdue my amusement, but I could not help myself. I laughed aloud. I gathered from his tone that this teacher of xingyi was not joking. I had no wish to enrage him further but, "killed for less?" Seriously?

"So are you going to come round and kill me, then?" I said through my laughter.

"No, I'm just saying," he muttered in a more conciliatory tone, either because his threat had been seen to have no fangs or, more likely, he regretted betraying his own frustrations with a statement so ludicrous. A few short exchanges later, the issue seemed to have been resolved without resorting to violence.

Speaking to Laoshi some time later, I asked him if his experience of advertising had exposed him to similar bizarre telephone encounters. Once again, Laoshi's reply was not necessarily the one I had anticipated: instead, it reminded me that the fingerprint of the Dao is on every experience, if only we had eyes to see.

"Do you think life is trying to draw your attention to anything by way of these encounters?" asked Laoshi.

"I don't know, Laoshi," I replied perplexed. "What could life be trying to tell me?"

"You don't like putting up leaflets, do you?" continued Laoshi. He often answered a question with a question.

"No, I can't stand it," I exclaimed with honest feeling.

"Hmm," mused Laoshi. I could tell a story was on its way. "One of my old teachers, Don, lived for a time in a Buddhist retreat center. He was searching for his Way in life and turned to Buddhism in the hope of finding direction. Don heard from other seekers that a venerable old Tibetan Buddhist master took on students at his retreat center in the rolling hills of Southern

Scotland. Don made a pilgrimage north to meet the master in person, whereupon he experienced such a vibration of peace and love that he stayed there for several years, under the guidance of the master. In return, Don worked in the center as payment for room and board.

"The master lived a simple disciplined life, eating one meager meal a day, a meal cooked by Don, whose duties included preparing and cooking all the master's food, whenever the master was resident in the center. At the appointed time each day, Don would lay a tray containing a single bowl of gruel and a glass of water at the master's door, returning an hour later to retrieve the tray and wash the glass and bowl. On returning for the tray one day, Don found the meal untouched. The glass was empty but the bowl remained full. As the old master ate nothing else throughout the day, it meant that he had gone hungry. Nothing was said in the course of the day's teaching, but Don was both disconcerted and concerned for the master's well-being. His unease and concern grew as the same scene greeted him at the master's door over the next three days. With growing apprehension, Don voiced his disquiet to the other center workers, who merely shrugged, providing neither solution nor consolation. Forced to confront the circumstance in which he found himself, he became aware of the intense feeling of hostility that he brought to his work in the kitchen. His introspection revealed the extent to which he despised the act of preparing and cooking food: he was looking for training in enlightenment, not to work in a kitchen. As a result of his resentment, he expended as little effort as possible in the food preparation, treating it as a hindrance to his more formal studies.

"Then, a moment of insight!" exclaimed Laoshi. "It occurred to Don that perhaps the master, due to his highly-developed awareness, sensed the contaminating spirit that accompanied the food's preparation in the kitchen. Don resolved to approach the next meal with due reverence and mindfulness, both in preparation and serving, in the hope that the food would be imbued with these qualities. That day, on returning to retrieve the tray, Don was rewarded with an empty bowl. From then on, every day, the master ate the meals prepared with this new, more wholesome attitude. From then on, Don paid great attention to every aspect of his work at the center, seeing even the dull and distasteful duties as Dao rather than drudgery."

"An interesting story," I conceded cautiously, before asking if Laoshi believed in the master's ability to sense Don's intention in the food.

"I have no idea," said Laoshi simply. "Don did possess a healthy imagination, but he learned something from the experience, nevertheless, and that was that the attitude brought to the task is as important as the task itself.

"When teaching taijiquan became my only means of income," added

29

Laoshi, returning to the point at hand, "I too hated the advertising aspect. I felt keenly that sharing the esteemed art of taijiquan would be a perfect occupation were it not for the irritation of having to advertise classes.

"When I could stand it no longer," added Laoshi, "I paid my students to carry out the necessary drudgery of advertising, just as you have, in order to rescue my time for the important work of teaching."

"In your own struggles with advertising, did the story of Don and the master inspire a fresh insight?" I asked eagerly.

"No," shrugged Laoshi, "I only thought about Don as we spoke just now. No, a turning point came when, after a morning tramping around the neighborhood with leaflets, I stopped for some tea in a local café. As I looked out at the damp, depressing streets of winter, I noticed a disheveled old man, carrying two huge plastic bags filled with empty drinks cans. He was wandering around, scanning the pavements for discarded cans. As my attention fixed on him, I recognized him as a man who, years previously, had visited my father. Accompanied by his wife, he had come to make an offer on my father's house, which I'm sure my father had no intention of selling. It seems he was entering the early stages of a mental illness, and we subsequently heard that, as his illness progressed, he was hospitalized and lost everything, including his home and wife.

"Anyway," continued Laoshi, after a brief pause, "I watched him from my concealed vantage point inside the cafe, as he laid down his overstuffed plastic bags and bent toward the pavement. He rose triumphantly, clutching in both hands an orange juice can of Italian manufacture, the type that you need a mortgage to buy and a bottle of mouthwash to scour the sugar from your teeth, once the contents have been drunk. Due to the expense, not many people buy these cans of juice, and so they are something of a rarity. The can collector lifted it delicately, held it to the dimming light, and examined the can as if he had found a ruby in a pile of pebbles. He smiled the broadest smile, opened up his jacket, and secreted his exotic prize in an inside pocket.

"As I watched," continued Laoshi, "a tear came to my eye."

"Yes, it's sad really how some people end up," I nodded trying to empathize with the can-man's predicament.

"No," rebuked Laoshi mildly, "It was a tear of poignancy, as I recognized the joy in another. I felt humbled. This man was happy. He had a Dao! To the casual observer, he was simply collecting junk, but to him, he was a prospector, or a hunter, or a biologist in the rain forest collecting specimens! In that instant, I was reminded that the Dao is in *everything*, even putting up unremarkable leaflets in shop windows on miserable, rainy days. Exercising the discipline of 'advertising' is part of the Way. Do not cut yourself off from it: this is a gift."

I confess it took me long enough to grasp this "gift" of Laoshi's reckoning. Anthony DeMello tells a story of a poverty-stricken rickshaw puller in India, who continued to work, in spite of a terminal disease, to provide for his family. He was so poor that he did not even own his own bones, having sold his skeleton, in advance, to make ends meet. And yet, the grinding poverty was not the key feature of this rickshaw wallah's story, rather it was the joyfulness that accompanied him as he made his way through life. (Things are not as they are; they are as we see them.)

Later as I meditated on the poor spirit with which I approached the more irritating aspects of teaching, the words of the *Zhongyong*, or "Doctrine of the Mean," came to me: "The Dao is that from which one cannot deviate; that from which one can deviate is not the Dao."

The next time I met Laoshi, as we were drinking some tea in his kitchen, I casually steered the conversation around to the topic of social media.

"Laoshi," I asked innocently, "do you remember telling me a while ago that the Dao is in everything?"

"Did I?" Laoshi replied mildly, but I knew his attention was keen. "I don't remember, but what of it?"

"Well," I began mischievously, "since the Dao is in everything, isn't the human 'cunning'—technology, invention—also part of the Dao? And, therefore, aren't Facebook and Twitter, and the rest of modern technological communications, all part of the Dao, as well?"

The twinkle in Laoshi's eye never faltered, but grew into a broad grin.

"Gottcha!" I thought, waiting for Laoshi to squirm. I was even more gratified, when he replied smilingly, "Good push, Grasshopper," a reference to the young Kwai-chang Caine in the TV series *Kung Fu*.

"Mind you," he continued with barely a pause, "a rattlesnake is also part of the Dao, but I tend to avoid one if I see it. I didn't say that Farce-book or Twister was not part of the Dao." I could only marvel at the sudden mysterious return of Laoshi's recollection. "I said I keep my distance from them."

"Bugger!" I thought to myself, "The old fox had slipped away again. He was as slippery as a salmon, as a good push-hands player should be."

I smiled and bowed my head. "Touché, Laoshi!"

No longer obliged to teach daily form classes, Laoshi was free to devote more time to his own practice and research. Sometimes, his investigation into the art amounted to no more than reading the classics and performing his regular routine of hand form and sword form, but Laoshi also set about a deep exploration of push-hands and fencing: those aspects of taijiquan that require a partner.

To Laoshi's mind, while sincere repetitions of the form provide the taijiquan enthusiast with much of the art, the full flavor of Zheng Manqing's teaching was available only through additional study of the twin disciplines of push-hands and fencing. Laoshi, therefore, needed an available accomplice, complete with time to practice and an intimate knowledge of the subtleties pertaining to the art. Instead, he had me. I had sufficient spare time to fulfill the first requirement, and Laoshi tolerated my limitations in the second. As a result, I became an ever more frequent visitor to Laoshi's house on the outskirts of Glasgow, alternating between the roles of taijiquan "guinea pig" and "research assistant," depending on the direction of Laoshi's musings.

Though delighted at the added contact time with Laoshi, I initially harbored a suspicion that my presence might serve a purpose other than mere assistance with his research. I wondered if there was a subtle move afoot to control, through me, a school which he was spending progressively less time supervising. No doubt sensing my concerns, Laoshi reassured me early on by saying, "In terms of how and what you teach, there is nothing you have to discuss with me, but there is also nothing which you cannot discuss with me." Laoshi was assuring me that, in matters pertaining to the school, I had carte blanche.

How much my presence assisted in Laoshi's continuing evolution is debatable, but for me, those hours spent exploring the mysteries of push-hands and fencing were a veritable *Eldorado*: they compensated for the burden of teaching, which, at times, weighed heavily. Whatever the cause, Laoshi's development, indeed, seemed to reach new levels. "I dream about snakes and crocodiles a lot more regularly these days," he reflected one afternoon, as we rested between bouts of push-hands. "And when I do, I notice that, a few days later, I have a breakthrough in understanding. The insights are coming so thick and fast, I barely have time to assimilate one before the next comes along."

Laoshi had told me before of his dreams. Although he paid scant attention to dream interpretation, he had noticed a correlation between reptilian-themed encounters during the night and improvement in his taijiquan on subsequent days. The dreams were rarely pleasant, with Laoshi frequently finding himself bitten by the snakes, or chased by alarmingly fast crocodiles.

A friend of mine, on hearing of Laoshi's herpetological dream adventures, commented thoughtfully, "Hmm... perhaps that is because the ancient, primitive, reptilian brain is breaking through the control of the cortex." Whatever the reason, Laoshi was indisputably improving in his push-hands and fencing, and I was to be privileged to witness his development first-hand. All I had to do was run his school.

Of course, witnessing his evolution was not the only benefit of increased time spent with Laoshi. Opportunities frequently presented themselves for me to solicit his advice on difficulties confronting me in my practice and my teaching.

"I'm having some trouble pushing these days," I confided to Laoshi during one of our sessions, "not only with you, but with some of the other students."

I broached this subject with Laoshi after encountering a stumbling block, which I felt threatened to derail my future progress. Although I was becoming increasingly proficient in the skill of "uprooting," and relished the prospect of launching colleagues against the wall, my early promise appeared to be floundering in frustration. My fellow students sought to stymie my pushing by adopting, to my mind, ever more outlandish defenses. It began to feel as if they measured "success" by the degree to which they could achieve an awkward obstinacy. Their progress in this direction easily outstripped my efforts to counter these apparently boorish tactics.

My ability to line up an attack on an opponent's center remained, as did my skill in issuing force through my forearm, wrist or hand. I could even employ the "press," one hand backing up the other, to deliver devastating power. However, in spite of my gains, I was having trouble with the more senior students, who would unceremoniously grab my arm and wrench me off balance, just as I steadied to "pull the trigger," and propel them into the wall with a satisfactory thump.

Worse, was the seeming undercurrent of smug satisfaction I encountered when pushing hands with those senior students, who, perhaps, felt usurped by my position. They had commenced their studies ahead of me, but now found themselves "overtaken," as I assumed the role of teacher. Through subtle little acts of defiance, they seemed to vent their feelings at being "passed over," adding to my growing list of negative and unforeseen consequences, resulting from my replacing Laoshi in class. Push-hands class was the arena where the thin veil of civility felt most fragile.

Jealousy exists in all fields of human endeavor, but, naively, I had

33

presumed Laoshi's students to be above such unworthy attitudes. Perhaps I should have been forewarned by Laoshi's descriptions of the strong emotions aroused even in Zheng Manqing's New York School, known as "The Hall of Happiness." According to Laoshi, Tam Gibbs was the target of hostility because of his close relationship with the Professor. These rumblings, evident at a minor level during the Professor's life, became volcanic upon his death.

Rather than be deterred from my path, I became doubly determined to deepen my understanding and gain the upper hand. Some years later, reflecting on lessons learned from Laoshi, I wondered if he had any inkling that my appointment as teacher would cause resentments, which I would have to salve. Was he trying to encourage senior students to improve by shocking them out of their complacency, or was he following Zheng Manqing's inclination to allow a competitive atmosphere to develop between his more senior students?

I remain unsure of his motivation, if any. But I recall Laoshi's response to a discussion concerning the strong feelings unleashed after Zheng Manqing's death. One senior student was fiercely critical in regard to the fallout after the Professor's death, finding both the Professor and his senior students to be equally at fault. Laoshi replied forcefully, "We are studying a martial art. What do you expect: sweetness and light at every turn? Our practice is to face conflict fearlessly, not scatter like rabbits frightened by our own shadows."

"But, all of Zheng Manqing's good work could have died as a result!" protested the student.

"If it died as a result," replied Laoshi coolly, "then it was not worthy of the name taijiquan."

When all was said and done, I knew I had no choice but to improve and develop my skill in order to counter the crude techniques employed against me. Still, tactics such as gross arm pulling only added to my annoyance, when I found myself rendered impotent in its clutches. Laoshi was sympathetic, which encouraged me. "Push-hands is an arms race, both metaphorically and literally. But you must develop your legs," he counseled.

"You should also expect the use of tactics," Laoshi added, "especially when dealing with the seniors of a school. They have been around a long time and know a few tricks. But in truth, using those tricks has caused some of them to stall in their own progress—they have developed a tactical mind—*if you do this, I'll do that*. A tactical mind is a narrow mind, a mind unable to improvise. A principled mind, meanwhile, is not constrained by specific responses to particular stimuli. Rooted in principle, one can remain open to all things.

"In the short-term, however," Laoshi added with a wink, "it may be helpful to fight fire with fire. You can utilize some tactics of your own, temporarily, of course, to get around the blockage that faces you. Have you heard me mention 'the three ropes'"?

It is not uncommon for taijiquan teachers to group ideas or techniques into threes. Zheng Manqing, for example, talks of "the three treasures" and "the three fearlessnesses." His classification of progress into stages also echoes the notion that "good things come in threes," with each of the three levels of development: heaven, earth, and human having three subdivisions. Other teachers have their own threes: "the three gates," "the three pushes," "the three nails," "the three dantians," and so forth. Furthermore, Zheng Manqing's taijiquan is based on the triad of form, push-hands, and sword. Not to be outdone, Laoshi had his own version of "the three pushes, which he taught to novices, but I had not heard mention of "the three ropes."

I said as much to Laoshi.

"An oversight!" he smiled. "Let us rectify that now." And so Laoshi proceeded to instruct me in three techniques to counter the tactic of arm pulling in push-hands.

Laoshi summarized the problem: "As you know, our *peng-lü-ji-an* method of push-hands is…" he paused, searching for the right word—"precise. It is not like pushing a stalled car. When pushing a car, we do not pay much attention to the position of the arms: we just shove and be done with it. In push-hands, however, a more refined method is called for."

Laoshi's insistence on this "precise" approach to pushing derived from Wang Lang's mantra of "attack with the idea of defending; defend with the idea of attacking." Accordingly, Laoshi stressed the need to develop skill in pushing, while, simultaneously, listening for and countering any defense enlisted by the opponent being pushed.

Laoshi continued. "In theory, to neutralize our push, the opponent should turn his waist to yield, while at the same time unbalancing us through the connection of our elbows. Neutralizing is easy to do, if we push with only one hand, however, it becomes a little more challenging when we employ two hands to push. But with the addition of a forearm and elbow, many find a simple turn of the waist ineffective in dealing with our push."

I was certainly one of the "many," especially when Laoshi pushed. As the pusher becomes subtler, the receiver finds increasing difficulty in making principle work. As Zheng Manqing said, "Neutralizing is ten times more difficult than pushing."

Unable to deal with a subtle push by turning the waist, the receiver frequently resorts to grabbing the pusher's wrist and elbow, and, with a yank, rips the pusher's body to the side. In effect, the pusher's own forearm is used as a lever against him. This was the problem I was currently experiencing, as I tried to push my partners.

Laoshi resumed: "Our method of pushing, which includes using the forearm, apparently leaves us vulnerable to a pull by the receiver. If, however, we push with sensitivity, we can overcome any pulling by the receiver. The idea is to imagine your forearm as being a rope as you push. With this image in mind, there are now various ways to respond as the receiver pulls on the rope.

"The first method is called 'ringing the bell.' Imagine those ropes in the church belfry, attached to huge wheels, which are in turn connected to massive bells. The pulled rope causes the wheel in the belfry to rock the bell to the side. Once the bell has reached its limit, its own massive weight then causes the bell to rotate in the other direction, pulling the rope back up to the ceiling. At that point, the bell-ringer had better let go, or he will be pulled heavenward as well. Similarly, in push-hands, the receiver is the bell-ringer, and as you push, your arm is the rope, and your waist is the wheel. You let your opponent pull, and then you turn your waist back again, returning to the position where you began, and resulting in the receiver being pulled off balance."

Laoshi then demonstrated, in order that I could analyze the technique. He added a touch of refinement to the proceedings by making a little looping movement at the end of my pulling motion, in order to create the sensation of continuous movement. As I pulled, Laoshi blended with my efforts, first rotating his waist, and then counter-rotating to return his arm to its original position, with surprising ease and minimal drama.

It was an impressive technique, and I wondered why I had not encountered it before. When I put the question to Laoshi, he merely replied; "I will explain later, but first we must look at the second idea: 'cutting the rope.'

"Have you ever lifted a heavy-looking object, only to find it surprisingly light?" Laoshi enquired.

"Of course, Laoshi. You put too much force into it, and it flies away."

"Exactly," he nodded. "That is identical to 'cutting the rope': when your opponent pulls, they expect a least some resistance, but instead, you add to their pull, using your forearm, and, as a result, they lose balance, while you capitalize by sending them into the wall for their trouble."

Once again, Laoshi demonstrated the effectiveness of this concept. Sure enough, this time my pull on his arm, combined with Laoshi's own force, pushed me back into the wall with bruising effect. But before I could ask any questions about this second technique, Laoshi continued, "Finally, we come to my favorite of 'the three ropes.' We might call it 'anchoring the rope.' It is, perhaps, the technique that is closest to principle.

"Consider the ability of your arms," said Laoshi. "You can use them to push something away from you, but equally, you can push away from an object more substantial than you. This is the basic idea behind 'anchoring the rope.' As your opponent pulls on your arm to redirect your push, you root into the ground and they find that, rather than pulling you, they are hauling themselves off balance."

Once more, Laoshi proceeded to familiarize me with the mechanics of this technique firsthand. My sincere attempt to pull his arm found me, rather than him, tipping forward, off-balance. Laoshi did, indeed, feel "anchored" to the ground, and I found my attempts to break his connection with the floor working against me, as I felt my heels rise and my weight tip forward. To an observer it might have been tricky to discern precisely who was pulling whom.

In comparison with the previous two techniques demonstrated, Laoshi's "anchoring the rope" felt considerably more subtle, more akin to Laoshi's customary way of managing his partner in regular push-hands sessions. I said as much to Laoshi.

"There is truth in what you observe," Laoshi acknowledged. "Ultimately, most techniques are tricks, and, unfortunately, they can encourage tactical thinking—the notion that there is a 'set response' to a 'set attack.' In this regard, they are limited. "Anchoring the rope," however, hints at something subtler: the notion that we attack the opponent's body and not their arms, their *center* and not the periphery. This is where we enter the realm of truly advanced push-hands. We dispense with crude ideas of pulling and shoving our opponent's arms, and instead, we go directly to the heart of the matter and control their center."

"Hmm... I think I begin to see why you do not over-emphasize 'the three ropes...'" I commented at the conclusion of Laoshi's demonstration, realizing how easily proceedings could degenerate into "arm wrestling."

"Indeed," Laoshi concurred.

"So why show me?" I was curious.

"Because, I think you may be ready." Laoshi's gaze was steady. "Such techniques have value if you understand how to make use of them, but not if you become used by them."

"I'm not sure how that works, Laoshi," I shook my head doubtfully.

Laoshi nodded in acknowledgement. "Okay, let me try to explain it like this: 'the three ropes' are a little like conversational ploys. 'Ringing the bell' is a bit like saying to someone, 'Yes... but...' You are agreeing, but also disagreeing at the same time. It is the 'I'm being perfectly reasonable...' approach.

"'Cutting the rope,' however, is a more forceful defense, not unlike saying, 'Who are you to talk?' This is a counter-attacking defense, or one which turns defense into attack.

"Then we come to 'anchoring the rope.' Frankly, this can be used as an undermining strategy. It is like saying, '*Are you sure you know what you are talking about?*' This is designed to unbalance the other person and gain advantage by encouraging their doubt and confusion."

Laoshi's point began to sink in: from a certain perspective, "the three ropes" could be seen to hint at a kind of cynicism, quite at odds with the philosophical underpinning of the taijiquan which Laoshi advocated: a taijiquan that fosters integrity in interpersonal relationships built on honesty and equity, not scheming and manipulation.

I now further appreciated Laoshi's care in introducing "the three ropes." If I had genuinely believed that progress was to be measured only in cunning, then I would have taken as my master a former work colleague, who, in spite of his morbid lack of enthusiasm for work, had remained in constant employment, when many a better man had fallen by the wayside. His favored survival strategy employed three stages in "the avoidance of blame." The first stage, he referred to as the "Bart Simpson" defense: a basic, all-bases covered denial as in: "I didn't do it; it wasn't I; it was like that when I got there." He assured me that this "deny all knowledge" strategy was an excellent first line of defense.

However, there were circumstances, my colleague counseled, where simple denial proved insufficient, at which point one should proceed directly to the "spread the blame" gambit. As my colleague kindly reminded me; "blame shared is blame halved." The "poor little me" variation on this particular tactic involved assuming the role of victim, unfairly hounded by the callous establishment.

Should the preceding strategies fail, my creative colleague would proceed immediately to his last line of defense: the "push the shit uphill" evasion. It was always possible, he assured me, to suggest that a superior was in fact to blame for not pointing out errors at an earlier stage. "This is *surely a failure of leadership!*" my colleague would protest.

Laoshi chuckled as I related my colleague's philosophy. "It is hard not to smile at his ingenuity. On the other hand, your friend's cultivated avoidance is also symptomatic of the tactical mind: it is clever, but it is spiritually vacant. To devote our energies to the avoidance of life is self-defeating: taken too far, there is nothing left to live *for*.

"Your friend is not so different to the push-hands players, who concentrate on tactics, while neglecting the study of principle. Did I ever tell you about my former teacher, Lenny, and his letter to Dr. Qin?"

"I don't think so, Laoshi," I replied with a shake of my head.

"So… Lenny made a month long visit to see Dr. Qin in Seattle. Now a

38

month is a very short time to spend with a master and, in that time, Lenny felt he had only managed to absorb the basics of Dr. Qin's instruction. When he returned home, he tried to put into practice the lessons from the trip, yet Lenny felt he still lacked depth in the intricacies of push-hands. Since another trip was financially beyond him, he wrote Dr. Qin a long letter, detailing various 'pushes' and requesting the details of 'counters' to each push. Lenny's letter ran to several pages.

"Some weeks later, a letter arrived on Lenny's doormat, bearing a United States post-mark. Lenny eagerly tore open the small envelope to discover a scrap of paper, bearing a one-line reply from Dr. Qin: 'Dear Len,' it read. 'When he push, you yield. Love, Qin.'

"Dr. Qin," laughed Laoshi, "got to the heart of the matter. Push-hands, and life in general, is perhaps best approached without a tactical mindset. In the end, to abandon tactical mind is the only sensible approach. As Wang Lang might say: 'Tactics work some of the time; principle works all of the time.'"

However, as I reflected upon Laoshi's words over the weeks that followed, I could not help but feel that they contained contradictions in regards to tactics, technique, and principle. Did not Laoshi himself insist on a "precise" application of the technique of push-hands? Were we not instructed to follow the Professor's advice to "study the form; it has meaning?" What was the precise relationship between tactics, technique, and principle? I pondered. It was, indeed, a koan.

With time, some degree of understanding arose from my ruminations. I began to see that sincere study of the technical aspects of the art could, indeed, lead to the experience of "flip" that Laoshi had previously described to me. On the other hand, there was always the danger of technique becoming empty ritual. This had been the reason why Wang Lang was reluctant to teach the two-person *dalü* exercise. "*Dalü*," he said, "is the part of our method which lends itself most easily to ritual."

Laoshi was similarly at pains to guard against providing technical "prescriptions" which might be applied without reference to the particulars of a given situation. Technical study, Laoshi believed, was not a "one-size-fits-all" formula to be applied indiscriminately and without sensitivity, rather, a sincere study of technique ought to lead to a refinement of sensitivity: to do the right thing, to the right extent, at the right time.

As to why Laoshi appeared selective, even reticent, in expressing this sentiment, I soon came to recognize, as a result of my own efforts at teaching, that *instruction is never delivered in a vacuum.* Each of us comes to our study with our own inclinations, predilections and preferences, and, as a result, our own unique imbalances. Each of us may require a nudge to left or right, depending on the state of those specific imbalances. The best teacher, sensitive to our divergence from "true," simply guides us by prompting us to balance yin and yang within ourselves.

Just as there is no algorithm to mastery in the performance of the art, there exists no single blueprint for effective transmission of the art from one to another.

Chapter 6: The Three Timings

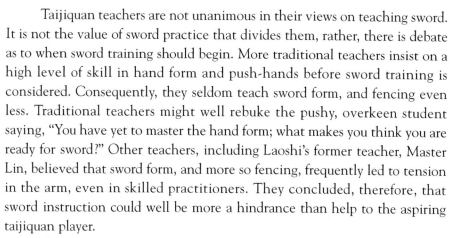

Taijiquan teachers are not unanimous in their views on teaching sword. It is not the value of sword practice that divides them, rather, there is debate as to when sword training should begin. More traditional teachers insist on a high level of skill in hand form and push-hands before sword training is considered. Consequently, they seldom teach sword form, and fencing even less. Traditional teachers might well rebuke the pushy, overkeen student saying, "You have yet to master the hand form; what makes you think you are ready for sword?" Other teachers, including Laoshi's former teacher, Master Lin, believed that sword form, and more so fencing, frequently led to tension in the arm, even in skilled practitioners. They concluded, therefore, that sword instruction could well be more a hindrance than help to the aspiring taijiquan player.

Zheng Manqing appears to have had varying views on the matter: in Taiwan, he taught very little sword, whereas in New York, he made both sword form and fencing pillars of his approach to taijiquan.

Coming from an aikido background, which viewed sword as an indispensable part of the art, I was heartened by Laoshi's view that taiji sword was an indispensible component of the complete art of taijiquan. More than once, he advised us: "What you discover in push-hands informs your fencing; what you discover in fencing, informs your push-hands. They are like legs: it is easier to walk than to hop, so use them both." To galvanize our flagging spirits when progress seemed remote and slow, Laoshi would also say: "When you find yourself stuck in push-hands, find the answer in fencing; when you find yourself stuck in fencing, find the answer in push-hands."

This was not to say that Laoshi tolerated slackness in technique, whether in sword form or fencing. "Sword form is not merely waving a stick in the air," Laoshi frequently admonished us. We were assured by word and deed that mastering the sword was a lifetime's undertaking. A student once asked Laoshi if he subscribed to the saying that "learning the saber takes one hundred days, whereas learning the sword takes ten thousand days." Laoshi replied crisply, "To master the sword might take ten thousand days, if you practice for several hours every day. If you practice only once a week, for a single hour, mastery will lie beyond your life-time."

Laoshi applied this uncompromising attitude to himself as much as his students. As a result, Laoshi was constantly seeking to improve his own understanding of sword form and its application in fencing. Just how much effort he put into sword study became clear to me during the hours we spent fencing in Laoshi's garden, often watched unblinkingly by his cat. These sessions were intense, as Laoshi was preparing me for my first attempt at teaching sword form to a group of students.

Interestingly, Laoshi's preferred method was to devote almost the entire session to fencing, Laoshi played with me like a mouse, the cat looking on with interest, seldom "cutting" me, but simply moving in and out of range with his sword, remaining connected to mine. His skill in slipping round the "yang" in my sword was sublime, if annoying, and I frequently found his sword sliding up my sleeve. When, laughingly, I demanded to know what allure my sleeve held for his sword, Laoshi replied simply, his eyes a-twinkle, that it was, "Just for fun." Cutting me was not sufficient challenge it seemed, and so he amused himself by targeting the gap between my wrist and sleeve. I began to appreciate the preposterous-sounding "pinnacle" of skill as proposed by Wang Lang: "Your skill in fencing should reach the point, where you can close distance with your partner, remove the glasses from his nose, clean them, and return them without him being able to stop you." Occasionally, I found myself wishing I wore glasses if only to see what Laoshi would do.

Although fencing with Laoshi was uniquely frustrating, it did seem to be bearing fruit. During regular fencing sessions in class, I felt my improvement gather pace, accompanied by a marked reduction in "advice" from more senior students. Lectures on my inadequacies were now replaced by a grim determination to "cut" me. I welcomed this as an indication of progress.

On the eve of teaching my first sword class, Laoshi halted our fencing practice and invited me to take a seat in his garden. He brought out some cool drinks as I relaxed in the sunshine.

"Your technique in sword is improving," he began after a mouthful of iced tea. "Fencing practice has put some feeling into your memorized choreography of the sword form, so the principles are in place and gradually being refined. To these basic ideas, you have added to your understanding of *yin* and *yang* on the sword blade, and you are beginning to exert some control over the opponent's sword. You are also on nodding terms with gaining *sente* (initiative). Now we must discuss timing."

Laoshi looked at me directly, "In fencing, faced with an opponent, what is your strategy?"

"Well…" I ventured carefully, unsure of my ground, "I guess, as a taijiquan player, I wait for him to attack me, and then I yield to his force."

"In which case," pressed Laoshi, "who has the *sente?*"

"Umm… I guess the opponent has," I offered, feeling myself grow hot under the sun and Laoshi's gaze. I knew I was out of my depth.

"Hmm… so that is why you will lose when you fence with me. You allow me the initiative, so I enter and take control, and you dance to my tune until I let you off the hook. Once I have the sente, the outcome has been decided: I either cut you, or let you escape, but I am in control. The battle is over, perhaps not when the swords cross, but certainly when one fencer has the initiative."

I could not argue. How many times had I already experienced Laoshi moving in to control my sword, pursuing me as if he were the cat and I was the mouse.

"So, should I attack you first, Laoshi?" I asked. But, even as the words left my mouth, I knew the answer to my own question. Instinctively, I understood that success in swordsmanship should not depend on who attacks first.

"Not necessarily," responded Laoshi, confirming me in my instincts.

"But what then?" My brow creased in puzzlement. "If you attack me first, how can I gain the initiative?"

"Ah well… By using *late initiative*," replied Laoshi. "Obviously!" he added, a mischievous glint in his eye. I had to smile. Laoshi was still fencing with me. I played along.

"Okay then, Laoshi," I grinned. "What is *late initiative?*"

"Ha! I thought you'd never ask," laughed Laoshi. "Well now… Did your aikido teacher ever mention *go-no-sen* or *sen-no-sen?*"

I thought for a moment. As it happened, I did recall Billy mentioning the terms *sen*, *sen-no-sen*, and *sen sen-no-sen* some years ago. Unfortunately, I had not mined that vein very deeply at the time, and so retained only a superficial understanding of the terms. I indicated as much to Laoshi.

"Not to worry," nodded Laoshi consolingly, "I will explain. There are three possible timings in fencing: for instance, should you attack me first, I can yield to that attack, deflect your blade with mine, then counterattack. You may have attacked first, but I still capture the *sente*. This is called *late initiative*. Your teacher would have referred to this as *sen* or, perhaps, *go-no-sen*.

"However, if you attack, and I counter at precisely the same time, this we can call *mutual initiative*. You are defeated just at the precise moment you thought you had won. This, the Japanese arts refer to as *sen-no-sen*.

42

"In the third scenario, I attack you just at the point when you are beginning your own attack, but have yet to deliver your thrust or cut. Being already committed to your intended action, you cannot react when I take advantage of the gap between action and thought. This I would call *prior initiative*. Your teacher would likely have referred to this as *sen sen-no-sen*."

Laoshi checked my expression to see if I was following his explanation. "You already understand *late initiative*, I think?" queried Laoshi. "You first deflect, then counter-attack. Yes?"

"Yes, Laoshi," I concurred. "But I thought that was what everybody did in taijiquan: wait for the attack, and then yield before responding. I'm not sure that I grasp the idea of *mutual initiative*. Are you saying that you can yield and respond at exactly the same time?"

"That is exactly what I am saying!" Laoshi confirmed. "Have faith—it will happen for you soon. When it does, you simply have to recognize what has occurred."

I shook my head in perplexity. "I'm not sure how it will happen, if I don't know what it is I am actually trying to do…"

"Ah well… fortunately," smiled Laoshi, "your heart-mind will do it for you. I only tell you this so that you might recognize it when it happens and build from there." His smile broadened, as he cast his mind back: "I can still vividly recall my first experience of mutual initiative. I had traveled to London to take some private instruction with Dr. Qin over a period of two weeks. Dr. Qin was a senior student of Zheng Manqing, who possessed a burning desire to understand the art of the sword. After a brief familiarization of basic sword principles, we would fence for three hours daily throughout the duration of my stay. Time and time again, Dr. Qin would batter my hand with his wooden sword, sometimes severely. I felt the blood of my anger rise, but controlled myself, and 'ate bitterness,' my desire to learn apparently matching Dr. Qin's desire 'to *make* me learn.'

"After ten days of Dr. Qin's close attention, 'it' happened. With our swords connected, Dr. Qin moved in to attack, his blade slicing perilously toward my already-bruised hand. Without the slightest thought, I slid my blade around his and hit him on the wrist at precisely the same time that I would customarily have received yet another painful blow from the edge of Dr. Qin's sword.

"Dr. Qin broke into a huge smile, breeching the intensity of his customary fencing demeanor. 'Wonderful!' he shouted, and hugged me. I actually felt moved emotionally. 'That is the feeling!' Dr. Qin continued to enthuse. 'Remember it well, each time it happens. Soon it will be yours to command.'"

"I don't know, Laoshi. It sounds more like mind reading than fencing,"

I exclaimed in mild exasperation, as Laoshi paused to take another long drink from his glass.

"It can seem that way," Laoshi acknowledged. "But the best is yet to come. When you have mastered *mutual initiative*, you will sense the merest hint of something even more amazing."

"You mean *sen sen no-sen?*" I supplied dryly, fearing for my capacity to ever make any real progress in this art.

"Precisely!" Laoshi remarked, brightly ignoring my depressed air, "although I prefer to use the term '*prior initiative.*'"

"*Prior initiative.*" I mulled the term over, trying to recall Billy's mention of *sen sen no sen* and wring out some meaning. "So… *prior initiative*," I added hesitantly. "That is when you sense the opponent is about to attack, then rush in quickly to get the advantage?"

The question mark hung in the air. "Hmm, you are half right," Laoshi smiled. "The truth is you cannot rely on being physically faster than your opponent. For example, as we age, we tend to slow down, so the speed of the body must be replaced by sensitivity. The power lies not in the ability to move quicker, but in the ability to attack between your opponent's movement and the thought that follows their movement."

"Sorry, Laoshi," I interrupted, my thoughts racing to keep up. "Don't you mean the movement that follows the thought?"

"Did I say 'the movement that follows the thought?'"

"Er… no, Laoshi, no you did not."

"Well then." Laoshi spread his palms as if that was explanation enough and repeated. "The movement comes *before* the thought."

So now I was thoroughly confused. Was Laoshi saying that the thought "attack" happens *after* the attack is underway? I sought Laoshi's confirmation.

"Indeed," Laoshi nodded. "It is entirely possible that we physically initiate the process which leads to an attack before we become consciously aware of doing so. The thinking mind only catches up with what is going on shortly afterwards."

"But how can that be!" I was incredulous. "Surely, we have to think about doing something first, then we do it?"

"*Do we?*" Laoshi smiled. "Or is the notion of voluntary action instead an illusion of the mind reacting to what the body is already doing?"

"Hold on, Laoshi," I protested: "I decide to move, then I move. It's common sense. How can I move *before* deciding to move?"

"Uh-huh. And how exactly do you *decide* to decide?" Laoshi was having a wonderful time, while my head was beginning to hurt. Laoshi pressed on: "In any case, there is a gap between movement and thought. In that gap, the opponent is as vulnerable as if they have come home and neglected to lock the front door. If you can wait until the right moment arrives, you may simply walk in. You then have *prior initiative*. Any reaction from your opponent is now 'a day late and a dollar short' as Wang Lang would say."

I was unable to make sense of Laoshi's assertion, conceptually speaking, so practically, I was no further ahead.

Months passed, and the lessons of that afternoon had begun to fade, until that is, I faced Tom one evening in class, fencing. Tom was a naturally talented fencer, whose skills tested mine to the limit. Until now, the ability to survive unmauled was the closest I could come to "victory." That particular evening, however, the concept of *mutual initiative*—out of nowhere—transformed into tangible reality. Near the beginning of our practice, Tom tried to slide his sword underneath mine in order to attack the right side of my chest. Bizarrely, as if a spectator to my own actions, I seemed merely to observe as my blade rolled around Tom's, and he walked into the point of my sword. Some slight and unknown adjustment on my part had effortlessly deflected his sword to one side, just as my sword point found its way to his chest.

Laoshi's words came immediately to mind: *"Your heart-mind will do it for you. I only tell you this so that you recognize it when it happens and build from there."* Tom also recognized "it," nodding simple acknowledgement, as we resumed our swordplay. Perhaps attempting to re-examine what had just happened, Tom made the same attack seconds later, with the same outcome. The only difference this time was the increased speed of Tom's attack, and the correspondingly deeper dig to his chest from my sword point. I muttered an apology, as Tom rubbed his ribs. "One moment…" Tom broke off our encounter and returned to his sword bag leaning against the wall. For a second, I feared he was injured. I felt some relief, then, when he returned to the floor, this time armed with a lighter, quicker sword. I smiled. Tom had assumed that the imprint of my sword point on his chest was due to a defect in his equipment, rather than his technique.

As it turned out, Tom may have felt vindicated, as he proceeded to give me a difficult time from there on in. Two instances of *mutual initiative*, in quick succession, it seemed was as much as my heart-mind would allow for one evening. Such is the way of things, but the reality of *mutual initiative* was now assured. As Laoshi had predicted, that reality became mine to command.

In the days following my moment of insight in fencing with Tom, I took to reading *Zheng Manqing's Thirteen Treatises*, as translated by Ben Lo and Martin Inn. The following extracts leapt from the page to imprint themselves on my mind:

45

"When you stick to him, then your qi and his qi make contact. Through this contact of qi you begin to anticipate his attempts. This is called *ting*. The Classics say "If he moves a little I move first" on which *ting* is based."

...and again...

"If my opponent moves even slightly, I can hear and comprehend him. When I comprehend his jin, then I can move first. Having the correct timing and position depends on me and not on him."

I felt certain I must have read those passages previously. Perhaps the significance had simply eluded me at the time. Now, I began to marvel at the possibilities of taijiquan: I speculated upon the mysterious upper levels of the art, where a slight movement in the opponent's energy would betray his intention and ensure his defeat. Though I still remained unsure as to whether movement preceded thought, or vice versa, I became determined to discover the secrets of "correct timing."

Chapter 7: Enter Like Water

Laoshi and I were fencing one afternoon in his garden. At the time, my estimation of my own fencing ability was growing, not because I found myself winning more than losing, but due to the increasingly devious tactics employed by fellow students to get the better of me. Faced with my improving skills, my colleagues ever more frequently resorted to the "evil twins" of fencing: speed and strength. Laoshi, of course, was another matter. As he effortlessly closed distance between us, I was obliged to employ increasingly desperate, if futile, means to avoid his advance. Within seconds of our swords engaging, Laoshi angled his blade into a position of dominance and controlled my sword with embarrassing ease. The almost magnetic connection, which seemed to bind my sword to his, had developed from an intermittent, almost casual occurrence, at our first meeting, to an ever-present, frustrating inevitability. I felt that I was not in command of my own sword; rather, I was a marionette dancing to the tune of Laoshi's swordplay.

And then I noticed a subtle but detectable change: instead of sliding past the yang point on my blade to position his sword point close to my throat, Laoshi began blocking and shoving my sword to the side. At first, I presumed that the fifteen minutes spent chasing me across the garden, as I attempted to evade his sword, had bored him into adjusting his strategy, but I was taken aback by the uncharacteristic forcefulness in his fencing and failed to react in any meaningful way.

"Why do you not enter when you have the chance?" Laoshi asked, after a few minutes of the new approach. "Do you not feel the push from my sword?"

"Well… yes, Laoshi," I replied uncertainly, "but I was unsure about what was going on: your fencing is usually less pushy."

"Well, *do it now*," Laoshi instructed, "When you feel the *yang* in my sword, attack the other side."

It was an underlying tenet of Laoshi's approach to the sword that a solid understanding of the defensive structure of sword and body should first be acquired. This foundation should then be followed by application of the concept of *yin* and *yang* as a means of attacking, even a secure defense. As Laoshi pointed out many times, "Understanding *yin* and *yang* 'trumps' the study of sword position." In our fencing practice, victory was seldom measured by Laoshi "cutting" me. Instead, he sought a higher level of skill, closing distance and controlling the *yang* point created in my blade by my ineffectual blocking and evasion. Once I was controlled and effectively "stuck," Laoshi's final cut, if he even bothered to deliver one, was a mere formality. Laoshi was now insisting that I utilize the *yin-yang* concept to counter his forcefulness.

However, it was not the theory that was beyond me, rather, I was unable to discern the precise moment at which the execution of that theory should take place. I had become sensitive enough to "hear" the blocking of other students as we fenced, and I was also now able to intuit the location of the vulnerable *yin* point on my opponent's sword, which arises mutually with the *yang* of blocking. No, the problem that presently confronted me was one of diminishing the delay between feeling the block, seeing the opening, and then, recognizing the existence of an opportunity, effectively executing an appropriate counterattack. I found myself unable to respond speedily enough for the "opportunity" to still be present by the time my riposte arrived. A habitual delay had insinuated itself between my recognition of the opportunity and grasping the moment as it presented.

Laoshi confirmed my assessment, when, in my frustration, I sought his wisdom on the matter. As I had come to learn, in asking for a master's insight, the question is often simply reflected straight back to you: *"You learn to do it by doing it,"* one might hear. Or else bizarrely, *"If I show you how it's done, you won't know how to do it."* I do not deny that the simple elegance of reflecting back the problem can provoke a breakthrough in understanding, albeit by adding to the underlying frustration, but sometimes you just want a straight answer. I once asked an aikido *shihan* why his feet were sometimes together when making a sword cut, and at other times apart. *"There is no Why,"* he informed me brusquely, leaving me torn between the brilliance of the response and the frustration of the question unanswered. Fortunately, for me on this occasion, Laoshi had something more concrete to offer.

As often, when pausing to explain a matter, Laoshi now cradled the blade of his wooden fencing sword in the crook of his left elbow, the hilt resting in his hand with the little finger wrapped round the hand guard, a pose I found myself copying unconsciously, "You are not unique in finding difficulty recognizing opportunity for 'attack,'" mused Laoshi. "It is common amongst students of sword. The difficulty arises due to a mistaken notion on our part."

"What notion is that Laoshi?" I pursued, my brows knitted in curiosity.

"Well… the notion that there is a difference between 'defense' and 'attack.'" He motioned for me to take a seat. "Nearly all students approach sword study with an assumption that these two ideas are separate, assuming that one follows the other. This is not so. Rather, we might say that there should always be 'defense' in 'attack,' and also that there should always be 'attack' in 'defense.' However, it is better not to burden a beginner with the truth of the matter, when they already have too much on their minds. Indeed, the effort to pry out a misconception sometimes only succeeds in entrenching it ever deeper. Like so much in teaching, it is better to wait until the student is tired of pressing 'dung' to their breast, mistaking it for gold. I see you are ready to drop some dung, so to speak," Laoshi observed dryly with a twinkle of mischief in his eye.

I had the urge to laugh at Laoshi's little joke but fearing to lose my thread, I shook my head in an effort to concentrate, and pressed the point: "So… Laoshi, how do we heal the division in our thinking between attack and defense? If I've understood correctly, how do we eliminate delay in seizing opportunity?"

"Ah, well now," Laoshi nodding enthusiastically…"Delay in grasping opportunity is not confined to the practice hall; it is present in our daily lives, as we procrastinate and allow opportunity to slip by. Often, we can see how to proceed, but delay action, and then opportunity passes.

Sensing a story-to-come, I remained quiet. I was not long in waiting, as Laoshi took up his theme "You recall I made mention of one of my former teachers, who lived in a Buddhist center in the Borders?"

I nodded in affirmation. "Well, one day my old teacher was dispatched to meet and greet a high-ranking Buddhist Lama, who was on his way to visit the retreat center. At the local train station, my teacher, Don, had no trouble in identifying the visitor, who was a large man, adorned in purple robes. Don introduced himself and deposited the Lama's bags in the back of the old van for the forty-minute journey though the remote Scottish uplands. Climbing aboard, the visiting lama seemed friendly enough, asking lots of questions, as he took in the scenery. Once off the main road and onto the narrow, twisting, country lanes typical of that part of Scotland, the Lama suddenly turned to Don and said, 'Do you want to fly?'

"Don was taken aback. He was a believer in the mysterious, and, furthermore, was absolutely certain that Tibetan lamas were custodians of mystical practices that enabled them to perform magic. So... he began to ponder whether the Lama had the power to physically transport them through the air to their destination, or whether there was some symbolic meaning in the question. For a few intense and pregnant moments, Don's mind tried to make sense of the offer presented to him. He considered the many possible and varied implications of what might happen next. Finally, he replied, 'yes.'"

"And, what happened next?" I pressed Laoshi eagerly.

"Nothing," replied Laoshi, "The Lama merely shook his head and remarked, 'Too heavy!' Don was left bemused and rather deflated. The remainder of the journey continued in silence. Later when he had some time to reflect, Don interpreted the Lama's response to mean that Don was too cerebral, over analytical. Don lamented the adventure his delay might have cost him."

"He was too heavy in his thinking?" I sought to clarify.

"Possibly," mused Laoshi. "You might also say too hesitant, too indecisive, too cautious."

"Double-weighted?" I offered.

"That could be," Laoshi nodded. "At any rate, he was not spontaneous. In your fencing, it is the same. There has to be spontaneity within the technique. That is to say not so much absence of technique, but freedom from rigid form."

"So, does spontaneity arise simply from practice, or can we coax it out of ourselves in any other way?" I queried. I was not entirely convinced that one could "coax" spontaneity.

"Well... when we practice with awareness, spontaneity is more likely to arise," offered Laoshi.

He must have noted my expression of continuing doubt, for he continued. "Okay, try thinking about it like this: the water in an aquarium is contained by the glass walls, yes?"

I nodded.

"And if the glass walls should shatter, the result would be that..."

"The water rushes out," I completed Laoshi's sentence without hesitation.

"Indeed," rejoined Laoshi. "And so consider: there is no delay. The

49

moment the aquarium wall cracks, the water is already through. In other words, the glass breaking and the water rushing through happen simultaneously. Why? Because the water is continually pressing against the wall of the aquarium: it is always testing the limits of its confinement.

"There are key lessons contained in this idea, not least being that we do not merely settle for our level of understanding at present, we are continually seeking the breakthrough which will lead us to the next level. Also, although *physically* we maintain softness in our sword arm, *mentally* we are constantly reaching out toward our attacker. Our intention—our qi—is directed outward. We are not simply 'in neutral,' waiting for our attacker to instigate action, we have already engaged."

"But," I broke in, fearing a flaw in Laoshi's reasoning, "didn't Zheng Manqing say something to the effect that *we wait for the attacker to move, and then take advantage of his energy?*" It would be a rare thing for Laoshi to contradict Zheng Manqing!

"Correct," concurred Laoshi unperturbed, "Zheng Manqing did indeed make such a declaration, although he did not dismiss the possibility of preemptive strike, when circumstances dictate."

"And so you are saying…" I invited Laoshi to explain further.

Laoshi smiled. "I am saying that *physically* we wait for the attacker to come to us, but *mentally* we are already engaged. We do not handicap our own defense by having to respond from a cold start, *energetically speaking*. By expanding our energy outward we are reaching out mentally, even though we are not moving outward *physically*. Or put another way, physically we remain *yin*; mentally we are already *yang*."

In the days that followed, I endeavored to put Laoshi's words into practice. At times, I thought I was making progress, but still felt that I was pursuing a technicality, rather than experiencing a meaningful feeling. Laoshi was both patient and sympathetic, seeking to shed light on his meaning from different angles: "Do you recall that I told you of the long hours spent in a car with Wang Lang, as he traveled around to his various classes?"

I nodded. I often compared Laoshi's stories of the time he had with Wang Lang with my own experiences spending time with Laoshi.

"Do you also remember," continued Laoshi, "that on the longer routes, I would drive his car?"

I nodded once again.

"Well, acting as Wang Lang's chauffeur was a tricky business. Apart from anything else, the stick shift, as they call it, was on the 'wrong' side for me, as was the traffic. More difficult, however, was Wang Lang's insistence that his car, an old Toyota, be driven in precisely the same way that he would drive it, even to the extent of changing gears at exactly the same time that he would change gears. His old Toyota had shared the road with him for many years, boasting a mileage of which two cars would have been proud. The engine was essentially sound and would remain so, in Wang Lang's view, if only the car was driven as he directed."

"The value of 'taiji' driving," I commented with a grin.

"Possibly," acknowledged Laoshi, smiling. "Anyway, with Wang Lang in the passenger seat, scrutinizing every move, chauffeuring him around was not at all a comfortable experience. Adding to the stress of driving on unfamiliar roads—traffic on the wrong side of the carriageway, and the gear stick in an unfamiliar position—was the feeling of near malevolence that would emanate from the passenger seat, whenever I changed gear a thousand revs too early or too late."

"Did Wang Lang ever say anything? Or was it just the feeling of his energy that you detected?" I asked, wondering if Laoshi's imagination was the real culprit.

"Well... I was not alone in experiencing a feeling of negativity," replied Laoshi. "Another student confided to me that she only ever drove his car once. 'Never again,' she told me, 'as the vibe in the car was so hostile!'"

"So what did you do, Laoshi?" I pursued, eager to cut to the chase.

"Do?!" laughed Laoshi. "The only thing I could do was, as I became aware of this cold, clammy energy seeping toward me across the space between us, I expanded my own energy and pushed back!"

I couldn't help but grin as I pictured an old car, barely containing Laoshi and Wang Lang and their dueling energies. Ridiculous as the image was, I was suddenly reminded of those times, when, dealing with a particularly difficult person, I could feel my own spirit recoiling before their, to me, negative, unpleasant presence. On such occasions, my spirit seemed to be cowering several feet behind me, leaving only my body in place, unable to escape, and enduring bad breath, boring company, or caustic comments, with a thin, forced smile on my face. I may not have conceded ground *physically*, but certainly I was being dominated *energetically*.

"I think I get it, Laoshi, about reaching out with energy, I mean. But how do I reach out when the other person's energy is so... off-putting?"

"Mmm, indeed," replied Laoshi with feeling. "So... imagine that you are looking at someone you truly love, standing a few feet away. But then imagine that the person you love suddenly changes into a dirty, down-and-out drunk, who smells from every orifice. Does the feeling change within you?"

I thought that the answer to that question was rather obvious, but I said nothing, fully expecting Laoshi to continue. "Have you ever wondered what it means to love everybody?" asked Laoshi quietly, as if musing to himself. "Perhaps it means that we do not hesitate to extend our energy towards that drunken bum, any less than we would toward the person we love. We don't have to hold hands, or give them money, or even utter a word, but simply extend toward them with our energy. Then do as we feel appropriate. Possibly to do so is more productive than fearfully contracting our energy in the face of difficult people or difficult situations. Possibly, 'loving others' does not mean contriving to be 'nice' or 'kind,' when we are not genuinely feeling it. Very possibly, extending love to another simply means being fully present before them and truly seeing who they are. No more, and no less: it is just you seeing the whole of them, with the whole of you."

It was not the first time I had heard love being mentioned in the context of martial arts. Did O'Sensei Ueshiba not say, "Budo is God's love?" But, at the time, Laoshi's assertion seemed astonishing to me, so much so, that I could make no cogent reply. I resumed fencing in order to cover the silence booming in my head. When I stole a glance at Laoshi, he seemed entirely at ease, neither perplexed nor impatient at my lack of response. His equanimity encouraged me to venture: "So... er... what you were saying is that the sort of reaching out we do when fencing?" I felt myself reluctant to mention love to Laoshi, even though he was the one who brought it up.

Laoshi never wavered from his fencing, but nodded assent. "Reach out with your qi, or intention, or feeling, whatever you want to call it—perhaps even love," he added with a wink.

Bloody Laoshi!

In spite of my initial resistance, something of Laoshi's words must have infiltrated my being, for in the weeks that followed, I found I that was able to detect slight pushes from Laoshi's sword and slip inside his guard. Gradually, as we practiced the gaps between my sensing the yang in his sword and the impulse to enter in became less stifled; opportunity and action were tending toward one. "I've got it!" I began thinking, though often a temporary thought when studying with Laoshi.

"Not bad," he remarked approvingly, "You are just a little too tense, too insistent. You are like a greyhound waiting for the rabbit at the racetrack," Laoshi grinned.

I felt the truth of Laoshi's words, yet also resolved to fill myself with positivity.

"Good!" I heard him say, "That's the way! Expand against my words. Listen to them, be guided by them, but don't be cowed by them.

"Remember the water in the aquarium?" Laoshi asked, as we continued to circle each other. "It may be pressing and probing for weaknesses in the walls of the aquarium, but there is no insistence in its probing. It is content to be contained." I grunted acknowledgement, as we continued fencing and I tried to reconcile "expansion" with "containment."

"The surface of the water is also calm, and like the surface of a loch on a very still, summer's day," continued Laoshi. "It reflects exactly what is there. It is a true reflection, not one distorted by agitation on the surface. So, you could say…" Laoshi caught my eye, "the impulse to enter must be balanced by the quality of… reflectiveness."

Interestingly, Laoshi's words nudged some memory inside of me, if only I could pin it down. The words "true reflection" reminded me of the early days of my aikido training. At the time, my teacher Billy Coyle called his aikido school *Kokoro E.* He explained that the meaning was "true reflection," an expression of the sincerity at the heart of our practice.

Another Japanese phrase came to mind, *mizu no kokoro*, which is usually translated as "mind like water," suggesting calmness in the face of the challenges of life, a calm mind, like the surface of the loch reflecting the entire sky without limits or distortion by thought.

It was at that moment that insight struck: on the surface, the loch is calm, but underneath, the tremendous weight of the volume of water, contained by the loch, is pressing down on the bed below, penetrating into every crevice, seeking for every opportunity to flow.

I put this new realization to Laoshi.

"Exactly so!" he beamed, "on the surface, we appear yin, yet inside, we are yang. The body is quiet and still, yet the qi inside is active. When applied to fencing, this idea means that to the onlooker, we may appear to be doing very little, yet *mentally*, through the point of contact with our opponent's sword, we are most decidedly active, always seeking for the *yang* on our opponent's blade and flowing around it, just as water parts when confronted by a rock in the river. We are unstoppable.

"As Zheng Manqing says, 'Study the *yin*, then the *yang*, and then put them together.' When we fill the *yin* of our sword with the *yang* of our mind, we are beginning to blend *yin* and *yang* into one."

Of course, with Laoshi, there was always another level. He finished the lesson by saying, "Once you have mastered this, we will talk about how to put the *yin* into the *yang*."

I simply nodded, "Yes, Laoshi." I had more than enough to think about for the time being.

Once, during a discussion concerning making progress in aikido, my old teacher Billy Coyle remarked: "If you attend class once a week, you will stay where you are; if you attend twice a week, then you improve slowly; if you attend three times a week you improve a little less slowly."

According to Billy, therefore, progress required a bare minimum of a two hours practice, twice a week. Over the years, I have reached a similar conclusion in respect of push-hands and fencing, and Laoshi, I believe, felt much the same. He told me once of a push-hands workshop he had conducted in Spain some years before, and the degree of disquiet that emerged over the price he charged for his instruction.

As Laoshi said of the incident, "At the time, I was surprised and a little irritated as the rumblings of discontent reached my ears. From my point of view, the quality of instruction was good, and I had pushed hands with each individual several times over the weekend. I had put in a 'good shift,' as they say, just not enough, it seemed, to satisfy a small group of students, who somehow felt 'short-changed.' Later, I realized that my limited grasp of the Spanish language had been responsible for a misunderstanding that was only corrected some years later.

"Many of those attending the course, including several teachers, had journeyed from the various regions of Spain. I had assumed that the skills I was teaching would be practiced diligently once they had returned to their own schools. Only later did I discover that, for the most part, those attending the workshop did no regular push-hands at all, but instead, only attending occasional weekend workshops, such as my own throughout the year. I had presumed that my instruction was to introduce ideas, which could be polished in regular practice time prior to the next workshop. I had not realized that these irregular weekend workshops were the only opportunity many had to push-hands at all. At home, meanwhile, they only practiced form, and so they wanted more time to practice whenever the opportunity presented."

So far, so understandable, I thought. But Laoshi's next comment took me aback at first: "They were wasting their time, you know."

It was not that Laoshi thought occasional weekend seminars were a waste of time per se, rather that, in isolation, the benefits of one-off seminars were limited, lacking as they did the solid foundation of regular push-hands practice. Nevertheless, when integrated with ongoing daily or weekly practice, additional seminars could prove invaluable. As a consequence, here in Glasgow, Laoshi conducted frequent push-hands and fencing workshops as supplements to the regular school curriculum, which allowed his students the opportunity to increase our "time on the court." Correspondingly, a supplementary fee was charged for these additional sessions, over and above the monthly class fee.

Although the fee was a relatively small sum, the matter of a few pounds, one of the students, possibly dealing with a financial crisis at the time, disclosed his irritation at the prospect of paying a supplement. Venting his displeasure at a weekend workshop, he appeared to challenge Laoshi with his tone: "So, Laoshi, is money so important to you?"

All at once, Laoshi's eyes narrowed in Rodney's direction, compelling the latter to seek reassurance by glancing toward me. As a recent recruit to push-hands class and more my student than Laoshi's, Rodney was yet to appreciate that Laoshi was not a man to shrink from implied criticism, no matter how subtle, or otherwise, the delivery. If Rodney was suddenly experiencing nervousness, perceiving that he had crossed the line of courtesy, then that was his own lookout. I felt he deserved whatever came next. And yet, by that time, I knew Laoshi to be both sincere and more generous than not in spirit. Amidst the moments of pregnant silence, I knew that Laoshi was coolly assessing the author of this impertinence, the unfortunate Rodney. I was intrigued, as was the entire room, to discover how Laoshi would deal with him.

Laoshi did not move from the spot where he was standing, but directed his full attention across the room towards Rodney, whose eyes were darting around the room as if seeking either allies or escape. Yet Laoshi's reply, when it came, was spoken softly and with a quiet energy, which reached into all four corners of the practice hall: "For me, money is the most important thing in the world." He paused dramatically, allowing an exchange of glances around the room. Laoshi's simple lifestyle belied so great an interest in money.

He continued, "And yet, at the same time, money is also the least important thing in the world. Money is important because, without it, I would not have the freedom to practice my art as I wish. I would have to take a job, and a 'job' is not the same as work. Work is what we do to make real what is in our heart, but a job is what we do for money. I am fortunate because the Dao has allowed me sufficient resources to pursue what is in my heart. Those resources are a gift from the Dao, and as such, they are important. They are not to be wasted, but treated with care in order that my heart's desire can remain alive."

A pin might have been heard to drop in the practice hall. We all were listening intently, as Laoshi addressed Rodney, struck by the calm and open tone of Laoshi's words.

"My relationship with money," continued Laoshi, now addressing his comments to us all, "is more direct than is yours. Most of you work for someone else, either a private company or for local government. I do not. I am, for legal purposes, termed 'self-employed.' This means that I am obliged to concern myself with the notion of profit and loss in a way that you, as an employee, do not: I set the price for my time, you do not; I take cash directly for my efforts, you do not; I decide when and for how long I work, you do not.

"Furthermore," he added, still with calm and quiet assurance, "I enjoy no holiday pay, sickness pay, or national insurance credits. My financial security is minimal, since a decline in student numbers results in dwindling income. I am obliged to maintain my affairs to the satisfaction of the Inland Revenue. I am further obliged to purchase, to my mind, redundant liability insurance each year in order to satisfy the health and safety requirements of those who rent halls to me. I have no built-in pension pot; I can never retire, and am obliged to teach until my last breath. I have no complaint, as this is my choice. Notwithstanding, the fulfillment found in following the Way, is accompanied by not insignificant insecurity.

Laoshi's final words on the matter still remain with me to this day:

"If money *wasn't* important, I *couldn't* teach taijiquan for a living.
If money *was* important, I *wouldn't* teach taijiquan for a living."

A number of the students, Rodney included, nodded in silent acknowledgement of his words. No more was said upon the matter. Class continued as usual.

I was not surprised that Laoshi's tone had been neither angry, nor bitter, nor whining, yet such revelations were rare in so private a man. I sensed in his disclosures an attempt to discuss honestly a subject, which still had the power to trouble him. Witnessing his discomfort, as uninformed or misguided students occasionally attempted to negotiate a reduction in fees, it was clear that Laoshi still struggled with the fiscal aspect of running a taijiquan school.

On one occasion, as I waited behind after class, I observed the scene, as a young professional woman was insisting on a discount. She had missed several classes over the previous months and was now advising Laoshi that she would miss a few more toward the end of the term. It was only fair, she declared, that a discount should be offered on the month's fees.

Laoshi regarded the young woman for a few moments without speaking before casually asking why she would miss so many classes. I was dumbstruck when she replied: "Well, I'll be away in the United States for a few weeks. There is this really great "Healing with Crystals" workshop I want to attend, but first I will be going to mine my own crystals in Arizona at this special crystal mine. It's so exciting! Then I will be going to Thailand to study qigong for a month, but, when I get back, I really want to study with you, as well."

Laoshi then asked who her teacher would be in Thailand. On hearing the teacher's name Laoshi commented dryly, "Mmm, I hear he is expensive."

"Oh, yes," she replied with no hint of irony, "but he's very, very good."

Laoshi insisted that she pay a full month's tuition, which represented a fraction of the sum she would be paying for her aforementioned travel, accommodation, workshop fees, and qigong instruction—not to mention crystal mining. Finally, after a few more failed attempts to negotiate a discount, she paid up, remarking tartly, "I suppose you are teaching me a lesson of some kind, although I'm not sure what it is."

After that incident, I approached Laoshi and suggested that, in future, I should collect class fees, reasoning that it is often easier to ask for payment on behalf of someone else. I wanted to save Laoshi discomfort. He smiled his thanks to me, but declined my offer, saying, "I appreciate your concern. Indeed, at one time I did have a student collect money for me, but I discontinued the practice."

"Why Laoshi?"

"Well… it is precisely because I have difficulty with money that I ought not to avoid the lesson of asking for it. As you will have gathered, I am not comfortable asking for money, nor do I enjoy pressing people over money, but I cannot avoid my responsibility. I need to address my arrogance in this regard."

I was even more dumbstruck. Was Laoshi telling me that asking for rightful payment was a form of arrogance? "I don't understand, Laoshi," I exclaimed, expressing my confusion, "How is it that you are arrogant because other people wriggle out of paying you?! Is it not they who are arrogant?"

"They may very well be," he replied softly, "but that is their problem. They must face their issues; I must face mine."

"So…" I asked, confusion turning to doubt, "what exactly is your problem with money?"

"The same as yours, I suspect," Laoshi replied with a smile.

"What!" I blurted out.

"I see that you and I have a common view of money: that is, we somehow feel that it is beneath us to have to ask for the money. We feel we ought to be above something as crass as money. Speaking for myself now, I was brought up with peculiar notions concerning money and wealth, notions that I find hard to shake off. My family credo included an unhealthy contempt for people with money. I imagine it is a common defense for poor-but-decent people, who find themselves on the wrong end of the economic disparity in our society. Together with a longing for matters to be rectified in heaven after death, they sought to inoculate themselves to financial inequality with a mixture of religion and disdain. It is as good a defense as any, I suppose, but it can leave a person bitter, or, in my case, with a chip on the shoulder, which seems to grow heavier whenever I have to assert my right to payment."

"Yes, but Laoshi," I protested, "you make it sound as if it is your fault when people try to avoid paying you your due. And, you make it sound like it is my fault, too, when I experience the same thing as you." I felt uneasy as to where Laoshi's reasoning was headed.

"Well… By making it my *fault*, if that is the word you wish to use, I am not allowing myself to become a victim. If it is my *fault* (you can also call it responsibility), I can take steps to address matters. If I do not, then I allow myself to be prey to my negative feelings whenever I confront those who would wriggle out of their obligations. Furthermore, I would be denying them the full measure of myself as a teacher, by not taking the opportunity to show them the 'tightness' in their own relationship with money." I had not thought of that and took a moment to ponder: was Laoshi suggesting that he felt his teaching remit to extend to reflecting back to us, his students, our own distortions regarding money? It seemed to me an onerous and unlooked for burden of responsibility, and a lesson I did not feel convinced my own students would either understand or appreciate, should I venture to offer it to them. At the same time, I knew that Laoshi was concerned with sincerity in all things and so felt compelled to listen to his point of view.

Laoshi expanded: "If I avoid feeling uncomfortable by always escaping whenever I am faced with an unpleasantness, then I make a victim of myself. I have given power to circumstances by running away from my reactions. In truth, we are our own worst enemy. It is we who make ourselves victims. I will not be a victim."

Laoshi's perspective on the "payment predicament" called to mind one of my old martial arts clubs in Glasgow. Customarily, at the end of practice, we the students would retire to the bar of the sports center, along with our sensei. As well as socializing together, we took the opportunity to pay sensei our mat fees, or, more accurately, most of us did. Alex, a class regular, was the exception, and more often than not, he paid nothing at all. His excuse followed the same weary old refrain: "Sorry sensei, I haven't got any money this month. I'll pay you next time." His words belied the reality of his situation, for he appeared to be always in sufficient funds to return from the bar with his pint of beer and twenty cigarettes. Needless to say, "next time" never arrived and never was he called to account.

"It is a common problem," sighed Laoshi, as I related the story. "Even Zheng Manqing had difficulties of this sort in New York. Wang Lang told me that, at one time, the Professor was obliged to appoint a student to collect unpaid fees. As it turned out, this student was unsuited to the task and so it fell to Tam Gibbs to take on the job, which he did conscientiously. One day Tam approached Wang Lang to ask whether he was up to date with paying class fees. Wang Lang's reply impressed me with its sincerity. He told Tam, *'The first dime I make goes to Zheng Manqing.'* Tam was perhaps equally impressed by Wang Lang's honorable stand, for the two of them seemed to bond thereafter. Nevertheless, the story suggests that Wang Lang's honorable attitude was more rare than it was common, even in the New York Shr Jung School."

In the weeks that followed, I was granted a further insight into Laoshi's attitude toward money. One day a student approached Laoshi with a proposition on behalf of a well-known Scottish football player, who, now retired, was suffering severe back problems. The former footballer, hearing of taijiquan, hoped that it might be an alternative to the surgery his doctor was recommending. He was prepared to pay for private lessons, if Laoshi was willing. Due to the fame he enjoyed, the ex-footballer was keen to avoid regular classes, so private lessons seemed a sensible route.

Being sympathetic to the former athlete's problems, Laoshi agreed to a meeting to carry out an initial assessment, prior to committing to anything further.

"Okay, but how much will you charge for private lessons?" asked the footballer's go-between. "You know, money will not be a problem, here," he added with a knowing glance.

"Same as for anybody else," responded Laoshi casually.

I was perplexed. I asked Laoshi why he had not increased the charge. The footballer was wealthy, due to his success on the football field and associated sponsorships. As the go-between had pointed out, money was not a problem. Laoshi looked frankly baffled: "I would not be providing him with anything I do not offer to my other students, so why would I charge him more?"

"Because he can afford it, Laoshi," I replied, with a hint of frustration, "obviously."

"It does not matter how much money he has, the Dao is not for sale. I simply charge for the time I spend with someone. I teach what I teach, they learn what they learn, and they practice what they practice. The magnitude of a person's bank account doesn't come into it."

"Well... that is a noble attitude, I suppose Laoshi," I allowed grudgingly. "Lots of people would just see the dollar signs."

"There is nothing noble about it," Laoshi scoffed. "If I allowed myself to become fixated with money, then I would deserve whatever came next."

"So... what do you mean, Laoshi?"

"Understand this," Laoshi intoned carefully, "If you venture down the path of over-charging wealthy people, then you sell yourself cheap. You are no longer charging for your skills, you are charging for *who they are*, and they know it! You have created your own trap. Now you must ensure that they are 'happy' with you at all times, or you risk being discarded like toilet paper. You can no longer be *who you are*, you are obliged to be *who they think you should be*. The prospect of being fired, and losing your 'meal ticket,' traps you into serfdom. Better not to become trapped in the first place. Pretty soon, you will be washing their car, collecting their shirts from the drycleaner, and who knows what else. They will have bought you—and for next to nothing."

I had not thought of it like that. I felt slightly queasy, with a vague sense of shame on my readiness to leap all over the dollar sign. But Laoshi seemed to be speaking from a place of personal conviction. He was not admonishing me.

"So... er, how's it going with him anyway, the footballer I mean? How's his back?"

"Who knows," shrugged Laoshi good-naturedly. "Things went no further. Apparently, I was too cheap." Laoshi winked at me. "As far as I know, he is happily ensconced with a teacher who is charging him lots of money. He assumes that the value is the same as the cost."

And with that, Laoshi wandered off laughing heartily.

Chapter 9: Senior Class

As a student, eyes firmly on Laoshi, I had been blind to the view from his side of the floor: a sea of blank faces massing into an energetic desert, seeking inspiration from the well of the master. As a teacher, I came to appreciate the extent to which I had drawn from the well that was Laoshi, both within his home and at his weekly senior class. I was grateful that amid the structural changes to the school, our Tuesday senior students class remained untouched. Senior class was a weekly touchstone for me amidst change, which threatened to overwhelm. It provided a two-hour oasis where, under the watchful eye of Laoshi, I was simply another student, struggling with the mystery of push-hands and fencing.

Driving to senior class one cold, damp Tuesday evening, I recalled my time as a regular at Billy Coyle's Tuesday night aikido class. The memory of the Habonim Boys Club on Glasgow's south side, where Billy's genius graced the mat, remained with me two decades later and provided a point of contrast with Laoshi's senior class.

Traveling to Laoshi's class that evening, I felt myself eager to immerse myself in the practice. I experienced a quiet excitement at the prospect of meeting and crossing swords with, literally and figuratively, the other senior students, not to mention Laoshi himself who, even after all these years, remained keenly participative. "These are the days when I learn!" he would tell the seniors with relish. "Have no compassion in this class: be selfish and push beyond your limits. This is the best way to help your comrades here. Strive to outstrip each other, outshine each other and compel your comrades to reach up to your level, or else, watch them fall by the wayside." It was an uncompromising message: unashamedly elitist and competitive, and a sharp contrast with the more gentle "inclusive" tone of the form classes Laoshi had relinquished to me.

In senior class, the rigorous approach Laoshi expected from his students was more than matched by the demands he placed upon himself: "As you become better," he insisted, "you push me onwards, and we all improve together. Don't take it easy on me!"

As a result, while we all respected Laoshi enormously, the injunction to "have at him" was wholeheartedly obeyed. Not one of the senior students ever consciously took it "easy" on Laoshi. Yet, since he effortlessly outmatched even the best in the school, our best efforts made little difference to the outcome. We found ourselves cut or pushed repeatedly, with scarcely a reply. Occasionally, a student would devise a new tactic, a "deviation," as Laoshi branded such sneaky maneuvers, and manage to push Laoshi. However, to catch our teacher once or twice was as much could be hoped for. Laoshi's seemingly endless ability to adapt evoked in us the sense of a giant game of snakes and ladders, where the snakes were long and the ladders short. As he adapted to each newly invented "deviation," Laoshi would laugh and exclaim, "Ah, the Borg has assimilated!" Laoshi loved a good sci-fi reference.

By way of contrast, Billy Coyle's aikido and iaido classes at the Habonim provoked a very different feeling in me. While they, too, embraced elitism, shunning a "pass-the-time" attitude to the art, we trained to excel, and the prospect of attending class created tension in me. The tension would intensify as I approached the Habonim dojo, and I became increasingly quiet as my focus turned inward.

It is possible that my feelings at the time resulted from my youth: I was still a teenager, the "baby" of the class. Yet the demeanor of my fellow aikidoka appeared to match my own, as I observed on those occasions when I was offered a ride to class in the company of seasoned veterans. The silence in the car on the way to class was deafening. No one spoke: we were all tense, the quiet before the storm. Such palpable collective tension is interesting in retrospect, as I cannot recall a significant injury despite the demands of the practice. Billy was also inspirational and encouraging, only scolding us occasionally, and seldom without good cause. Looking back, perhaps I accepted the tension as appropriate, arising from my expectation of a grueling practice session, wedded to the commitment to touch the very depth of my soul. At the time, an earnest teenager, I felt myself to be on a path of spiritual and mental purification, aimed at releasing within me the power that was my birthright. I believed that the goal of total spiritual transformation and limitless martial power lay at the extreme of what body and mind could tolerate, and I was prepared for the arduous struggle. It is possible that some of my comrades shared my youthful fervor. On the other hand, I imagine that most of them just wanted to be good at fighting.

The car ride home was always loud and boisterous. We emerged from class energized-though-exhausted, after three hours of hard physical and mental training. We had survived the heat of the furnace and felt the camaraderie of those whose body and spirit had been collectively scorched.

Meanwhile, attendance at Laoshi's senior class was by invitation only. Assessing his students keenly, Laoshi would wait until he was satisfied as to the student's readiness before discreetly passing on an invitation. There was no great mystery, no oath of secrecy, but nevertheless, senior students seldom discussed senior class openly. In general, there was no obvious sign as to who was or was not a senior student. By definition, students whose interest did not extend to push-hands or fencing excluded themselves from consideration, since senior class focused entirely on the partner aspect of the *quan*, i.e., push-hands and fencing. This focus reflected Laoshi's regard for the importance of the partner aspects of the art. Nevertheless, Laoshi also continued to value those advanced students whose interest never ventured beyond the form, recognizing that the school benefited from a balance in contrasting energies, talents, and contributions.

"The senior class," Laoshi informed me at the time of my own invitation to join, "was created to offer intensive push-hands and fencing practice. It is not open to all the students: it is selective. However, anyone who genuinely seeks to join the class is offered opportunity the moment that their skills reach an appropriate level. Mind you, skill is not the vital factor: the key requirement is that the student must be willing to bear the heat that intense practice brings."

Laoshi's school syllabus might have been considered limited in comparison with other taijiquan schools, where progress was more likely to be measured by the number of form variations and assorted qigong exercises that a student might acquire. While Laoshi did teach saber, stick and applications, the main focus of the school was the study of Zheng Manqing's form, the *peng-lü-ji-an* method of push hands, plus sword form and fencing—tackled in that order. In this way, a student might become eligible for senior class after two years of regular class practice, provided that their enthusiasm for push-hands and fencing had not withered in the meantime.

Since we fenced without armor in Laoshi's school, student safety was a significant consideration. Laoshi took the welfare of his students seriously having experienced, from his own training, the cost of unnecessary injury. Not that Laoshi's efforts in this regard were always appreciated. Every so often, an irate student, unwilling to engage in push-hands and, therefore, discouraged from fencing, would demand of Laoshi, "Why do I need to push-hands when I only want to fence?"

"For very sound reasons," Laoshi once replied coolly: "When, sword in hand, you face an opponent for the first time, you are unpredictable. In centuries past, there were many one-eyed fencing masters who lost sight (pardon the pun) of the fact that novices are dangerous."

A chuckle of recognition rippled around the practice hall. "A novice being over-timid is one thing, but a beginner who flips and *goes on a berkie* is a whole other problem."

"Goes on a what?" muttered one of the students, who hailed from south of the Border.

"A berkie," the student next to him replied helpfully. "You know: *take a flakie, go on the raj.*" His enquiring comrade merely looked bewildered.

"Going on a berkie"—another student, taking pity, translated: "It means going berserk."

"One of Wang Lang's students," continued Laoshi, "taught me something of the dangers inherent in fencing one evening while at sword class. This fellow was a tall, strongly built young man who was a teacher at a boys' school somewhere in New England. He was an exceptionally polite and congenial young man, whom I had met several times at form class. So when I partnered him for the first time in fencing, I anticipated no problems, as he seemed to be a sincere, sensitive taijiquan player. As a result, my guard was down as we connected swords. All was fine for a few minutes, until I pressed in on him, trying to close distance. Now, it must be admitted that, at the time, my skill level was still rudimentary, relying too much on force rather than skill. Nevertheless, his response to my advance was shocking: my hitherto mild-mannered opponent abruptly disconnected his wooden sword and swung it at my face, hitting me hard in the mouth.

"I was astonished. With my tongue, I swiftly checked to see how many of my teeth were missing, and reassured to find them all still posted in my gums, looked to my partner for some show of concern or apology. None was forthcoming. Instead, his eyes shone with a devilish glee, and a less-than-benign smile played upon his lips. 'He could not have meant to do that,' I reasoned with myself. After all, this was a friendly taijiquan environment, overseen by Wang Lang, who certainly did not endorse hacking at another student's face, whatever the perceived provocation. So I said nothing.

"We connected swords again, and passed a few moments in jockeying for position. Feeling I had the angle, I pressed forward once again, only to be greeted by my opponent's sword once more abruptly disconnecting and the tip arcing toward my mouth for a second time. Instinctively, I arched backward out of range, but the point of his sword still grazed my upper lip.

"This time, my accusatory gaze was met with a distinctly menacing glean in my opponent's eye, and a cruel smile creased his lips. As Goldfinger once advised James Bond: 'Once is happenstance, twice is coincidence, the third time, it's enemy action!' I was not about to let him define himself as an 'enemy' at the expense of my face, and so I simply determined not to give him the slightest opening for another attempt at rearranging my features."

"But I'm not like that!" exclaimed the would-be fencer. "I would never do something like that."

"How do I know what you might do?" countered Laoshi. "In the school, we begin with push-hands in order that you might have the opportunity to find out who you are before you pick up a sword. Push-hands reveals who you are—that is the 'real' you, not who you think you are, nor indeed, who you would like to be. You may not even be aware of your own reaction when someone comes at you with a sword for the first time. Many of us underestimate the rigidity present in our arms and the tension which arises when we feel attacked."

As with other students, I had spent some considerable time learning about myself through the medium of push-hands before my introduction to fencing. It was some time before Laoshi approached me to discuss senior class.

"Of course," Laoshi declared, casually following my eager expression of interest in joining the senior class, "there is an entrance test."

"What kind of test?" I had asked, surprised.

"Well... You are required to find out and accept the four conditions," Laoshi offered neutrally.

"So, what are the four conditions, Laoshi?" I asked automatically.

"It's not for me to tell you," Laoshi smiled. "As I said, you should seek them out for yourself."

"*What?*" I replied in growing confusion. "How do I do that?"

"Well, that's up to you," responded Laoshi mildly, as he wandered off in characteristic fashion, leaving me to my confusion.

Fortunately, it turned out that discovery of the four conditions was as simple as asking one of the senior students. Interestingly, however, it soon became clear that the more senior the student, the less assured their recollection of the conditions, Laoshi having originally outlined these conditions upon the creation of the senior class. Most students had readily agreed to them, and then promptly paid them little attention. The conditions themselves were common sense rules, designed to remind senior students that with greater seniority comes greater responsibility, both to Laoshi and their fellow students. By obliging a prospective student to discover these conditions for themselves, Laoshi had hoped that the effort to do so would leave an impression on the psyche.

It was not my first experience of an entrance test prior to joining a martial arts class. For a while, admittance to Billy's aikido class at the Habonim Dojo depended on the completion of an entrance test, although "ritual" might be the more accurate term here, since the willingness to participate in the ritual was more important than passing or failing a "test," as such.

At the time, Billy's reputation attracted many of the most talented martial artists in Central Scotland. The dozen or so men and women who made up the regulars of the class were impressive individuals in their own right, many of them being teachers themselves. All were in their physical prime, and mostly ten years my senior. There was no shortage of *dan* grades in Japanese martial arts: mainly shotokan and shotokai karate, kendo, and aikido. I felt myself to be a child in such company and strove to meet the high standards of the group.

The entrance test itself consisted of performing one thousand *suburi*, i.e., one thousand sword cuts with a *bokken*. As well as being a statement of commitment to the group, a newcomer's willingness to complete the task demonstrated of the possession of fighting spirit. Though not impossibly difficult, executing one thousand *suburi* was not at all comfortable, especially when Billy demanded that each sword cut be performed with full intention. Lasting thirty minutes or so, the test put muscle on the shoulders and arms, while stripping the skin from soft hands. Billy also demanded regular attendance: to miss three practices in succession would result in expulsion from the class.

In truth, the execution of a thousand *suburi* is perfectly achievable, if the will is present, though less than exciting to deliver. For me, the truly testing part of the *suburi* ritual was the requirement that the entire student body, including Billy, should execute one thousand *suburi* each time a new student sought admittance to class. As a result, the appearance of any potential class members was greeted with mixed emotion, as we knew that our three-hour class would begin with a thousand sword cuts. Worse still, one thousand *suburi* was the *minimum* requirement. The total number to be executed was calculated at one hundred times the number of us in attendance. On one unlucky occasion, a would-be student chose to arrive when eighteen bodies were present, obliging us all to perform nineteen hundred suburi. Annoyingly, our potential classmate never returned.

Being a member of that class was invigorating, though not always easy, but like all good things, and all bad things for that matter, it was of its time. People moved on, sometimes due to disagreements, sometimes because they had their fill of that particular well. Most of the "old guard" found that their way led them in other directions, and something of the piquancy of that period was lost.

Reminiscing has a habit of raising questions, and my memories of the long-distant aikido class at the Habonim aroused my curiosity as to the tensions I experienced prior to and during Billy Coyle's class, as compared with Laoshi's senior class. I resolved to consult Laoshi at the first opportunity.

Laoshi listened patiently to my account before responding thoughtfully: "Training in martial arts is ostensibly about learning techniques for self-defense, but as you know, martial arts are also about managing fear. Some teachers deliberately engineer an atmosphere in class to heighten the tension, even anxiety, you describe in order to mimic the feelings that arise when you must defend yourself in real life. That edge of danger upon entering the dojo is a part of the process. Winning the first fight of the evening is entering into the dojo to begin. The forge must be hot enough to melt the metal, or what good is it. The purpose of the class is to forge spirit, as much as to teach technique, for when confronted by an opponent, your natural inclination will be to avoid conflict and escape. Your training, therefore, had to contain something of that edgy energy: there had to be some voltage to push the current."

This made sense to me, in relation to my old aikido training, but I still wanted to know why Laoshi did not overtly "push the current" in that way. I knew Laoshi well enough to suspect that there must be some kind of compensatory idea, but I was hard pressed to articulate what that might be.

After relating my thoughts to Laoshi, he nodded in acknowledgment. "Do you remember Zheng Manqing's advice on confronting a man with a knife?" he asked.

"Of course," I answered, "Zheng Manqing said, think of the knife as a feather duster."

Laoshi smiled. "Strange piece of advice, don't you think? A man pulls a knife on you, and you are supposed to respond as if he is armed with a cleaning implement. Now, who among us can manage that? Not many, for sure. So... is Zheng Manqing's advice, then, useless?" I knew this to be a rhetorical question.

"The Professor," continued Laoshi, "also advised that, when confronted by a man with a weapon, or a man attempting to take your life, you should *get mean*. Do you recall hearing that?"

"Yes, Laoshi," I replied, now a little puzzled, "but I can't say I ever thought of the two statements together."

"Quite so," acknowledged Laoshi, "but now that they are placed side by side, which is the correct advice? Should you *get mean*, or should you think of the weapon as a feather duster? And, if *it is a feather duster*, would you need to get mean in the first place?"

I could not help but laugh. Laoshi had posed a good question. But I also knew that he would have given thought to the apparent contradiction and might be about to share some insight.

"Is Zheng Manqing contradicting himself then?" I ventured.

"I don't think so." Laoshi confirmed my inkling.

"Then how do you reconcile the two statements?" I pressed.

"Well... 'getting mean' has to do with *what you do*," explained Laoshi, "seeing the knife as a 'feather duster' has to do with *what you think*."

I nodded cautiously, but remained silent, knowing that Laoshi would elaborate.

"The Hindu sage Shankara tells the story of a man walking along a road on a dark night. Suddenly the man sees a snake coiled in the road and feels himself recoil in terror. His hands begin to sweat, and his insides churn, as his body prepares to fight or flee. Just then, the moon emerging from cloud casts light on the snake which is revealed to be nothing more than a piece of coiled rope. The man's bodily functions quickly return to normal.

"Although Shankara was making the point about life being an illusion, the story also reminds us of the fact that thinking affects our bodies. For a taijiquan player, in order for our method to work, we require to remain relaxed at the very point that the *fight/flight* response kicks in. As Wang Lang used to say, just at the very point when you need your taijiquan, it doesn't work. Your fear gets in the way, and tension rushes in."

"Ah so, has this got something to do with the difference between following a *do* and following a *jutsu*? You know, studying the art for self-cultivation, as compared with training for combat effectiveness?" I interrupted enthusiastically, sensing a glimmer of meaning.

"In a way," agreed Laoshi. "More subtly, the question is one of how we train our thinking mind to face fear. Your old teacher's method had the value of providing you with the opportunity to face the fear of the dojo and inure yourself to that particular fear. It is a type of inoculation, where constant exposure to a stimulus blunts the effect of the stimulus. The stimulus might be heightened gradually, at the discretion of the teacher. However, too much fear stimulus can also decimate the class by desertion or by revolt.

"Here, in taijiquan class, we focus more on the idea that the reaction in the mind to Shankara's snake, for example, causes physical reaction in the body: i.e., a tensing of muscles and a raising of the qi in the body, resulting in crude blocking and shoving. Here, we train to eliminate physical tension when a sword is thrust at us, or when our partner attempts to launch us into the wall. Consciously, *we invest in loss*, not just to learn the technique of how to yield, but to remain mentally relaxed in the face of hostility. The extent to which we resist or insist, when pushed or stabbed at, is the extent to which our mind tightens up and resists life, insists on its own way. Our aim is to be not only capable of 'being mean,' should the need arise, but also to be able to calibrate the extent of our 'meanness' from a place of relaxation. We aspire to the sentiment of Mencius who said, 'Mt. Tai could collapse before me, and I would not change my countenance.'"

As I began to realize the enormity of Laoshi's meaning, I experienced an involuntary reaction, as a chill ran through the entire length of my body. The art I was committed to, at its deepest level, demanded no less than complete relaxation in the face of a threat, whether that threat was to livelihood, relationship, self-esteem, or even my very existence. Laoshi was saying that practicing fluidity and sensitivity in push-hands and fencing could lead to the dissolving of involuntary and rigid responses to fear.

"That seems so difficult as to be virtually impossible," I lamented.

"Nevertheless," Laoshi persisted, "It is what our art demands, and it can be achieved. Simply remember: the more you sincerely practice to 'invest in loss,' the closer you will come."

Chapter 10: Touching Buttocks

Over time, I grew into my role as teacher. Class numbers were steady, and I discovered that teaching did indeed deepen my understanding of taijiquan, as Laoshi had predicted. More importantly, teaching was becoming enjoyable, and I dared to hope that at last the gods were on my side.

Perhaps the gods are capricious though. Passing a local newsagent's window one sunny spring morning, my eye was drawn to an unfamiliar flyer advertising a taijiquan class. On closer inspection, I felt my hackles rise, as I discovered that an interloper had set up in "my" area, and was offering classes in competition with my own. The scoundrel had not even had the common decency to hang his shingle a respectable distance from my own venue and had chosen a location directly across the street.

My hackles remained, even when I learned that the competition was teaching the 24-step form rather than Zheng Manqing's version. Among Laoshi's students authorized to teach, a "gentleman's agreement" prevailed, where each honored their comrade's "patch," and did not encroach upon it. On this occasion, however, the object of my ire was a new arrival in the city, with allegiance to another school. As such, he was free of any obligation to respect a comrade's territory.

Laoshi was unperturbed as I relayed the news. "Relax," he counseled, "Tend your own garden, and let things play out. If the Dao wants you to teach, then no one can push you out. Of course, you may have to share the pitch for a while." Yet Laoshi's counsel brought scant comfort, and I found myself adopting a "siege mentality," as I contemplated the battle of attrition to come, a battle with a "24-step man" for students.

As things turned out, out "24-step man" abandoned his location within the year. Indeed, as I later discovered, he abandoned the practice of taijiquan altogether. He had departed without our paths ever crossing. Though initially successful in attracting students, he was gone as suddenly as he had arrived. A chance meeting with one of his former students supplied the apparent reason: "He just seemed to run out of stuff to teach, once he taught the movements of the form," shrugged the former student.

Laoshi was unmoved on hearing the news. "It is a trap into which the novice teacher can easily fall. There is more to teaching taijiquan than simply instructing groups of students to perform a series of movements. The form might be thought of as an instruction manual for self-development. Learning the postures and stringing them together into sequence is only the first step, akin to collecting and binding pages together to construct the manual: only once the manual has been created can the true work of deciphering its message begin."

Laoshi sought to impress this point on his students, once the initial instruction of the Zheng Manqing form was complete, by recounting one Professor Zheng's stories:

A long time ago, dragons were plentiful on the earth and roamed freely, until humans decimated their numbers. Though it took many years, eventually a single dragon was all that remained of a once proud and noble species. The gods, in desperation, summoned this sole survivor to heaven. Having sympathy for the plight of the dragon, and wishing to preserve the species on earth, the gods gifted the dragon a peach from the tree of immortality.

As you may know, the peach is sometimes referred to as the 'Daoist' fruit, with its soft flesh concealing a hard stone center, a living yin/yang symbol. A peach from the tree of immortality, moreover, was reputed to confer immortality on any creature that consumed it. The gods directed the dragon to eat the peach immediately on returning to earth, in order to ensure the survival of its kind for all time. The dragon, however, was so fascinated by the fruit that it could not bring itself to take even one bite from such a delight. Plucked from the tree of immortality, the peach was immortal, and, therefore, immune to decay. The dragon, captivated by the marvelous gift, spent hours gazing upon its treasure. The more enchanted the dragon became, the less inclined it was to attempt even a nibble at the skin of its 'prize.' As a result, the true prize of immortality went unclaimed and the last of the great dragons died.

Laoshi drew a comparison between the form, whose postures had so recently been learned, and the peach of immortality: it was not enough to possess knowledge of the movements, rather it was vital that the form be practiced daily in order to reap the true benefits. The form had to be internalized, "consumed," if we were to know its full blessing. If not actual immortality, then at least health, happiness, and martial skill would flow from it.

For Laoshi, familiarization with the choreography of the form was no more than the initial step. "Consuming" the form required continual study and refinement, polishing of the movements and principles in order to tease out the mysteries contained within. Laoshi believed that the secrets were only divulged to those who sincerely looked. If one was not fulsome in their attention to the form, then the form would remain dry and abstract, and one's relationship with it would inevitably cool.

"But, where do we look for the secrets?" asked one student.

"Hmm, well let's look at the answer to that question in stages," said Laoshi. "*Taijiquan* means, literally, the method that uses the principle of yin and yang. Initially, it is enough to know that forward motion is 'yang,' and backward motion is 'yin.' Later, as our understanding ripens, we begin to recognize one side of the body as expressing yang energy, while the other side is yin. We may also come to regard the upper body as manifesting yin, while the lower body manifests yang energy. However, at a further stage, the realization dawns that the body as a whole is yin, while the energy, the qi, or the spirit of the form is yang in quality.

"From this revelation, we might begin to regard the body as a vessel, and the qi as the contents of that vessel. Accordingly, to improve, we can either concentrate on making the vessel more accommodating to the qi, or else we can begin the process of encouraging the qi to circulate more freely within that vessel.

"Imagine a garden hose left lying all winter in a garden shed. Come springtime, it had become kinked and twisted, with the result that the flow of water through the hose has been reduced. To facilitate the flow of water, we might try to smooth out the kinks in the hose in order to reduce blockages, but we could also turn the tap further to increase the flow of water."

One of the students asked mischievously, "Does that mean we have to become less kinky?"

"Yeah," another chipped in, "but more turned on!"

Laoshi smiled, "Indeed. Less kinky in that we smooth out the structure of our bodies; more turned on in that we encourage the flow in our bodies."

In this manner, in his periodic advanced form class, Laoshi directed our attention back and forth between first studying the structure of the body, and then studying improvement in the flow of qi. However, for myself, and for the time being, I limited my own instruction to correcting the structure of the body, as I did not yet feel qualified to discuss the workings of qi in the body.

In essence, the optimum structure of the "taijiquan body" is achieved by loosening each of the major joints of the body, or opening "the nine gates of the qi," to quote Wang Lang. To open the gates is like unkinking the hose. Opening the first three sets of joints: the wrists, elbows, and shoulders is relatively straightforward to comprehend, but still requires significant practice if consistent looseness is to be achieved. Opening the next three sets of joints: the hips, knees, and ankles demands a deeper level of understanding, since the simple removal of muscular tension would have us fall to the ground. More difficult still to approach, are the three gates of the spine: the sacrum, the middle of the back, and the crown of the head, not least because they are, as Zheng Manqing pointed out, "not purely physical" in their relation to the qi.

It was challenging enough to remain sensitive to any present tension in one's body, in order to relax and dissolve the same, but it felt an almost impossible task to be sensitive to who-knew-what, to be aware of what one had no inkling, and the suggestion that the inkling might be "not purely physical" helped me not one jot.

I had been toiling at the task of loosening my spine for some time, trying sincerely to respond to Laoshi's regular refrain: "relax the sacrum." Simply replying, "Yes, Laoshi," to repeated instruction served me not at all, as I was ignorant of the slightest notion as to how one relaxed the sacrum, not least because, to my mind, the sacrum was comprised of several vertebrae fused together. Hoping for revelation through practice, and reluctant to admit my ignorance, I chose not the press Laoshi for further guidance.

One day, however, my frustration rose to new heights in response to yet another directive aimed at my sacral tension, and I sighed audibly. "I know, I know, you keep telling me Laoshi, but what exactly does relax the sacrum mean? How do you relax a bone?"

Laoshi paused for a moment before replying, as if to himself, "Hmm... perhaps a change of tack is in order. Okay, so first of all, when we talk of the sacrum in this context, we do not specifically mean the bone at the base of the spine. The language is misleading, and, as you have pointed out, the sacrum is a bone composed of five vertebrae fused into one. It is more accurate, for taijiquan purposes, to think of the 'sacrum' as the 'lower spine and pelvis,' in the same way that we understand that the 'waist' is not only the belly, but the whole area between the hips.

"Some teachers prefer the phrase 'drop the sacrum,' and others 'tuck in the lower spine,'" continued Laoshi. "But these phrases often create their own confusion. Like you, I struggled with the notion of 'relaxing the sacrum,' and only began to make progress under the tutelage of Master Lin. By the time I met Master Lin, I had acquired some understanding of how to loosen the joints of the arms and legs by following Wang Lang's instruction.

"Like you, however, the matter of relaxing the spine remained a mystery to me. It was Master Lin, who led me to realize that relaxing the spine is to be accomplished by aligning the vertebrae correctly."

"Wait... So 'relaxing the spine' really just means 'aligning the spine?' So why not say that then?" I asked huffily. "Why do taijiquan teachers seem to delight in disguising what they really mean?"

"Don't be too hard on us," soothed Laoshi. "These concepts are challenging, both for student and teacher. 'Alignment of the spine' is here concerned with dissolving tension, rather than imposing a specific shape upon the vertebrae. After all, there is significant variation in the shape of human spinal columns: some appear serpentine, whereas others are straight like Greek columns. Attempting to force the spine into a 'one-shape-fits-all' template would be ill-advised."

Laoshi's words reminded me of the efforts of a previous teacher to remedy my "calamitous posture."

"Stand next to a wall," he commanded. "Now place the base of your spine against the wall, and then with the base of your spine still against the wall, place the middle of your back against the wall. Finally, with both the middle of and the back of the spine against the wall, touch the wall with the back of your head. And there you have it: perfect alignment."

It may be the case that for those fortunate enough not to have misshapen their spines over the years with slouching and stooping, this advice is helpful.

However, speaking for myself, the moment I had complied with these instructions, and then moved away from the wall, I looked and felt as if the proverbial poker was well and truly in its proverbial place.

Laoshi continued, drawing my attention back to what he was saying. "Do you recall me telling of how Master Lin's students appeared to have no qualms about feeling my buttocks when I was holding postures to check my relaxation?"

Laoshi occasionally entertained his students with anecdotes concerning his studies in Taiwan. The cultural differences highlighted in such tales amused him greatly. "A couple of Master Lin's students approached me as I stood in single whip, moving minimally, trying to fathom Master Lin's corrections. They looked me over for a moment before one of them reached out and promptly fondled my buttocks. Well…" Laoshi would look askance around the room at his student audience, "I mean hands-on instruction is one thing, but we hadn't even been introduced!"

As Laoshi recounted to us, assessing the quality of relaxation in the gluteus maximus by fondling the backside seemed unremarkable to Master Lin's students. Indeed, Master Lin made his own buttocks available in order that his students could likewise ascertain the master's level of relaxation. Laoshi, however, had respectfully declined the kind offer: "It was a cultural bridge too far for a Glaswegian," he confided to the empathetic student body.

"Whether you are standing in front or back posture," continued Laoshi, more seriously, "ideally, the buttock muscles are relaxed, because if they are not relaxed, you are almost certainly leaning forward."

"Er… can I check for relaxation myself, Laoshi?"

Laoshi may have caught something in my anxious tone. "Certainly! Certainly!" he reassured. "Try this: stand with your feet parallel, shoulder-width apart. Now, place your hands on the lower part of you buttocks, just where they meet the back of the leg. You should feel the cheeks to be soft—relaxed—when you are standing upright. Is that so?"

I did as instructed and speedily concurred that, indeed, my lower buttocks were soft and relaxed.

"Now," resumed Laoshi, "gradually tilt forward from the hips and notice how the band of muscle in your buttocks gradually begins to tighten as you incline your spine forward." I did as I was bid and again nodded my agreement. "So… as you can feel for yourself, any tightening of that band of muscle is an indication that your spine is no longer upright."

"Hmm… So Laoshi," I pursued, "does that mean that the lower buttocks should remain soft when we practice our form?"

"Indeed," rejoined Laoshi.

"And is that on the weighted leg or on the unweighted leg?" I queried.

"Both," Laoshi replied emphatically.

"*Both?*" I challenged. "Even in front-stance?"

"Especially in front-stance," confirmed Laoshi. "I have observed that a slight forward tilt in front-stance is common in the posture of even experienced students. To be fair, however, to these students, many taijiquan teachers contend that a *straight* spine does not necessarily have to be *upright*. But I have come to believe that this misses the point. Master Lin was unequivocal on this matter. For him, the crucial test of straightness was to be found in the relaxation of the lower buttocks.

"In regards to his own struggle to embody this principle, Master Lin reported that he would check his alignment frequently, and sometimes even outside of class. Once, while queuing for a bus, Master Lin had the notion to check out his alignment. A fellow standing in the same queue observed with interest after noticing the Master's subtle self-examination. Approaching, he enquired politely if Master Lin was a student of martial arts. Master Lin nodded a confirmation, but refrained from asking how the fellow knew. However, his fellow traveler was already, obligingly, indicating his own buttocks. "We do the same thing in judo," he nodded sagely.

I tried to imagine the same exchange taking place at a Glasgow bus shelter, but quickly dismissed the idea as unlikely. Instead, I took up a front-stance, attempting to apply the test only to discover that the softness I had previously felt in the lower buttocks, when I was standing upright, was now missing. By rotating my pelvis up and under, I found that the softness had returned. I experimented with a few adjustments of my spine, until, in addition, the sense of connection through my feet to the floor now felt radically different: the soles of my feet seemed much more strongly connected to the ground than I had ever previously experienced.

Laoshi nodded unsurprised: "Relaxing and dropping of the sacrum not only opens the gate of the qi at the base of the spine, it also stimulates the *yongquan* point, the bubbling well, more efficiently. You may notice that the bubbling sensation in the *yongquan* point becomes more pronounced for a time."

Laoshi's words were borne out. I soon found that the tingling sensation in the *yongquan* (located at the center and just behind the ball of the foot) was a constant companion in the months that followed, and not just when I was practicing taijiquan. True to form, while genuinely pleased with my improvement, Laoshi did not allow me to rest on my laurels. "Now... relax the *middle of your spine*," he directed. And again, some time later, when I had somewhat succeeded in dissolving the tension in the middle of my back, Laoshi drew my attention further up: "Put your head on straight. The crown of the

74

head rises to heaven."

I began to understand that each adjustment in the lower part of the spine required a complementary fine-tuning in the remainder of the spine, all the way up to the head. I also discovered that, over time, and as I lowered my posture, the entire process of alignment had to begin afresh: the upper gates of the spine responded to even minimal change in alignment of sacrum or pelvis. "Touching buttocks" became a regular exercise at home, but never in public. Furthermore, I never sought to test the buttocks of any student: this was Glasgow after all.

Chapter 11: Shortcuts

"You have good karma," said a former teacher one afternoon, as we chatted alone after class. I was flattered despite my skepticism in respect of karma: a mighty ledger of good and ill maintained by the great deity seemed unlikely to me if for no other reason than the tedium implicit in such a project. Fortunately, any smug satisfaction threatening to surface was abruptly cut short as he added, "because you have me as your teacher."

Possibly feeling underappreciated, my then teacher was highlighting his own competence, rather than the flawless conduct of my past lives. And yet his comment was nevertheless accurate: he was indeed a competent teacher amid a mass of mediocrity at the time. However, despite his inspiration and instruction, few of his students approached his expectations in either effort or application. It is sobering to recognize that good quality teaching alone cannot guarantee success in taijiquan, even for the truly gifted student, blessed with talent and a love for the art. Significant progress requires equally, if not more so, a healthy dose of patience.

Laoshi was making something of the same point, when he repeated Wang Lang's tale of a chance encounter on a railway platform while on his way to class. "Wang Lang had been waiting for a replacement train at a New York station due to a technical difficulty," reported Laoshi. "He noticed a police officer some dozen or so feet away, assessing him closely. Recognizing that he had been spotted, the officer approached Wang Lang and declared, 'You study taijiquan, am I right?' Wang Lang nodded before asking the officer how he had arrived at his conclusion. 'To some extent it was your age and physique, but the clincher,' the officer revealed, 'was your sword bag.' In the ensuing conversation, Wang Lang discovered that the officer had studied taijiquan for more than a decade before quitting in favor of a less baffling art. Wang Lang responded, 'Lost patience, then, eh?' Indeed he had."

For the taijiquan player, the time needed to make progress is measured, not in months, nor years, but in decades: one of the reasons why the ranks of taijiquan teachers are thick with relative novices. Given the requirement of twenty to thirty years of sincere study to gain even a modicum of understanding, most give up. Of those who do persevere, many find the amount of "it" attained can seem frustratingly inadequate, given the resources spent on "its" acquisition. Not surprisingly then, many of us speculate about the existence of shortcuts.

Feeling the lack in my own abilities, heightened by some insecurity in my new role as teacher, I began wondering if progress by less traditional means was possible. Were there, as it were, "performance enhancing" methods for taijiquan? As usual, I put the question to Laoshi, despite some concern that my question might suggest I was tempted by the "dark side."

"I asked Wang Lang the same thing," replied Laoshi on a warm summer afternoon as I broached the subject while acting as his chauffeur.

"And… what did he say?" I asked, relaxing a little at his apparent willingness to engage with a possibly foolish question.

"His reply was very interesting," continued Laoshi. "He told me that there were indeed potential shortcuts to progress."

"Really?" I exclaimed, "Then why don't we use them?"

"My very words to Wang Lang," he laughed. I sighed a little. Laoshi's habit of addressing an issue indirectly had been less evident for a while, but he still indulged himself from time to time.

"So, what did Wang Lang say?" I pressed him, growing impatient.

"Oh, he said that although these methods did exist, they had downsides and were potentially harmful. The method of Zheng Manqing may be slow but is safe."

This was getting interesting. "Right, so what methods are we talking about?"

"Wang Lang," added Laoshi, "told me that drugs, alcohol, and certain kinds of qigong can stimulate our energy and improve our insight. However, he was unequivocal in warning of the addictive nature of drugs and alcohol, and the damage excessive amounts of these substances can do to the body."

"Okay, but what about the qigong methods?" I pressed him further.

"Well, two problems are inherent with the qigong methods we are talking about here. Some methods advocate unnaturally tensing areas of the body, while others employ reverse breathing to achieve results, both practices which Zheng Manqing categorically advised against. These methods may have some benefits, but they lead to imbalances."

"What do you mean by imbalances?"

"What I mean is," added Laoshi emphatically, "what I mean is that they cause imbalance in the body by diverting energy to some parts of our organism, while depleting other parts. In effect, they rob Peter to pay Paul."

As I sat quietly for a moment digesting this new information, a well-known qigong teacher from Southeast Asia came to mind. I mentioned the name to Laoshi, who confirmed that this master promoted the very techniques that Wang Lang considered either dubious, dangerous, or both.

I had not met this qigong master personally, knowing him only by reputation. He had been busy on the workshop circuit in London many years before. His qigong methods, he claimed, had a proven record in relieving a range of physical and psychological problems. His techniques, however, were far from uncontroversial. Former students reported rather distressing internal conditions arising from seriously adhering to his regime, while others decried his system as fanciful. My own reservations centered on the financial circus that accompanied his workshops. Whatever his skills as a healer or qigong master, he was certainly a businessman.

"He, and others like him," nodded Laoshi. "But, there is a still greater danger in obsessing over shortcuts, a kind of trap which is hard to escape once caught."

"Really! What kind of trap?" It was a captivating topic, and I was desperate to hear more.

"The trap that makes us think there is a destination."

"But..., isn't there a destination? Are we not trying to improve our taijiquan?"

"That is not a destination," smiled Laoshi. "That is growth, and growth is so precious because it grows in its own way: no two trees are identical, and no two rivers follow the same course. Have you ever seen two identical valleys? So too, taijiquan reveals itself to each of us uniquely. To have a shortcut is to have a destination, but the Dao is not a destination: it is a happening, a flowering. Can you have a shortcut to a flowering? More to the point, do you want a shortcut to a flowering?"

Laoshi paused momentarily, assessing my muted reaction to his words. He then continued, "Once a confrontational student questioned my abilities in taijiquan. He was a young man, new to our classes, and very sure of himself. He asked, 'This taijiquan you do, are you any good at it?' A gift from the gods, I thought, as I replied, 'Well... when you consider the teachers I have had, my natural abilities in this direction, the amount I have practiced, the limitations of my body, the injuries I have suffered over the years, and the distractions life has thrown at me—when you consider all these factors, I am just about as good as I should be."

Laoshi laughed, as he recalled the scene, and before more could be said, we arrived at our destination. "Thanks for the lift," he said opening the door, "see you next time." And I was once again alone.

I shook my head a little and smiled as he sauntered away in the afternoon sunshine, apparently not a care in the world. I sat behind the wheel, allowing Laoshi's words to settle. He was reminding me to remain patient and not "forsake the near for the far." Progress would come, not only in its own good time, but also in measure and direction of its own choosing. A carbon copy of another's journey was a fake, just like a copied Rembrandt. The original is valuable because it is original. It is the potency and essence of the Dao expressed and encapsulated in form at a particular time and a particular shape.

Then a moment of insight: Laoshi's irritating propensity to explore tangents, sometimes so involved that the initial question was forgotten, coincided with my attempts to impose a methodology on advancement, to systemize progress into a hierarchy of principles and map out a route to mastery. It was almost as if my attempts to codify taijiquan triggered in him an opposite reaction, an escape from the straightjacket my views of achievement might impose on him, and by extension, me and my students. I doubted a conscious design in his evasions, rather a reaction against my own definite ideas on the nature of progress, ideas which would constrain progress, rather than allow it to mature and flower according to the will of the Dao.

It was then that I began to value patience for its own sake, the yin from which the yang emerges, the mundane that leads to the majestic, and the simplicity, which is the source of the profound.

Chapter 12: The Chashaobao Push

I was never happier than listening to Laoshi's stories on long, lazy Sunday afternoons at his home on the outskirts of Glasgow. Often, as Laoshi revisited tales from his past, little details would change, but the gist remained constant. Blending significant anecdotal material concerning Professor Zheng and other taijiquan luminaries, along with candid accounts of his own experiences, Laoshi gradually constructed a "cultural identity" for us, his students. We were able to fix ourselves within the taijiquan firmament and our position relative to the many schools of taijiquan that emerged following the Professor's death.

I particularly enjoyed hearing of Master Lin, Laoshi's teacher in Taiwan. Master Lin, after many years as a senior student of the Professor in Taipei, became a renowned taijiquan teacher in his own right. "By the time I made the journey to Taiwan to meet Master Lin," reminisced Laoshi, "he was no longer teaching form, only the *kugong* exercises, which contained the essence of his accumulated taijiquan experience, distilled down to a sort of 'physical elixir.' Once the elixir had been sipped, so to speak, Master Lin would reveal the full potential of the exercises, through his sublime skill in push-hands.

"However, infusing push-hands with the spirit of Master Lin's *kugong* exercises was no easy task: not for me, nor for Master Lin's regular students, some of whom were veterans of his approach. At our first meeting, Master Lin, referring to his students, advised me to 'listen to what they say, but do only as I do.' I soon came to understand his meaning, for repeating his instructions only requires a passable memory, but the execution of the method is infinitely subtler. I did as instructed, watching him closely, and burning his image into my mind in minute detail. At the same time, I listened closely to and filled notebooks with the oral guidance of his students.

"That short time in Taiwan was my Damascene moment," continued Laoshi, "I amended my whole approach to push-hands, as a result. In particular, I glimpsed what push-hands could be: a seamless catching, blending, and rerouting of a push. Arriving in Taiwan that autumn, I was certainly no novice. I had already been shown the importance of turning the waist in successfully neutralizing a push, emptying one side of the body while simultaneously filling the other. It is not to say that my understanding was flawed. It was, however, incomplete.

"I struggled with a specific push, which my 'empty-fill technique' failed to manage. My study of the peng-lü-ji-an approach to push-hands had shown me that my response to a push should resemble the turret of a tank revolving to deflect the push away from my center. Simultaneously, my arm, like a gun barrel rotating with the turret, should sweep the pusher to the side. While effective against a push aimed at my chest, problems arose when the pusher directed his force on to my arm, to 'lock me up,' before delivering a strong shove. Continuing with the analogy, I found myself helpless if the pusher pushed on the gun barrel as well as the turret."

"Was Wang Lang not able to show you how to counter that sort of push?" I interrupted.

"It was my view at the time," answered Laoshi candidly, "that Wang Lang himself struggled with this type of push. On several occasions I questioned him on the matter, but remained unconvinced by his answer."

"So, what kind of advice did Wang Lang offer about this kind of push?" I was eager to hear more of Laoshi's early frustration with push-hands.

Laoshi paused for a few seconds before replying, "You must understand that Wang Lang's push-hands ability was considerable, but he limited his study to concentrate on a very narrow set of parameters. In part, this restriction was a conscious attempt to promote soft technique over physical force. Unfortunately, however, imposing too many restrictions reduces the applicability of the method in all situations. Ultimately, as Wang Lang himself believed, the method we study must be relevant universally, and not be successful only with people 'playing the same game' as we. To be worthy of the name taijiquan, our art must be equally effective against those who are non-compliant, as it is with those who harmonize with our movement.

"I remember," added Laoshi, as he recalled an incident from his past, "one occasion when my frustration with this particular push was threatening to boil over. I had asked Wang Lang a specific question relating to this type of push—the push that will not be neutralized. The occasion was a summer camp in Virginia, where Wang Lang had been invited to conduct a weeklong series of push-hands sessions. One of my own students, Benny, a gentle soul, though big, strong, and well rooted, had made the trip to drink from the source that was Wang Lang. Benny had been innocently provoking a silent, seething rage within me for some time prior to the trip, with his excellent rounded-arms push. He afforded me no room to maneuver and advanced till I was trapped by a seemingly huge beach ball, pressing against me. I felt like Patrick McGoohan in *The Prisoner*, being chased by a massive, unrelenting, suffocating balloon. My every attempt at escape was swallowed up by Benny's inflated presence. Wang Lang described Benny's push as the 'chashaobao' push."

"Wait a minute… *Chashaobao*? Did you say, *chashaobao*?"

Laoshi nodded.

"What on earth is a chashaobao?" I asked.

"It's a Chinese-style pork bun, but also the name Zheng Manqing gave to a push that comes at you like a big, sensitive, well-rooted, doughnut. You've heard of a doughnut, I presume."

I nodded, and patting my belly, replied, "And eaten a few lately, as well."

"The very roundness of the 'doughnut'" continued Laoshi, "allows it to push back against wherever the receiver fills up. With Benny, any attempt to sweep his push to the side only succeeded in making him root more effectively. Wang Lang quoted Zheng Manqing's recommendation for dealing with this push: 'Let it roll off the table.'

"Wang Lang took me to the push-hands floor to demonstrate this let-it-roll-off-the-table technique," added Laoshi. "As I pushed, using a *chashaobao* smothering style of attack, he yielded further and further back, sitting down deeper and deeper into his back leg, and bending forward, till our foreheads almost touched, waiting for me to become vulnerable by overextending. I became aware of the crowd of curious students, who had assembled to witness

80

the spectacle, sensing something of importance was occurring. I aborted my push, though I knew he had not escaped. My desire to know was overridden by a reluctance to cause embarrassment to my teacher by forcing him over in front of the other students. I have no doubt that he was aware of the limited success of his demonstration, for he commented loudly, 'Of course, there are not many people who can do the *chashaobao* push as well as you can.' Ironically, that was the very problem: I knew a few who could and, worse still, one of them called *me* teacher."

Listening to Laoshi's tale, I sympathized with both him and Wang Lang. Laoshi had not felt able to pursue his question to its limits, and Wang Lang, no doubt, felt his response to be wanting.

Laoshi's voice recalled me from my thoughts, "Of course, on meeting Master Lin, the problem evaporated. I employed the same *chashaobao* push as we touched hands and found, in his simple movements, an expertise at 'moving the table,' and I was neutralized. He was adept at catching the energy of a push and rolling it around on itself before guiding it away."

Although hard to envisage solely from the written word, the method that Laoshi observed in his short time with Master Lin formed the basis of his subsequent study and teaching of push-hands. Conceptually, the idea is deceptively simple, and not dissimilar from catching a stone that has been forcibly thrown. Simply placing a hand in the path of a speeding stone results in the painful impact of hard rock on tender flesh. Softening the hand and arm to blend with the incoming missile for a short distance takes out much of the sting. Catching a push has much the same flavor.

"When pushing Master Lin," recalled Laoshi, "I became aware that he responded to my push by instantly 'dropping' his weight into his rear leg. The quality of this 'dropping' of weight was different from smoothly transferring weight on the back leg, as we do in the form. Once noticed, the 'drop' was as unmistakable as it was consistent. Before any other action was taken, Master Lin would 'drop' his weight back. At first, I assumed he was simply establishing a stable root on which to rotate his hips. Further observation of his movement revealed the subtle yielding, which accompanied the 'dropping' of weight onto his rear leg. This almost imperceptible yielding compelled me, the pusher, to fall very slightly toward Master Lin. Once falling, it was only a matter of directing my fall to the side by turning the waist."

Listening to Laoshi brought to mind my encounter with a crowd control barrier many years before in an Edinburgh train station. I was in the company of Billy Coyle and several of his students en route to a showing of the Kurasawa movie, *Kagemusha*. Emerging from the platform, we were confronted by metal barriers channeling us off to the side. While my comrades complied with circumstances, I used the opportunity to show off my vaulting skills. Unfortunately, I had not realized the barrier was an expert in taijiquan. Built in the manner of a track hurdle, it displayed its solid yang quality when pushed from the front but, when pressed from the rear, it allowed only so much pressure before giving way. Allowing my hand enough solidity to commence my vault, it collapsed as my weight bore down at the wrong angle. I was left an ignominious mess on the floor, fouled by a toppled barrier. My recollection triggered a rush of blood to my face, and I refocused on Laoshi's words.

"Of course," Laoshi clarified as I nodded seriously, "it was only later that I saw the full implications: not only must we catch the push, but also the energy of the push."

"When you say 'catch the energy of the push,' is that similar to Zheng Manqing's comment about answering the energy of a question?" I interrupted once again.

"Indeed so," nodded Laoshi. "Push-hands and conversation have much in common. Like the Professor, we must not be held captive by a questioner's words, no matter how eloquent. Like the Professor, we must speak to the heart of the matter. In the United States, Professor Zheng may have been aided by his lack of English, and relied more heavily on the 'total energy statement' of the questioner. Nevertheless, we can apply the idea to push-hands. The hands and arms of the pusher are like the words we use in conversation. The meaning lies behind the words, as the force of body is behind the strength in the arms. If you can catch an attacker's arm, you sometimes catch their center; but if you catch their center you always have their arms."

It was not that Laoshi was advising that we ignore an incoming push, or punch for that matter. He was repeating a principle of martial arts: to control the center is to control the periphery. And, by extension, his preference in dealing with people was to look beyond the words for the true content behind what is said.

"Okay, Laoshi," I protested. "I kind of know what you are asking me to do… in theory at least. But I really have no idea how to go about catching another person's center in push-hands."

"Ah, well then, in that case," suggested Laoshi, "you should begin with this idea. Watch your partner's chest carefully when they push toward you. Soon you will see that they are leaning, perhaps ever so slightly, but leaning they will be. In time, you will recognize that this leaning is falling by another name. In time, you will be able to help those who push you to fall more efficiently." He chuckled a little before adding, "Critically, your efforts must not oppose the fall or you become a fence post for them to lean on."

"That reminds me of something Billy once said," I interrupted spontaneously. "He advised his students to 'never throw someone who is not already falling.'"

"Well put," nodded Laoshi. "The skill is not in the throw, but leading the attacker to a point where the throw is inevitable. Dealing with a push is similar: catch the body falling, and you can lead the fall away from you."

I pursed my lips a little as I considered his suggestion.

"I see a question forms," said Laoshi, gauging my reaction.

"Yes Laoshi. But what happens if they are not falling? How do I catch the center then?"

He laughed a little, shaking his head as if I was missing something entirely obvious. My face flushed once again, and I felt a tinge of embarrassment. What could I be missing?

"Your partner is always falling," he stated emphatically. "As long as they are standing, they are falling."

"Really?" I queried. "How can that be, Laoshi?"

"Because," he revealed, "we are all continually falling and continually compensating to remain upright: all of us, all of the time. I have heard the phenomenon described as 'the small dance.' We have to make adjustments to remain standing. We may be unaware that we do this, but nevertheless, we constantly readjust just to remain upright. Taijiquan makes use of this phenomenon to catch those tiny corrections of balance and topple an opponent.

"And," added Laoshi, developing his theme, "if we are falling while standing still, how much more so when we are pushing. The decision to push mobilizes the qi, or intention, if you prefer, and the fall is directed toward a target. If the target is missed, balance is lost and has to be regained before a fresh target can be acquired. The very intention, the very extension of qi, leads the pusher out of balance. As your sensitivity to the qi becomes finer, you will, by capturing its movement, catch the opponent's center. This is not mysticism: this is sensitivity. If you cannot sense their fall, you must pay attention till you do."

In this context what might appear mysterious is no more than sensitivity in ever-finer gradations. The skill lay in ever more acutely sensing the very intention, the qi of the pusher, and catching it to lead it where we wished.

"How sensitive do I need to become, Laoshi?"

"No more than the leaf of a tree."

"What?"

Laoshi led me to an old sycamore tree in his garden and challenged me to touch a leaf without moving it. I was surprised to discover that it is an impossible task: to touch the leaf is to have already moved it, to have already pushed it. Laoshi's analogy had much in common with the classics, which bid us to strive for such sensitivity that a fly landing on us would set us in motion. Much later, as my own students protested that they were not pushing, although their hands were on mine, I would similarly challenge them to touch a leaf while leaving it at rest.

Just as standing upright implies continual falling, connecting hands with our partner is effectively pushing. Letting the *chashaobao* push roll off the table depends on the sensitively to tilt the table in the right direction at the right time, like the game of rolling a ball bearing through a maze to drop it through a hole in the middle. Without sensitivity, what hope can there be!

Chapter 13: Reincarnation

Though infrequent, the world is occasionally blessed by the birth of a martial arts genius. These savants reach the pinnacle of their respective arts in the blink of an eye, while the rest of us wander lost in the foothills, mistaking stone for silver and granite for gold.

One of Zheng Manqing's Taiwan students had something of this genius, and according to the Professor, grasped the essence of taijiquan in less than a year. Of his skills, the Professor said, "Even though there were people who had been studying for decades, no one could touch his shadow… It was impossible to talk about his talent."

Despite his capabilities, this prodigy gave up the study of taijiquan to pursue a business career and, seeing Zheng Manqing on the street, crossed to the other side to avoid a meeting. Perhaps it is the price paid by the phenom: the ease of attainment devalues the achievement.

Genius on the level of the Professor's student is the exception, but many of us value our own worth too highly and, in regard to our teachers, make swans out of pigeons, as Robert Smith might say. I recognized the same temptation in me, although Laoshi was a great deal more modest in appraising his worth, once asserting that, "this stuff is difficult. I'll need, at least, three lifetimes to get it." Despite employing a figure of speech to weigh the difficulty in learning taijiquan, his comment, nevertheless, provoked a question in me: is reincarnation real, and to what extent can we access the knowledge of a previous lifetime to advance our training in the here and now?

"Laoshi," I asked one glorious April morning, the spring sun warming the land and promising rebirth, "Do you believe in reincarnation?"

"No, not really." This was a disappointing and slightly offhand reply from an apparently disinterested Laoshi, who was purposefully spooning tea leaves into a pot in his kitchen.

"So, you don't think we can come back in some form to pick up where we left off in a previous life?"

"Haven't you heard that it is wise to live in the present?" he said, looking up after depositing the rooibos leaves into a plain Japanese style tea-pot and adding hot water.

"Yes, Laoshi," I persisted, "but you yourself talk about getting it in three lifetimes."

He took a seat at the table and carefully set down the teapot on a straw tablemat, then leaned back saying, "Reincarnation... who cares! You will find out whether you come back or not when the time comes. Or there again, maybe you won't." He chuckled a little before continuing. "Of course, you do not have to wait till you die before your life changes. I think a major change occurs every seven years. Even if it is not so regular an event, change on a smaller scale happens constantly. You are not the same person you were yesterday and you are not the same person you will be tomorrow.

"Reincarnation may simply be an idea to help us manage the fear of death. If something of you were to survive death, that would be a comforting notion would it not, if a little egotistical?"

"Egotistical, how is that egotistical, Laoshi?" I asked, a shadow of doubt masking my face. "Surely it is human nature to want to survive death in one form or another?"

"Ha!" exclaimed Laoshi. "No, not human nature at all: ego-nature maybe, or that part of you which identifies itself as separate from the universe. Of course, the danger is not in the need to distinguish us as separate, but in the desire for our separateness to be something 'special.'

"I am different from you, that is true. But to persuade myself that I am so special that the universe must keep 'me' alive after the body is worn out, leads to a great deal of tension. What makes me, or any of us, so important that we cannot be let go when our time has come?"

The discussion had veered off in an unexpected direction, but was, perhaps, all the more entertaining, and I was forced to admit that, practically speaking, Laoshi was correct: life will be perfectly capable of carrying on despite my eventual demise. As I reflected on Laoshi's analysis, the subject might have been quietly dropped, with some of the wind knocked from my sails, and reincarnation something of a non-issue, but then, unbidden, Laoshi picked up the thread once more: "Perhaps, I am being too harsh and too quick to dismiss these beliefs. If the idea of reincarnation is comforting, who am I to criticize? After all, Zheng Manqing did not completely dismiss the idea out of hand."

I was astonished. It was news to me that Zheng Manqing had voiced an opinion of the reality of reincarnation. "Ahmm... How do you know Zheng

Manqing's view on reincarnation, Laoshi?" I asked, perhaps a little skeptical.

"Oh, it was something Master Lin said."

"Yes… and what did he say?"

"Well, let's see, my memory of the time is a little hazy,"

"Yes, Laoshi?" I encouraged him.

"I seem to recall Master Lin mentioning that a friend of Zheng Manqing had insisted to the Professor that his artwork bore a striking resemblance to the work of a monk, who had died a little before Professor Zheng was born. The friend suggested that Zheng Manqing was a reincarnation of this monk, an idea not entirely dismissed by the Professor on hearing that the monk in question was disabled and could not walk. Master Lin explained that the young Zheng Manqing could not walk till he was five years old. He also quoted Zheng Manqing as saying, 'one life sitting, one life standing' referring to the amount of time he spent working his legs in his present incarnation. Furthermore, when the Professor was shown where the monk had lived and worked, he had a sense of 'recollection of the place.'"

"But that does not convince you of the reality of reincarnation?" I asked.

"It's just a story," shrugged Laoshi. "At one time, I had a student who was a famous spiritual healer. His name was known and respected throughout the healing community in Scotland. I apprenticed myself to him for a while to learn his methods. There was a time, you see, when I imagined myself as a famous healer. I spent much time with this master of the healing arts, who also claimed ability in mediumship and channeled communications from another world. He fascinated me with descriptions of my spirit guides and amused me with tales of my past lives as a Cavalier fighting the Roundheads and a Roman legionnaire battling the Picts in the far North."

"Wow, that's really something, Laoshi" I mused aloud.

"Well," shrugged Laoshi, "a good yarn is a good yarn. At least I wasn't a shit-shoveler in Sheffield." Laoshi laughed, causing me to sigh. He was not taking this too seriously, but I persisted, "Why did you give up Laoshi, the healing I mean?"

"I soon came to realize that I wasn't truly interested in the healing arts, only in the mantle of the mysterious master of the medical arts. Neither did I have a vocation to minister to the sick. The final nail in the coffin, so to speak, was hammered home when my spirit guides, all five of them (it seems I needed a lot of guidance) turned out to be unreliable."

"Unreliable… in what way unreliable?" I had not heard before of Laoshi's brief fling with healing, and I was more than a little curious.

"My spirit guides apparently informed my mentor that the knee injury, which had troubled me on and off for years, would spontaneously disappear in exactly three months from that date."

"Do spirit guides usually give time frames?"

"The very question I asked myself," smiled Laoshi. "My master agreed that such precision was unusual, but was adamant that the three month term was correct. So, I marked in my diary the day when my old knee problem would be history, found no change the following day, and never returned."

"You lost faith?" I said in understanding.

"I suppose so," he nodded with a smile. "What use have I for guides, who cannot tell time? Nor for psychics whose contacts from the other worlds 'know' intimate details of past lives, but don't know your name. Once, through a bizarre, and as yet unexplained coincidence, I felt the need to seek out my dead sister's spirit. I asked around and was put in touch with a well-respected professional clairvoyant. After I paid the hefty fee for her services, the unremarkable middle-aged woman, who introduced herself as a seer, claimed to have made contact with my deceased sister. My sister was anxious for the seer to relay a message to me regarding important documents under the stairs of her old house. It was odd, however, that my sister apparently 'knew' documents were under the stairs, but could not remember the address and, even more bizarrely, could not remember her own name, a detail I withheld from the medium as a test of authenticity."

"But," I insisted, cutting Laoshi short, "shouldn't you be prepared to accept the possibility of reincarnation if someone like Zheng Manqing thought there was something to it?"

Laoshi considered my question before answering. "You have heard me talk before about the difference between faith and belief, have you not?"

I nodded.

"Well," continued Laoshi, "we are on something of the same ground here. On first hearing that faith and belief are not the same thing, I felt the truth of the matter intuitively, but later, as I thought more deeply, I wondered about that difference. I wondered where and how beliefs arose. I had assumed their origin was in the heart-mind, as was the capacity of faith. It was only after much reflection that I came to understand that belief is just as much a part of the rational mind as are other thoughts."

"Whoa, hang on a minute, Laoshi," I said, holding up my hands to emphasize the point. "Surely belief and rational thought are different things entirely. Isn't that what is meant by "rational"? It is not random belief. Rational thought is, surely, arrived at by reason and deduction from facts?"

"You would suppose so, and I understand some psychologists argue as you do," acknowledged Laoshi, unfazed by my objection. "But as they say with computers 'garbage in, garbage out.' Many, if not all, of our most cherished beliefs are nothing more than cultural or social conditioning, the ideas that we have taken in with our mother's milk. Have you heard the story of the monastery, where the monks' daily meditation was routinely disturbed by a wandering cat?"

"No Laoshi, but I've a feeling I'll be hearing it now."

"Quite so," smiled Laoshi. "Well, the master, it seems, in order to stop the cat from interrupting meditation, ordered a senior monk to take the cat and tie it up outside the hall for the duration of the session. The following session saw the cat similarly tied up outside the hall. In fact, the cat was regularly tied up to allow the monks to meditate in peace. When the aged master died, the practice of tying up the cat outside continued. Then, later when the cat died, the monks, accustomed to seeing a cat tied up at meditation time, found a replacement cat and continued the tradition. Over the years, monks came and went, and so did a succession of cats, until one day a senior monk wrote a doctrine on the spiritual necessity of tying up cats prior to meditation."

Returning to the thoughts of Zheng Manqing, Laoshi added, "The Professor, as with all of us, was raised in a specific cultural environment and, as such, interpreted the world in keeping with those ideas. We must distinguish between what is cultural and what is essence. For instance, the Professor refused to wear shirts or jackets with collars, believing they were a symbol of slavery. Does that mean we have to tailor our wardrobe to follow his lead? Aspects of his behavior arose from his cultural perspective and may not be relevant in our culture or time. As Wang Lang said, 'You do not have to do anything the Professor said.' Instead, take the Professor's teachings and practice them to find out where they are alive for you. The principles may be immutable, but our environment is ever changing.

"We have to be careful of beliefs suckled from society's breast to avoid being imprisoned by those very same beliefs. We can find our minds trapped in the 'empty husk of true faith.'"

Laoshi was referring to one of his favorite passages from the *Daodejing*:

> When the Dao is lost, there is goodness.
> When goodness is lost, there is morality.
> When morality is lost, there is ritual.
> Ritual is the husk of true faith, the beginning of chaos.

"But surely beliefs are important to us?" I argued, acutely aware of my own cherished beliefs. "Surely, if we are to live together harmoniously we must have common ideas of what is right and wrong?"

Laoshi smiled broadly and nodded before explaining further.

"Well said. We must not throw out the baby with the bathwater. You are right to argue for commonly held beliefs to bind society together. We must, however, guard against the notion of accepting them as absolute truths, rather than relative truths. Does this make sense to you?"

"Yes Laoshi, it does begin to make sense, but seems rather abstract."

"Well," he said looking upward for inspiration. "Think of the form. Let us restrict ourselves to Zheng Manqing's form for the time being, the one we know best."

I nodded.

"Now," he asked. "As you watch students from other schools demonstrating the form, how can you judge if their form is competent?"

"Well, if they maintain the principles, then it is correct. If they break the principles, then it is wrong."

"Almost," he corrected, "nobody totally embodies the principles, but you are essentially correct: the closer the adherence to the key ideas of upright body, separation of weight, body as one unit, turning at the waist, and beautiful lady's hand, the better. But have you not also seen me correct students who are not breaking the principles? Do I not instruct students to copy my movements more closely, even when their own movements are consistent with principle? You have also seen me correct the form of a student from another teacher, who has a good grasp of fundamentals."

"Yes Laoshi, I guess so," I replied cautiously, "like in rollback, where some teachers teach that the arms open up as the waist is turned to the right, whereas you teach that the hands don't move relative to the body."

"And so, am I justified in making these corrections?" asked Laoshi.

"I guess so," I ventured, remaining on alert, "since you are my teacher, you are correct."

"A politic answer," nodded Laoshi with a smile. "When principle is not compromised, slight differences in the form are irrelevant, but you should know what you are doing. You should know your own school's tradition and stick with it."

"That does not make much sense, Laoshi," I queried. "Surely if the differences are irrelevant, it doesn't matter how you do it?"

"Think of driving a car," said Laoshi without a pause, as if anticipating my question. "Think of the actual mechanics of driving the car as principle: the use of the accelerator pedal, the use of the gear stick, the use of the steering wheel. Knowledge of how to operate a car is essential to make the car go. Now, think of the Highway Code: we drive on the left but the Americans and Europeans drive on the right. This difference is a matter of tradition. It does not matter to the car which side of the road you are on, but if you want to avoid a crash, you follow the same rules as everyone else.

"Beliefs are like the rules of the road: we need them to get along with each other. Ironically, the more complex our society becomes, the more important these beliefs seem to be, but they are conditioning, not heart-mind. In the form we have to understand the provenance of what we are doing and know if it is essence or tradition. The same is true of our thinking: we must learn to distinguish what is heart-mind and what is unexamined belief."

Laoshi's explanation was a little dismaying. It seems that I had not fully understood the heart-mind concept. The internal programming infused in me by parents, schools, and culture was not heart-mind, but rather the internal policeman, which society imbeds in us to keep us from straying beyond society's use. It was all a little depressing: how was I to gain freedom when I was scarcely aware of my imprisonment?

Laoshi, unsurprisingly, seemed to be reading my mind. "Trust the heart-mind," he said.

"But," I protested, "I don't know what the heart-mind is; how can I trust it to guide me?"

"Find what brings you joy and follow it: not what is pleasurable, but what makes you feel truly content. Learn to recognize the feelings, which arise when you love what you are doing. Compare these feelings with the temporary satisfaction of pleasing others. Unless you can recognize and free yourself from society's approval of you, then you will be a hostage forever and never know freedom."

"But I will make mistakes and do stupid things."

Laoshi seemed to find this comment particularly amusing and laughingly replied, "Welcome to the human race." Then, more seriously, "Invest in loss. Gradually you will learn to distinguish between the short-term glow of society's approval and the genuine path of the heart."

As a final piece of advice, Laoshi offered, "If you feel personally attacked, when a belief you hold is challenged, then know you are acting as society's proxy. You are defending what is your culture's preference for how things should be. What is true needs no defense. As the *Daodejing* says, 'Those who justify themselves do not convince.' Like gravity, which speaks for itself every time something falls to the floor, the heart-mind needs no defense. My 'truth' does not rely on 'opinions for or against' by those other than myself."

Returning to the question of re-incarnation, I began to understand Laoshi's view: In the company of the heart-mind, who cares!

To engage conscientiously in push-hands or fencing is to observe that "like leads to like," where force and aggression are concerned. A forceful approach by an opponent provokes a similar response in oneself. Zheng Manqing did not approve, commenting that, "Double strength: ox-strength versus ox-strength, becomes muddy water." This muddying of the waters is commonplace and the norm in many push-hands environments.

It is perplexing, however, to discover that the reverse is not equally true: like does not routinely lead to like when we encounter softness, especially when softness renders our force impotent. Being neutralized by a skillful, sensitive, and soft response to a push does not inspire a reciprocal sensitivity in subsequent attempts to deliver a telling push. Indeed, the opposite is a more likely outcome. The softer the deflection of our forcefulness, the greater the tendency to add rather than subtract force in subsequent pushes. Thus, many a taijiquan player abandons the push-hands scene altogether, or seeks a ritualized push-hands environment, so as to avoid feeling polluted by those who would emulate the ox.

Fencing without armor does, to an extent, inhibit the prevalence of forcefulness out of a sense of self-preservation. We instinctively acknowledge the risk of a mutual massacre if unchecked aggression, stoked by the actions of a belligerent opponent, escalates to dangerous levels. However, within the fencing scenario, there is still enough scope for rigid resistance to arouse a sense of unease, as sword presses firmly against sword. "Is this how it is meant to be?" we ask and seldom find an answer convincing.

In searching for the means to overcome the bullish manner of a few of my comrades, I adopted similar tactics when fencing with Laoshi. Forsaking all attempt at finesse, I greeted the subtlety of his offense with rudimentary blocks and cheap jabs. There was no comfort to be had in this approach, as his repertoire of responses was a match for my forcefulness, and he nullified my cloddish efforts, even the more devious.

"I just don't get it, Laoshi," I sighed holding my hands up in resignation, "how do you manage to control my sword, even when I try to power out of my stuckness using force?"

"Oh, is *that* what you were doing?" Laoshi affected surprise, "I thought you were constipated or something today."

I shook my head a little as Laoshi chuckled. I rolled my eyes and sighed loudly in response, only to provoke more laughter from Laoshi.

"You are really so childish sometimes, Laoshi," I mumbled peevishly.

"And you are always so mature," he responded with mock seriousness.

Then more pointedly, "Feeling sorry for yourself is puerile. You do yourself a disservice. Remember the golden rule of push-hands applies equally to fencing: it is never your opponent's fault when they cut or push you, whether the means be fair or foul."

"Sorry Laoshi," I sighed, "It's just the frustration. I'm getting really frustrated fencing with the guys."

"Don't be," he smiled, "they are paying you a complement."

"How so?"

"They are acknowledging," he reassured me, "in their own way, that you are catching them. Their ego recoils at the realization that you can get the better of them, and so they engage in denial by forcing their way out of trouble. Believe me, however, deep down, they know. That is their koan."

"But, what about my koan, Laoshi?" I questioned. "What kind of fencing skill only works with compliant opponents?"

"Ah! The age-old question," replied Laoshi. "Come inside and have some tea." He led me into the warmth of the kitchen. The tea, once brewed, was set down on the wooden dining table. He gazed absently out of the window before, once again, illuminating the path before me, as only he could.

"Now," he began, "your fencing has improved rapidly over the past couple of years: your basics are sound, your ability to feel the yang of your opponent through your sword has reached a significant level, you are no stranger to gaining the sente; and the subtleties of timing are no longer a mystery. You agree?"

"Yes Laoshi, I'd like to think what you say it true," I hoped to convey a sense of modesty but very much welcomed Laoshi's recognition of my progress.

"Well," he continued, "all that you have learned is only preparation for the next stage."

"Another stage. Who'd have thought it?" I felt an urge to express my sarcasm but remained silent. Laoshi, however, appeared to accurately assess my feelings, and added, "As always, there is another stage. Even the very best of us, or more accurately, especially the very best of us, acknowledge the vastness of the art and the impossibility of reaching the end of knowledge. Remember, the great Ben Lo likened the extent of his expertise in taijiquan to 'a single hair on the back of a water buffalo.' How much less is our own?"

"This next stage," continued Laoshi, "we can call 'connection.' It is an idea common to all martial arts. In Chinese, the term is, *lian*. Some in the Japanese arts call it *musubi*."

"Oh, I'm sure I've heard of *musubi*," I interrupted, "Billy said it meant contact, but also implied the notion of harmonizing with the opponent."

"Indeed," nodded Laoshi, "but usually we use the word connection rather than harmonizing. Remember, Zheng Manqing advised students to consider the four ideas of sticking, adhering, connecting, and following. These words come from the 'Song of Push Hands,' and each represents a core concept in our art. Of course, as with so much in taijiquan, there are several possible interpretations of these concepts.

"Crucially," added Laoshi, refreshing our cups with more tea, "in terms of our present discussion, the concept of connecting is more easily studied in fencing than push-hands. Correct connection can be identified easily, as there is a sense of sword sticking to sword. You are familiar with the feeling, yes? It's almost as if the swords had become magnetized."

This type of connection was indeed familiar, but the experience was exclusive to fencing with Laoshi: none of us could bind another's sword to our own in quite the same manner. Indeed, our lack of skill in this department was betrayed by the sound of wood clacking against wood: "the sound of incompetence," according to Wang Lang.

I recognized that Laoshi's ability to "magnetize" my sword was sticking at an advanced level, a feature of his fencing, which was becoming ever present as we dueled together. Whatever he was doing, he was getting better at it. The moment our swords crossed, I was controlled, and found it impossible to escape. The only variable seemed to be in the length of time he found it amusing to chase me around the garden before ending it by "cutting" me on the hand or body. As I listened to Laoshi, I grew hopeful: perhaps the time had come when he would reveal the secret of the magnetic contact.

Resuming his explanation, Laoshi advised, "Imagine two spacecraft docking: first there were two, then there is one. Once you have docked, so to speak, with your opponent through the connection with their sword, you can control them, as the classics say, like 'leading a thousand pound bull by the ring in its nose.' At this point, the opponent still has the ability to move, but you are most decidedly in control; you have successfully combined yin and yang in a very particular way. There is no resisting the force from the opponent's blade, but your intention, your qi, is alive, very yang, directing the opponent's attacks in the direction you chose. You are relentless. Once you have docked, they are at your mercy."

I had reservations. I was clear on the premise: *lian* or *musubi* implies a marriage of power with sensitivity: once contact is made, our sensitivity informs us as to the direction and strength of our opponent's intention, which is then controlled using our own intention. A question formed like a thorn in my mind, "But Laoshi, how is that different from using force to overpower the opponent's force?"

"Ah ha!" he exclaimed loudly, as if waiting for my objection, "because, you only apply yang on your opponent's yin. The connection itself reveals, with crystal clarity, the energy of the opponent, where they are resisting and in what direction. We then blend, or harmonize, as your former teacher might say, with that resistance, before leading it in the direction we chose. It is called, 'turning resistance into non-resistance.' Once this principle is mastered, it can be applied in all situations, forceful or not."

The phrase, "turning resistance into non-resistance," was the catalyst to my comprehension. Like so many taijiquan aphorisms, the words, although familiar, had previously brought forth little insight. This time, however, the meaning resonated within me, evoking a sense of wonder in the power of true connection. Blending with an incoming force, we are not victims to its whim. By pressing softly on the inevitable yin point, we take control over speed and direction, leading a hostile energy as we choose, until its force is spent. A sensitive opponent will, of course, realize that the trajectory and force of his blade has been hijacked and will compensate. But, sensitive to the connection, we readjust once more to catch the force and make it our servant.

Clearly, simply hearing of the principle does not confer mastery, but we do glimpse what is possible. The rest is in practicing, until connecting is instantaneous. Ironically, the very forcefulness used by our comrades to power out of stuckness dramatically reveals the yin and yang on their blade and aids our attempts to blend and lead their force as we choose.

Chapter 15: Stone Balancing

In an age where travel is increasingly speedy and communication is effectively instantaneous, progress in push-hands remains undeniably obstinate in resisting the trend. An ability to utilize the *jin* energy to push an opponent is, for some, the project of a lifetime, and, frustratingly, in common with the proverbial "black belt" of Japanese arts, only a beginning. The ability to uproot another is not the holy grail of push-hands, merely the first step in a search for ultimate principle. As a first step, however, it motivates many an aspirant to become consumed by the treasure it appears to offer.

Laoshi often commented how he, in the company of Wang Lang's senior students, tended to obsess over the prospect of pushing effectively using the soft energy of taijiquan. "In those early days," he recalled over tea one morning, "I was desperate to learn the skill of uprooting. I assumed that once the skill was mine, none would stand long before me, until I acquainted their backs with the brickwork. Imagine my disappointment as I faced up to the reality: despite acquiring something of the power, even a novice could frustrate me as I labored to launch them powerfully against the wall. In learning to uproot, I had not reached the end of the game, but had only thrown a six to get on the board."

I was sympathetic since any progress I made in mastering the uprooting ability was accompanied by the same dissatisfaction alluded to by Laoshi. My discomfort was not ameliorated by Laoshi's constant admonition that discovering *fajin*, the uprooting push, meant we had only entered the courtyard of taijiquan.

Entering the courtyard, for me at least, depended on the willingness of my partner to hold the door open for me. When pushing with a gentle soul, who favored a sweetness of technique above crude resistance, I could deliver a strong, well-timed push, capable of sending them to the wall with a satisfying thud. Such purists were a rare dish, indeed: the haute cuisine at the table of push-hands. More often I found myself served up an assortment of wrigglers, bracers, and blockers, leaving me with a frustrating indigestion.

In fairness, I must own to the fact that, at times, my own resistance and insistence was on a par with anyone. Several senior students, frustrated in their attempts to push me, resorted to holding me fast with a strong grip, forcing me to remain compliant, in order to deliver their own version of the uprooting push. The situation was unsatisfactory for all, but the mantra of "don't insist, don't resist" was so inconsistent with our norm, that we had little choice but to indulge our baser instincts. We longed for the days when our pushing would be worthy of the name taijiquan, relying solely on the intrinsic energy that the Professor had mastered.

A previous complaint to Laoshi did elicit sympathy and some welcome instruction in three techniques to assist in pushing a non-cooperative opponent. These three methods, dubbed "the three ropes," were only offered with some reticence. On asking him, some months later, the extent to which he relied on "the three ropes," Laoshi replied somewhat offhandedly, "That stuff? That's for children."

His reply, I presumed, was less a dismissal of the "three ropes" and more a warning against becoming enthralled by technique, a sentiment he shared with Wang Lang, who reminded his students that, "technique works some of the time, principle works all of the time." My suspicions were confirmed when, sometime later, as we readied ourselves for a practice session, Laoshi asked, "Do you remember 'the three ropes' idea I mentioned to you before?"

"Yes Laoshi," I nodded, "I have been really trying to practice those ideas."

"Excellent," he replied before adding, without a trace of irony, "Now, forget about the ropes. It is time to put childish things behind you."

A smile played on my lips, as I celebrated my elevation in Laoshi's opinion.

"At least I'm moving up in the world," I mused before Laoshi continued. "You should now use a more... how should we say, a more discerning idea when pushing."

"But what about 'the three ropes?'" I enquired.

"They are useful for a time, but they tend to tie you up," he chuckled, before adding, "Get it... ropes, tie you up?"

I had missed the pun in my eagerness to learn more, so I simply stared blankly ahead. Seeing his joke miss the mark, he resumed, "Well anyway, back to the point. 'The three ropes' are like tactics, and so are of limited use. They are, at best, preparatory exercises. It's not that they are completely redundant, but they remain blunt instruments: they force something to happen rather than harness what is already happening. In push-hands, as with life, we progress by using what has been given. This, in itself, is a deeply spiritual idea: we must not miss out on the life we have by fixating on the life we wished we had."

I nodded, as this wisdom recalled the C. S. Lewis admonition, "to live the adventure that is sent."

"Now, have you ever heard of "stone balancing?" asked Laoshi.

"No Laoshi. I can't say that I have."

"Neither had I, until some years ago, when I was about to dine out with a friend. Arriving early at his house, I found him absorbed in a television program about the coastline of the British Isles. The subject did not interest me, so I scanned a newspaper, as I waiting for the program to end. My prompt arrival turned out to be fortuitous, for my attention was seized by a comment from the television: 'It's the paradox between fragility and solidity.'

"I immediately looked up from the paper. The phrase hit me hard. Those few words described exactly the subtly of the feeling I was searching for in push-hands and fencing. The phrase was exquisite: 'The paradox between fragility and solidity' is something a push-hands or fencing master might say. I looked at the screen, eager to see what they were talking about. I heard the voice continue, 'You have two very big, heavy stones, and they are balanced in a very fragile way.' I was amazed, as the same could be said about two push-hands players, as they seek out each other's center.

"The speaker turned out to be Aidrian Gray, an artist, who specializes in stone-balancing, the art of balancing hefty stones on each other at implausible angles without glue, sand, or other medium to fix them in place. He was able to create barely believable sculptures with only the friction of stone on stone and a precise sense of balance to maintain these compositions in a condition of fragile solidity.

"He outlined his method further: 'You focus in completely. You close out everything else because you have to have stillness within you. You listen to the rocks. You listen with your hands, and you move them very, very gently. Then when you get the feel for it, you find a weightlessness....'"

Laoshi was becoming quite animated, as his hands seemed to be pushing a boulder, searching for weightlessness. He continued miming the method, as he developed his explanation. "To listen with your hands, moving them very, very gently, seeking a kind of weightlessness is the exact method of the highly skilled push-hands player, homing in on the yin point of the opponent. The metaphor is clear: my opponent is a huge rock or stone, and I gently feel for their point of balance: their yin and yang, their strength and weakness, their heaviness and lightness. When I locate the yin point, which must always exist, if there is even the hint of resistance, my partner feels weightless, or at least lighter, and I need very little force to take their balance completely.

"Does this make sense?" he asked, insuring I was following. "Do you understand? To find the soft spot, look for the lightness which comes with heaviness."

Laoshi's metaphor had indeed hit home, as I told him. Laoshi then suggested we practice. I cannot report that my pushing was transformed dramatically and instantly, but as I began to search for the soft, indefensible yin spot, I realized that precisely because yang is heavy, it is more obvious, and so the yin is habitually ignored. Our attention, being captured exclusively by the yang, we remain unaware of the yin, which is where our opponent's real weakness lies. It is another expression of the figure/ground phenomenon. We see the figure, not the background; we are so compelled by the black letters on the page, that we totally ignore the white paper on which the letters are printed.

Laoshi was directing my attention to the weakness in my partner's position by feeling where they are light, where they feel empty. It is that emptiness that we can then fill with a push. Laoshi also showed me that locating and filling the emptiness does not have to be a rapid, violent, brutish act. It can be achieved with slowness and sensitivity, even allowing the receiver the freedom to attempt an escape. Each evasion creates another yin spot, which is filled once again. Such evasions are limited, as each one renders the opponent closer to the point of no return, when they will be stuck and at the mercy of the pusher. An image came to my mind as I experienced Laoshi's slow, deliberate unbalancing. I felt I was trapped in the coils of a giant anaconda, squeezing the life out of its prey with each attempted escape.

As we finished the session, Laoshi turned toward me, "Do you see why this method is superior to 'the three ropes' and other tactics or tricks?"

"I do Laoshi," I replied sincerely, "those methods are about doing it, rather than allowing it. They are a kind of forcing. I see that now. They are techniques to engineer a particular outcome. The anaconda idea is about following our partner, until they become stuck. It is more like *wuwei* (nonaction) in action."

He smiled approvingly. "Absolutely right, you have it. To mix metaphors, 'the three ropes' are like the glue, sand, or wires that some might use to force the stones to balance. We must learn to discard these devices and rely purely on feeling. In terms of pushing, there is not much more to say. You already know *how* to uproot, and now you know where to uproot. You are as, Wang Lang would say, 'a dangerous man.'"

My delight at Laoshi's praise was as welcome as it was brief, for he added casually, "Of course, now we must work on your yielding."

Chapter 16: Professor's Secret

Laoshi tended not to mix with the wider taijiquan community, following Wang Lang's preference to "tend my own garden," but as Ramakrishna observed, "When the flower blooms, the bees come uninvited."

And so, visiting "bees" from other schools were a regular occurrence at Laoshi's classes. Some came only once, others stayed, having found a class in accord with their needs. Normally, those who arrived to test the waters did so alone, like samurai of old on a musha shugyo pilgrimage. I was taken aback, therefore, one spring evening, by the arrival of three new faces at Laoshi's push-hands class. As a senior student of the school, I welcomed visitors with a mixture of excitement and apprehension: new blood in push-hands class is always welcome, provided it is not spilled by the over-eager, or the out-right hostile. Any disquiet I experience at the arrival of guests is heightened when they appear mob-handed.

I was reassured to discover, therefore, that our visitors were unknown to each other and their synchronistic arrival signaled nothing sinister. All claimed several years of experience in taijiquan. Two had a Yang style background, one having studied in England, the other in Mainland China. The oldest of the three was a seasoned veteran of Zheng Manqing's taijiquan, with a solid foundation in form and push-hands. Despite skills acquired in differing settings, all three were united in one respect: they all adopted a significant forward lean as they lined up with a partner for push-hands. I expected as much from the Yang style students, but the lean was equally, if not more pronounced, in the Zheng Manqing trained man.

As was his custom, Laoshi made not even the slightest mention of the spinal inclination of our guests, preferring to involve them in our practice, without imposing his view of correct principle. As our visitors became regular students, however, Laoshi began to offer his understanding of how postural alignment was an important part of our study: "One of the key aspects of Master Lin's taijiquan," began Laoshi one evening, "is that the spine be upright and the front of the pelvis be rotated slightly upwards to drop the sacrum."

Master Lin, Laoshi's teacher in Taiwan, had a well-deserved reputation for outstanding push-hands ability, characterized by his commitment to a soft, non-competitive approach and a determination to place yielding ahead of overpowering an opponent.

"Master Lin," Laoshi continued, "was not in favor of leaning forward while pushing hands for two very good reasons. First, and perhaps foremost, the waist cannot be turned effectively if the spine is inclined forward. Turning while leaning causes the shoulder to dip downward, leading to a loss of equilibrium. Secondly, there is a tendency to drop the chin, a fault he was at pains to correct in my own practice. Master Lin admonished me saying that I 'should not be afraid of being hit or pushed and must keep my head up, so I can see what is to be yielded to.' Master Lin went on to assert that, 'Muhammad Ali could dance around and not be hit because he had his head up and could see the blows coming.' Indeed, Master Lin went further declaring that, 'generally in boxing, the one who kept his head up would be the winner.'"

"But…" questioned one of the new students, "that advice is counter to the fundamentals of boxing: chin down, hands up."

"I understand that," replied Laoshi, "but the young Ali, prior to his rope-a-dope technique, was a master of fighting with his head up and hands down. This is what Master Lin was referring to. Crucially, Master Lin also revealed that Zheng Manqing's secret was to look at the opponents chin, not in an intense way, but to notice when the chin dropped."

Not having hitherto heard of the Professor's "secret," I was weighing the implications, when my thoughts were interrupted by the Zheng Manqing enthusiast, who had joined us only a few weeks previously. Perhaps reluctant to eradicate the forward lean from his posture, he raised his hand and politely asked, "Excuse me, but does it matter all that much since even Wang Lang said that push-hands was mostly about rooting?"

Laoshi eyed the newcomer for a few moments before querying, "I was not aware that you had met Wang Lang."

"Well… to be fair, I haven't, but one of his students told me…"

"I am not sure you are doing justice to Wang Lang's view," interrupted Laoshi. "Perhaps your friend's opinion is based on a story Wang Lang recounted after meeting an old comrade some years on from their Shr Jung School days."

"Which story is that?" asked another student, encouraging Laoshi to tell all.

"It seems," replied Laoshi, "that on a trip to the southern states, Wang Lang took the opportunity to visit an old taijiquan comrade, who had moved out of New York some years before. His friend, Joe, was still practicing form, but unable to find like-minded partners had not pushed hands in years. Wang Lang assumed that Joe's standard would have declined sharply due to his lack of regular partner practice.

"Wang Lang was in for a surprise: Joe's ability in push-hands had improved markedly, despite not even touching another taijiquan player in the interim. Responding to Wang Lang's compliments on his ability, Joe revealed his routine which included serious rooting practice: one hour a day."

Laoshi paused, allowing us to draw our own conclusions from the anecdote.

"From this story," added Laoshi, scanning our faces, "it could be argued that after a certain level of technique has been achieved in push-hands, the rest is solely a matter of rooting power.

"However," he added by way of clarification, "I do not believe that Wang Lang would take such a restrictive view. His approach was based primarily on developing sensitivity, the improvement of root being a secondary, though significant consideration. I am equally certain that Master Lin would not regard root development as the primary means of assessing skill in push-hands."

"How then did Master Lin measure ability in push-hands?" I asked.

"Good question," Laoshi replied. "How do we measure ability in push-hands? So much depends on why we practice taijiquan at all. Master Lin's approach was much more spiritual than some others. He was clear that, 'Our taijiquan is not about fighting, but self-cultivation, which means it is about relaxing, yielding, having a sincere heart, and not going against another's force.'"

Laoshi paused for a moment, as if remembering his old teacher, before resuming, "Master Lin's words suggest an approach far removed from a comparison of root against root."

Class ended on that note, and over the next few weeks I mulled over Master Lin's revelation concerning Zheng Manqing's "secret." Laoshi typically made no mention of the opponent's chin in class, instead advising students to watch the opponent's chest, so as not to be deceived by feints. I only recall one instance where Laoshi described the method of an Olympic caliber judoka who pounced as soon as the slightest tilt of the head revealed an imbalance in an opponent's structure. Laoshi habitually warned against being transfixed by an opponent's eyes, and recommended that our gaze fall on the chest.

As I considered the matter ever deeper, I wondered if Zheng Manqing was simply making use of a "tell" in taking notice of the chin dipping, or was there a deeper principle at play. After all, the Professor did deduce much from a fine examination of a patient in his medical capacity, once advising Wang Lang that frequent sighing was a sign of excessive yin, while pronounced half-moon shapes beneath the fingernails was indicative of excessive yang.

Bearing in mind that mind and body are indeed one, it would be unsurprising if the body should reveal aspects of our deeper being. It would be equally unsurprising if Master Lin, a deeply spiritual man, who spent several days a month in meditation at a Buddhist retreat center, should have a posture in harmony with his spirituality, that is, relaxed, upright, centered, and balanced.

I began to suspect that the aspiration toward a straight, upright spine was not only vital for developing our qi and improving push-hands, but also had a role to play in deepening our spirituality.

I asked Laoshi for an opinion. He considered my question briefly before replying, "Qi development, deepening spirituality, improved push-hands—it's the same thing."

Chapter 17: It's a Two-Game Thing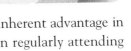

Zheng Manqing's assertion that women have an inherent advantage in push-hands was not reflected in the number of women regularly attending Laoshi's push-hands class. While his form classes contained a roughly even split between genders, Laoshi's push-hands class attracted very few women.

Watching some push-hands exchanges, it is easy to empathize with women, reluctant to engage with a process where their advantage takes so long to materialize. The blessing of softness and sensitivity, which many men struggle to develop over years, does not prevent a smaller woman being rag-dolled by a less skillful but physically stronger man. Being pushed around by less sensitive partners in order to learn is known in taijiquan circles as "investing in loss." The gift of softness women bring to push-hands must be combined with an immense capacity to invest in loss, perhaps to a greater extent than required by men.

Laoshi did little to make things easier for the women and those sensitive men who found the experience of push-hands overwhelming. When asked why, he replied, "If you take the grit from the oyster, it does not produce the pearl. If you make push-hands easier, you lose the very thing that makes it worth pursuing.

"Besides," he added wryly, "the strong, physical guys who enjoy 'success' early in push-hands will soon enough face their own trials: they simply don't know it yet. As nature depletes them, or they face even stronger opponents, they will discover what the women learn from the start. Perhaps the real advantage that women possess is not one of superior sensitivity, but an insight into the reality of push-hands right from the start. Men's delusions result in wasted time."

"Yes, Laoshi," protested a student, "but that means many women will give up immediately, their enthusiasm killed by forceful opponents, who quit later anyway. Isn't there something to be done about this?"

Laoshi nodded slowly, acknowledging the point before conceding, "I know of no way." To be sure, Laoshi discouraged use of excessive force in favor of subtlety in respect of push-hands, but, for the most part, we were deaf to his entreaties.

Nevertheless, women took to fencing with greater alacrity and persistence. Though still outnumbered, women made a significant contribution to sword class, fencing on equal terms with men. In my new role of teacher, I pondered this apparent inconsistency, wondering if perhaps fencing was a way to encourage greater participation in push-hands. Traditionally, the taijiquan student is introduced to push-hands before sword, but I wondered if there was merit in reversing the order.

Inevitably the topic came up for discussion with Laoshi. Attempting to solicit his views concerning the order in which push-hands and fencing are taught, I remarked on the dearth of women actively participating in push-hands, compared to those who took up fencing.

Laoshi replied quite casually, "I am sure the answer to that question stems from the fact that, to use Wang Lang's words, 'fencing is a *one-game thing* while push hands is a *two-game thing*.'"

I was taken by surprise, as the phrase now attributed to Wang Lang was new to me. I had presumed, by this stage, that I would be familiar with the entire lexicon of Wang Lang's injunctions and axioms.

"What does that mean, Laoshi: a one-game thing or a two-game thing?"

Laoshi took his time replying, "How strange… idioms once used on a daily basis can fall out of use. I haven't thought in those terms for a long time, perhaps because 'game' suggests something trivial.

"Wang Lang," he continued without further prompting, "was inclined to characterize some of the crucial differences between fencing and push-hands by using the 'one-game/two-game' analogy. He also applied the same classification to distinguish the approach favored by him as opposed to other teachers."

"Has this," I interrupted, "something to do with our custom of taking turns as pusher and neutralizer in push-hands, while our fencing is more of a free-for-all? Is that why push hands is a two-game thing: because we play the role of pusher then receiver?"

"Hmm… a day of strangeness," mused Laoshi. "I've never thought of it that way." Pausing for a moment, he considered my analysis, before returning to his own explanation. "Regardless… that's not what Wang Lang had in mind. The difference is more important and fundamental. It relates to an essential difference in the nature of our fencing practice, as compared with our push-hands.

"First, we must not forget," he cautioned, "that our fencing exchanges are far removed from an authentic sword fight in many ways. For example, that we are accustomed to acknowledge a cut immediately on being touched by the opponent's blade. This is not realistic in terms of a real duel with live blades, but, then again, we are not training to rival Lin Chong (one of the heroes of *Water Margin*) or Musashi (samurai swordsman)."

"So, Laoshi. How would you categorize our approach to fencing?"

"Well… I take the view that, at a fundamental level, we are studying yin and yang in relation to martial arts, and so, by extension, to life itself.

"To inflict a debilitating cut on an opponent requires more than the tickle of a blade on skin or clothing. As Wang Lang often pointed out, 'our swords are not electrified.' When we practice our brand of fencing, however, every touch is recognized as a 'hit' regardless of whether the pressure is sufficient to injure. This is why our fencing can be described as 'a one-game thing': once the sword blade touches the opponent at all, the game is over.

"The rationale in push hands is very different. We begin with a touch, the touch of hands on hands.

"Using the hands and arms as antennae, we detect, intercept, and deflect the attacks of our partner. A novice often fails to appreciate that our arms are, first and foremost, preventing an opponent's force from reaching the vital organs of our body. If push-hands becomes over ritualized, we can be misled into thinking that an aggressor simply wants to arm-wrestle. Remember, the real target in push-hands is our body or head, which we defend with our hands and arms to prevent a blow becoming debilitating."

Laoshi was reminding me of the ease with which the ritualized nature of a practice can blind us to the *raison d'être* of that practice.

Laoshi continued, "After all, an attacker whose evil intent amounts to no more than pushing my arm is not someone to trouble my peace of mind very much. Push-hands, however, is a training device to prepare for a deliberate and focused attack by an aggressor intent on causing severe injury, hence the injunction to avoid rigidity in our arms when faced with a pusher. To hold out a rigid arm and brace against an anticipated push is as farcical and ineffective for a self-defense system as was the Maginot Line in World War II.

The attacker is perfectly free to disconnect and attack us directly onto the body. Should this occur, we must remain loose and alert, sticking to our opponent's hands ensuring no direct contact with our body.

"This, then, is the first game of push-hands: the arms and hands remain in contact, each partner trying to either get past, or control, the other's defenses. Of course, at some point, the attacker may penetrate the screen that our arms provide and reach our body; now we enter the realm of the second game. The arms may be the first line of defense, but, should these defenses be breached, we must defend by employing principle in a modified form."

Laoshi paused for a while, as he gathered his thoughts, so I used the opportunity to ask, "Laoshi, would it be true to say that Wang Lang was predominately concerned with the first game?"

"He was," confirmed Laoshi.

"And we too concentrate on the first game, as well, do we not?"

Laoshi nodded and waited for the inevitable question, which I was bursting to ask. I did not have him wait long. "So, Laoshi, why do we spend so much time on the first game and so little on the second?"

"I cannot speak for Wang Lang, here," answered Laoshi, "I can only tell you of my own opinion on the matter. Will that do?"

"Certainly Laoshi. You are my teacher."

He nodded, then addressed my point, "It is not that the second game is not worthy of study, but I would submit that unless you know the first game intimately, the second game tends to encourage a reliance on 'bracing.' We all come to the push-hands floor as accomplished bracers already: we resist in virtually every aspect of our lives. We instinctively meet force with equal or greater force: an attitude first learned in the playground and relied on for the rest of our lives. In common with everyone else, I came to study taijiquan well versed in resisting: physically, psychologically, and spiritually. I had no need of a teacher to encourage greater resisting. Intuitively, I knew I needed to seek something new, something that would negate the bracer within.

"This is one reason why I do not support competitive push hands: it cultivates a like-for-like response. Faced with the kind of opponents that Zheng Manqing describes as people "who love combat and never fail to use stiff and brutish force… or fast techniques to grapple…" it is easy to respond in kind, and thus become those very same people. The argument is sometimes made that in fighting an opponent, you become as they are. Perhaps the real cost of fighting is how we become someone detached from our real selves. I do not want to be someone else—I want to become the true me."

"But, Laoshi, people really seem to enjoy the rough and tumble of competitive push hands. Are they maybe practicing who they are?"

104

"Maybe," conceded Laoshi with a shrug, "but I suspect, they mostly enjoy winning, which is not the same thing. Doing something because the practice is itself uplifting is one thing; doing something for the glorification of the ego is something else. When the adulation of victory means more than the joy of participation, then you are not gaining much. After all, the adulation, which is so prized, will be soon lost. And while no one loves a loser, there is little real respect for a winner: mainly a simmering resentment of a boil on our backside we cannot quite reach."

"This reminds me of the saying," I interrupted; "Whatever you practice, you become?"

"Indeed," agreed Laoshi, "whatever you practice you become, for good or bad. Push-hands is far more important than pushing or not being pushed. As Zheng Manqing reminds us, it is Dao we are studying here: the Dao that reveals the heart-mind. And if a sense of the Dao is not discovered in the first game, you will not find it in the second."

Chapter 18: String of Pearls

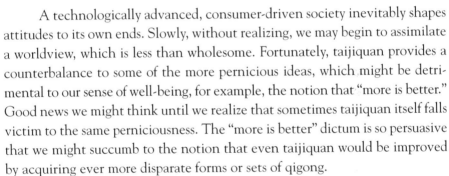

A technologically advanced, consumer-driven society inevitably shapes attitudes to its own ends. Slowly, without realizing, we may begin to assimilate a worldview, which is less than wholesome. Fortunately, taijiquan provides a counterbalance to some of the more pernicious ideas, which might be detrimental to our sense of well-being, for example, the notion that "more is better." Good news we might think until we realize that sometimes taijiquan itself falls victim to the same perniciousness. The "more is better" dictum is so persuasive that we might succumb to the notion that even taijiquan would be improved by acquiring ever more disparate forms or sets of qigong.

Laoshi, predictably, recoiled from such a proposition, preferring to limit the school syllabus to promote a deeper understanding. Nor was he enamored of the idea that bashing out form after form to the point of mental paralysis would result in significant progress. When questioned about the limited nature of his school syllabus, he would reply, "More understanding, not more forms." A sentiment in agreement with Dunraj Seth, one of John F. Gilbey's fanciful friends, who observed: "One technique mastered is worth a thousand sampled."

Unsurprisingly, as Laoshi's student, I embraced his commitment to deepen understanding within a limited syllabus, although I did retain some sympathy for those who sought to measure progress by memorizing an increasing corpus of forms and exercises. My first taijiquan teacher favored the acquisition of forms and, perhaps inadvertently, emphasized quantity over quality. As a beginner, I welcomed his broad syllabus approach, due to the intense feeling of anti-climax I experienced on finally completing the Zheng Manqing form. I could detect no significant enrichment in my sense of well-being, despite committing to memory a string of movements containing thirty-seven distinct postures. I was advised that progress was to be won by learning the long form: the original Yang form as performed by Yang Chengfu. Needless to say, having added the long form to the "toolbox" of exercises available, I remained unconvinced as to the overall improvement in my gongfu. Over time, as my toolbox expanded and my wallet contracted, I was able to demonstrate, in addition to the Zheng Manqing and Yang forms, the following: three sets of qigong exercises (Eight Strands, *Shibashi*, and the "Vancouver" sequence); *makko ho*, a Japanese system of "meridian" stretching; numerous self-massage techniques; three methods for push hands; *dalü*; a sword form; pushing swords; a saber form; and assorted "Daoist" health exercises— all of which I could perform, albeit without any true understanding of what I was doing.

"'Coffee-table' taijiquan," remarked Laoshi when I recounted the list one day over tea.

"Sorry Laoshi." I countered playfully, "I've never heard of 'coffee-table' style."

"You haven't?" Laoshi feigned surprise. "You were doing it long enough," he added with a smile. "'Coffee-table' taijiquan is like the books seen on coffee tables or in waiting rooms, just for skimming through, not for reading. There to distract you a while and take your mind off what the dentist will be doing to you shortly.

"Nor will we make much progress mindlessly repeating form after form after form. A contemporary of mine, becoming dissatisfied with his progress, decided to hurry things along by performing 78 forms per week: one for each of the cards in a tarot deck."

"And... did it work? Did he get better?" I asked.

"I doubt it," shrugged Laoshi, "although it is a few years since we last met, and he may, even now, be levitating on a cushion of qi, lost in rapturous peace, in company with High Priestesses, Hanged Men and Magicians, but I doubt it. I have heard from one of the vultures wishing to inherit his school on his demise, that his level is much as before."

"So..." I interrupted, "how do we make progress in the form then, if not by learning more stuff or doing it more often? Do we practice quicker, or slower, or is doing the form just like brushing your teeth; it doesn't matter too much how you do it, as long as you do it?"

"Paradoxical, isn't it," said Laoshi thoughtfully. "We must put in great effort, but relax completely. It is like a koan: not unlike learning to push without pushing."

"It's certainly confusing, Laoshi," I agreed.

"Yes," added Laoshi after a brief pause. "How do we progress? What does progress even mean? If we leave the answer to the rational mind, it will resort to the twin levers it thinks it can control: namely, learning more methods or doing them more often. However, it is my belief that progress in taijiquan is of the heart-mind. It is about insight."

"So how do you prompt insight?"

"A very good question," replied Laoshi. "Think of bacon and eggs— that venerable British breakfast institution. The saying goes: 'the hen is involved, but the pig is committed.' I believe it is the same with the form. You can be like the hen, blithely pushing out form after form, or you can be like the pig, each form cut straight from your very being, every form a rasher."

"That is a very… hmm… unique way of looking at it, Laoshi," I laughed. "Are you saying we must practice like pigs?"

"What do you think?" smiled Laoshi—yet another koan?

Years passed, and now a teacher myself, I returned to the question of how to nurture insight in teaching taijiquan form. Analyzing Laoshi's teaching style, I began to sense how insight and the form might relate to one another. In classes, particularly advanced form classes, Laoshi alternated between emphasizing the body's structure, and abruptly changing to concentrate on aspects of flow and internal movement. It appeared Laoshi was applying the concept of yin and yang to the teaching process itself, an emphasis on removing tension in the structure of the body—yin, followed by directing awareness to the circulation of energy within the body—yang.

Laoshi was inclined to liken his teaching method to preparing a garden hose for use after leaving it neglected in a shed over winter, unwinding and straightening out the hose, then turning the tap on fully to ensure a plentiful flow.

Laoshi deliberately kept these two aspects: structure and flow, separate when teaching. While emphasizing the importance of body structure, he did not mention flow; while encouraging flow of energy, he rarely mentioned structure. It was while considering Laoshi's teaching pattern that I had a moment of insight. By concentrating on one aspect of practice, then ignoring it completely, he was empowering the heart-mind to internalize the lesson he wished to convey. In effect, while he was teaching structure, we were assimilating flow; while he was teaching flow, we were assimilating structure.

A second insight arrived almost immediately: Laoshi's yin/yang approach to teaching the principles of structure and flow was a variant of the "learn and forget" method he employed in beginner's class. This was a thorough exposition of the physical postures of the form, followed by anecdotes, philosophy, and witty asides to relax the rational mind and let the instruction become internalized without strain.

One question remained, which I put to Laoshi, when we next met. How did he decide when to change emphasis from structure to flow and back again?

"I wait till I am tired with one, then change to the other," he replied casually as if further explanation was superfluous. I pressed him to amplify his thoughts, and he obliged saying, "Sometimes the intricacy of the postures and the precise alignment of the body captivate my attention, but their luster fades with the examination. It is a quirk of nature that the more you admire something, the less admirable it becomes. In essence, we become bored. When I am in danger of becoming sick and tired of taijiquan technique, I turn to ideas of flow to reinvigorate me. In time, of course, a type of fascination with the technical aspects returns, often with additional insights, which deepen my understanding. Have you heard the form described as a 'string of pearls?'"

"Yes, many times, Laoshi. The pearls are like the postures put together in a necklace."

"Correct," he nodded, "The postures are like the pearls: each one perfect, elegant, and with a beauty of their own. We can appreciate their majesty, but, if not linked together, they can become like marbles in a box. To be worn and shown to best advantage, we thread them together with a piece of string. The string is ordinary in comparison, easily replaced, and relatively inexpensive. The chief requisite is that the string be sturdy enough to do the job, while not detracting from the pearls, to remain understated and in service to the pearls. And yet, without the string, the least valuable part of the ensemble, the pearls could not be displayed to their fullest.

"The old Daoists truly understood the inherent value of things. Often we overlook the vital role played by what appears to be worthless or empty. We do not live in the walls but in the nothingness, which the walls enclose. Likewise, without holes for doors, a room would be useless, no one able to enter or leave, no matter how magnificent the construction.

"As Laozi points out:

> We join spokes together in a wheel,
> but it is the center hole
> that makes the wagon move.
> We shape clay into a pot,
> but it is the emptiness inside
> that holds whatever we want.

We hammer wood for a house,
but it is the inner space
that makes it livable.
We work with being,
but not-being is what we use.

"Do you see?" asked Laoshi. "The postures are what we work with, but it is the flow that we use. The postures are magnificent and contribute to the deepening of our power, but the flow from posture to posture brings life to the form and nourishes our soul. Holding postures may make us more powerful, but the flowing quality of the form is spiritually fulfilling. The true joy in life is to be found in the plain, humble, and ordinary. In golf they say: drive for show, putt for dough. In taijiquan, we could say: postures make us grow, flow makes us glow."

Chapter 19: Revenue Streams

To me the ideal work scenario is to be paid to do the thing I love.

If one loves to study taijiquan, however, this means one must teach. There is no taijiquan tournament circuit (thankfully, I might argue) with baying, paying spectators cheering on their favorites. Demonstration of form is more likely to send the crowd to sleep than it is to persuade them into parting with their money. And, to my knowledge, the "taijiquan busker" is extinct, if ever such a species existed. It's strange when one thinks of all those street artists standing immobile on plinths, imitating statues, who would seem to make sufficient money in order to make it worth the effort. Taijiquan cannot even compete with statue imitation when it comes to parting an audience from their spare change.

Although, arguably best pursued only as a vocation, teaching taijiquan can help to fill the rice bowl, while endeavoring to pursue the art. Unless one has independent means, the alternatives are limited: the choice is to undertake a "real" job, or else embrace the threadbare existence of a "taijiquan bum." Salaried employment, if you are fortunate enough to have it, may separate earning from learning, but the modern day workplace can also be a black hole for energy and enthusiasm. Once the demands of relationship and family claim their share, there is little left for practice. The taijiquan bum, however, may channel his entire being into perfecting his art, but he must be prepared to become a latter day knight-errant or *shugyosha*, except with less travel involved, since bus fares are expensive.

Having embarked on the path of professional taijiquan teacher, and despite having undertaken the short course in business planning, financial forecasting, and profit/loss analysis, I was faced with an uncomfortable truth: there is not much money to be made in teaching taijiquan. A professional musician, an infrequent student of mine due to his uncertain finances, was sympathetic to a point. His own tales of woe as a jobbing piano player put matters in perspective: "Too many piano players chasing too few gigs, man."

"How do you keep going?" I asked him, hoping for a glimmer of inspirational light in the financial darkness.

"You just gotta out-starve the other guy," he shrugged. Somehow, I did not feel comforted.

Before long, the would-be taijiquan professional is compelled to increase the size of the rice bowl by exploring other "revenue streams," as business-speak would have it. In plain English, this means selling stuff. Some taijiquan professionals of my acquaintance, committed (or fool-hardy enough) to brave the uncertain waters of teaching full-time, sold stuff by variously introducing membership fees, or offering school-branded clothing, or newsletters, or gift vouchers to their students. Laoshi, by contrast, vehemently rejected any such notions, a reaction, no doubt, to his early experience as Scottish representative for the Still Lotus School, upon whose insistence he had unenthusiastically peddled clothing and other items.

His views on the matter were forthright: "Why bleed the same students all the time? They already pay for class! Memberships offer nothing real in return for the money, and clothing can be bought cheaper locally and without the wart-like school logo offending the eye." For Laoshi, appropriate taijiquan clothing was, simply, anything loose and comfortable. He eschewed the notion of profiting from the need of individuals to identify with a cultural subgroup by wearing a uniform.

When I took on Laoshi's teaching responsibilities, I felt bound by his preference to forsake the merchandizing route. In truth, sales not being my forte, I was not unhappy with the situation. There was one exception, however: in the early days, at the request of his students, Laoshi had produced an instructional video, long before YouTube was born. Indeed, in those days, VHS had just beaten Betamax to become the industry standard in the age of magnetic tape.

Laoshi's videocassette was professionally made and of good quality. It featured Laoshi demonstrating both the regular form and sword form. It had sold conservatively over the years, fulfilling the role of aide-memoire for some students, and acting as a catch-up resource for those with sporadic attendance. Being even less enthusiastic about sales than I, Laoshi was content when I inherited the role of taijiquan instructional video salesman. We agreed to split any profits fifty-fifty, which was marginally better than nothing in terms of income. However, even this most modest means of rice bowl enhancement was not without pitfalls.

After a while, I decided to tweak Laoshi's business model slightly, by sourcing a cheaper electronics outlet to produce the videos I would sell on Laoshi's behalf. The new supplier could do the job for less than half the price of Laoshi's man. Now, it has to be said that my new business associate was the walking definition of shifty, apt to change business premises regularly on account of his singular bad luck: a flood in one of his shops had "destroyed all his equipment;" a fire has apparently done the same in another; and then thieves targeted him, immediately upon replacing all his previously "destroyed" equipment. The fact that he managed to re-equip with rapidity after each catastrophe, with identical machinery bearing eerily similar scratches and dents to his previous "destroyed" or "stolen" equipment was, I told myself, none of my business.

The point was that he could do a quick, cheap job lot for me whenever I required. He was indifferent to the signed letter I proffered from Laoshi stating that there was no copyright infringement. "Cash on delivery" was his creed, and our business relationship seemed to run smoothly enough.

I found myself both wholehearted and qualm-free in recommending Laoshi's video to my students. My "enterprising" self, which remained repressed and uncomfortable when selling my own merchandise, was now turned up a notch, when hustling on Laoshi's behalf. Indeed, I considered it noble to put a little extra cash Laoshi's way, and, in time, I became a decent salesman.

One evening after class, an elderly lady approached me to inquire, "Err... What exactly is supposed to be on that instructional video you sold me last week?" Without hesitation, I explained that the hand form and sword form were demonstrated by Laoshi, front view and back view, with accompanying verbal instructions. "Why do you ask?" I queried.

"Ahm... No reason," she replied hastily, which only made her enquiry seem all the more curious. However, the matter did not catch up with me until a month later.

I had arranged to dine with my very first aikido teacher, Wes. Although no longer his student, I had kept in touch with Wes over the years and now considered him a friend as well as former teacher. We met up regularly to indulge in the Glaswegian culinary passion for curry. Apparently, there were more Indian and Pakistani restaurants in Glasgow than anywhere outside the Indian subcontinent, and it seemed Wes was well acquainted with them all.

I was running late when Wes appeared at my flat one Sunday evening.

Unusually punctual, Wes had caught me unprepared: It was usually I who had to wait for Wes, and so I found myself a little flustered by his unexpectedly early arrival. I needed a further fifteen minutes to get ready. I suggested Wes amuse himself by watching the Zheng Manqing film I had recently bought from a supplier in the US. At the time, the UK standard was PAL, while videos from the USA were formatted in NTSC. In order to be able to view the video, I had taken this precious film of the Professor to my erstwhile video producer contact and paid a surprisingly small sum for a conversion to PAL.

I inserted the video into my video player, pressed play, and left Wes to his viewing as I resumed my preparations for dinner. Now, Wes was a genuinely upright man, who held himself to the highest standards in both his personal and professional life. He was a testament to clean living: he neither smoked nor drank alcohol; he lived a life of celibacy, and seldom uttered an unkind word about anyone, regardless of the provocation. He was, in short, the closest man to a saint amongst my acquaintances.

Wes had been quietly watching the film for several minutes, when I entered the room in search of a watch I had mislaid. I happened to glance at the TV screen, and to my confusion and mortification, glimpsed two writhing bodies engaged in what can only be described as pornography. My brain tried to compute what was happening: I knew that I did not own such material, and yet, somehow, I had managed to set up an embarrassing "private viewing" for the saintly Wes.

My hand flew to the remote control, all the while with apologies and protestations of bewilderment as to how such a tape had come to be in my possession. To his credit, although perhaps it was shock, Wes maintained a Zen-like expression and remained silent. I ejected the videocassette and looked hard at the label to confirm that this was, indeed, the Zheng Manqing film from the States. What was going on?! Closer examination of the cassette offered up the answer; after last viewing the film, I had not rewound the tape to the beginning. The Zheng Manqing portion of the tape must have been dubbed over some previous, less edifying material, which had not been entirely erased.

Just to check, I rewound the tape to the beginning and pressed "play" in order to demonstrate to Wes that Zheng Manqing was indeed on the tape. I had no knowledge of the video "extras," I told Wes with feeling. I could only surmise that my seedy copying contact had run out of blank tapes and simply re-used one, which had previously contained more salacious (and no doubt) illegal content. It was at that moment that I suddenly broke out in a cold sweat, recalling the curious inquiry of the elderly lady student, "Err... What exactly is supposed to be on that video you sold me last week?"

"Shit!" I blurted out, clapping my hand to my forehead. "Have I been selling porno tapes to my students?"

I was not in the habit of checking each and every tape I bought from the dodgy media man: instead, I checked one in each batch selected at random, and even then only for the a couple of minutes, before setting them out on my stall at class. The thought that I might have inadvertently been selling pornography to my students tormented me throughout my dinner with Wes that evening. I feared that scores of students had received more than they bargained for, but were simply too embarrassed to tell me. I was practically catatonic with terror, when it further dawned upon me that I had implicated Laoshi, if only by association. My head fell into my hands: I had dishonored Laoshi! Would the students think that it was Laoshi who had, wittingly or otherwise, dubbed over some old porn films? I fairly cringed with shame and embarrassment. But I knew I had no choice: I needed to tell Laoshi at once.

I went to see Laoshi the next day, following a phone call in which I stuttered out my desperate need to see him and explain something important. I arrived in an agitated state and refused his customary offer of tea before launching into my sordid tale, and barely drawing breath, apologized to him profusely for possibly tarnishing his reputation. Laoshi looked stern and remained quiet as I told him the story. When I eventually stumbled to a halt, there felt to be an eternity of silence before Laoshi suddenly burst out laughing. "Is that all? I thought from your incoherent ramblings on the phone that it was something serious. I thought you were giving up taijiquan."

"Aren't you angry then, Laoshi?" I asked warily. I was astonished at his reaction. Relieved too, but still a little guarded. "Err… aren't you worried that people might think you are a porn freak or something?"

Laoshi simply smiled. "People can think what they like. I think what I like, and so do you. It makes no difference to me what people choose to dwell upon, and it should make no difference to you what people choose to think."

"But, what about your reputation, Laoshi," I insisted. "What about your good name in the taijiquan community? Doesn't it worry you?"

"My *good name*?" Laoshi looked skeptical. "Listen, anyone who wishes to think ill of me will do so regardless of the facts, and anyone inclined to think well of me will do so, in spite of the facts. And, by the way, anyone daft enough to believe that we are deliberately selling pornography will have poor estimation of us already. I mean, apart from anything else, we are selling those videos at a pittance."

Laoshi fell about laughing once more.

I laughed too, only nervously. I still could not comprehend Laoshi's levity in the face of a potential threat, as I saw it, to his reputation. Still keen to atone for messing up, I pressed Laoshi as to whether he was simply being kind to me: was he truly unconcerned about his reputation? Sensing my ongoing discomfort, Laoshi grew solemn for a moment, looked me straight in the eyes, and responded with characteristic obliqueness: "Did you know that Zheng Manqing once broke his hip?"

"Err... No Laoshi. I heard that he once injured his hip through a fall on an icy New York street. Is that what you mean?"

"Indeed," Laoshi nodded. "The fact that Zheng Manqing's hip was fractured was concealed by the senior students. You understand why?" he asked meaningfully, his gaze never leaving my face.

"Er... well, I guess maybe they did not want their esteemed teacher to be seen as vulnerable, to be just as prone to injury as the rest of us, despite his skill in taijiquan."

"Precisely," replied Laoshi quickly. "But you understand because of your own reactions earlier. You want to protect me, just as Zheng Manqing's students instinctively wanted to protect the reputation of their teacher. Entirely understandable, commendable even. However, it is also wholly unnecessary. I, for one, am genuinely impressed by Zheng Manqing's ability to stand up in spite of a broken hip! Not to mention, then returning home to heal *himself* of so severe an injury."

I pondered Laoshi's perspective in silence for a few moments. "So... should I mention to the students that there might have been a mix up in the copying process?"

"Not at all," Laoshi smiled, "As Laozi says, 'He who would justify does not convince.' Listen, relax. Things are not always what they seem—and you cannot spend your life running around correcting everybody's lack of clarity in what they see.

"Did I ever tell you the story of the Argyll and Sutherland Highlanders assaulting a heavily fortified hill position during the Korean War?"

I never failed to be amazed at Laoshi's capacity to pluck a quirky tale from thin air.

"Umm... No Laoshi. I don't recall you mentioning that." I smiled, relaxing at last, and settling back to enjoy the story.

"Ah, well then," mused Laoshi drifting into story-mode: "I will tell you... At one point in the campaign, the Argylls were ordered to capture a hilltop position, which was strongly defended by regular Chinese troops. The first battalion started up the hill, only to be met with murderous fire from the enemy machine-gunners. They were forced to retreat. Then, the second battalion was ordered forward: they advanced courageously, under intense fire, only to be pushed back, in turn. Finally, in one desperate all-out bid for glory, the colonel himself led the third battalion up the hill. Under enemy fire and suffering serious casualties, these brave lads were also being forced into retreat when, suddenly, Regimental Sergeant-Major McTavish about-turned and stormed back up the hill to the astonishment of all who witnessed him. The sight of the RSM fearlessly storming up that hill galvanized the men, who turned retreat into attack and captured the position!"

You had to love the way Laoshi got totally immersed in his story telling. I swear I glimpsed a tear in his eye, as he recounted this tale of heroism. But he was not finished: "After the battle, the Colonel who had witnessed the RSM's bravery, first hand, congratulated McTavish heartily: 'RSM, that was the single most impressive thing I have seen in thirty years of soldiering. But tell me, what on earth possessed you to go back up the hill into the teeth of the enemy?' There was a slight pause as McTavish shrugged and replied nonchalantly, 'Aye, well Sir, it was like this: I was halfway down the hill, you see, when I realized that I'd dropped half-a-crown up there.'"

And with that, Laoshi broke into hearty laughter once more and headed off into the garden, leaving me sitting there, bemused.

I continued to sell Laoshi's videos. However, from that day onward I put my trust, and money, in the hands of Laoshi's original supplier. We made less money, but at least I had confidence in every cassette's "suitability."

Chapter 20: Turf Wars

Having decided to commit to taijiquan as a professional teacher, I now needed to offer additional classes to make the rice bowl bigger. Although simple in theory—find a hall, do some advertising, and begin—establishing a new class was not as easy as I had thought. Not all areas were suitable and, of those that were, many were already colonized by teachers from other schools. Forging a presence in those areas would involve a degree of competition for new students with incumbent teachers. Two veteran students of Laoshi were already teaching part-time in the better locations outside the West End of Glasgow: Jonny and Ethan occupied the south side of Glasgow and the Stirling area, respectively.

Examining a map like a military commander assessing the terrain, I identified the nearby town of Paisley, which adjoins Glasgow to the west, as a possibility. It was distant enough to be distinct from Glasgow, and yet near enough for easy access along the motorway. The usual etiquette accompanying a move to a new location was to ask for Laoshi's approval. This was because it made little sense for Laoshi's students to compete with each other by teaching in the same area: some method of arbitration was necessary in order to avoid turf wars between existing and aspiring teachers. Laoshi, therefore, acted as informal arbiter to balance existing teachers' interests with opportunities for new teachers to carve out their own territory.

In Laoshi's school, there were no formal strictures compelling the fledgling teacher to remain with the school. Any "regulation" was centered on Laoshi's guidance as to what was appropriate in the circumstances. In essence then, we were more a loose federation of teachers, who understood the benefit of remaining connected to Laoshi. Nevertheless, I often wondered what would happen when Laoshi's unifying presence was no more.

Judging the right time to approach Laoshi, I outlined my plans for expansion and sought his blessing. Not only did Laoshi endorse my plan, he surprised me by revealing that Paisley had been an early location for his own classes prior to retrenching to Glasgow in order to concentrate his efforts in a more central area.

It came as surprise, therefore, to receive a phone call from Nora, whom I had only briefly encountered at Laoshi's push-hands and fencing classes in my early days with the school. I knew very little of Nora beyond a reputation for bellicosity and a fondness for tobacco. It was rare to hear a good word spoken of Nora by the senior students; her moniker in those circles was "Dragon Lady," referring to her belligerent attitude in dealing with other students. I was about to discover first-hand how she merited such a reputation.

"Are you the person putting up leaflets advertising classes in Saint Andrews Church Hall?" There were no niceties, no preamble with Nora; it was straight to business with a superior tone, which suggested she was speaking to an underling.

"Er... yes," I answered hesitantly. I was caught off-guard, expecting the call might be from a potential student seeking information on costs or clothing for class. "I am starting a new class in Paisley next month," I followed up, in as pleasant a manner as I could muster.

"No you are not!" hissed Nora. "This is my territory, and you are not allowed to teach here."

The rest of our conversation remains with me only in snatches: me mumbling something about Laoshi agreeing to the plan and about my ignorance of her presence in the area. Her parting shot, however, was un-equivocal: "Get your posters taken down at the earliest opportunity, or else!"

Once the line was clear of Dragon's breath, I called Laoshi and relayed, as best I could, both the gist and the tone of Nora's communiqué. "Ah," replied Laoshi, on a long outbreath, as if divining the nub of the problem instantly. "Listen, just disregard what Nora says and carry on as you had planned. Just give me a day or so to pave the way. Rest assured, you will have no more trouble from Nora."

In spite of Laoshi's reassurance, over the next few days, I considered cancelling the new Paisley class in the interests of maintaining harmony within the wider taijiquan fraternity. In the end, though, I decided that I was within my rights to stick to my course. I proceeded as originally intended and received no more communication from Nora on the subject. However, I remained curious to discover the cause of Nora's hostility, not to mention, the mechanism employed by Laoshi to smooth her ruffled feathers.

Thinking that Jonny might have insight on the matter, which he might also be persuaded to share, I told him of the exchange between Nora and me. Jonny laughed heartily before replying, "Typical Nora! Her cork was always in too tight. She was always quick to make up her mind about you, and then equally quick to let you know what she decided. She always said that, in her book, someone was either a 'good guy or a wanker,' her words by the way. And 'she never changed her mind.' Well... I guess you know what she thinks of you!" Perhaps, mindful of appearing reasonable, Jonny then added, "To be fair to Nora though, if she thought you were a good guy, like Sundance, she could be very generous. It's just that most of us never experienced her benevolent side."

"Who's Sundance?" I asked.

"You know... Sundance," he repeated as if that would assist my understanding. My expression remained blank.

"If you met Nora, when you first started, you must have met Sundance, too. They were pretty much joined at the hip at that time. We called him Sundance, but his real name is Lachlan. He was 'honorable number one student' up until the time he and Nora split from the school to join another teacher."

The penny dropped. I did remember Lachlan, a tall, strongly built man in his mid-thirties, who was invariably to be found attached to Nora on their frequent smoking breaks outside the hall. Lachlan was rarely mentioned by Laoshi's senior students, as they refraining from gossiping with anyone who was not of their immediate circle. Today, however, I was being indulged.

"Why was he called Sundance?"

"In those days, we gave nicknames to each other for a laugh," replied Jonny. "Lachlan was called 'Sundance' because he was Laoshi's right-hand man, see, like Butch Cassidy and the Sundance Kid. His taijiquan was ahead of ours, and he was a good guy. Still... none of us could see why Laoshi or Sundance tolerated Nora, when the rest of us couldn't stand her. If taijiquan is supposed to be about relaxation, why Laoshi ever allowed her to teach is a mystery, since Nora is the furthest thing from relaxation you could imagine!"

Now my curiosity was raised further, and Jonny's mention of the early days of the school intrigued me about Nora and her relationship with Laoshi. Though keen to hear more, I bided my time until I judged that Laoshi was amenable to talk about the matter. The time came one lazy summer afternoon, as we sat drinking tea in his garden, "Laoshi," I asked causally. "What was going on with Nora and that phone call a few months ago?"

Laoshi regarded me in thoughtful silence for a few moments before seeming to reach a decision: "You have the right to know, I suppose, since you were on the receiving end of her anger for matters that were not of your making. The fact is, her issues are with me, not with you, but anger is often unleashed upon the nearest available target, regardless of appropriateness, or otherwise."

Laoshi took a sip of tea then sighed deeply before resuming: "When I began teaching, Nora was my first student. In fact, we were both originally students of Lenny, but it was Nora who encouraged me to start my own class. She helped me to find a hall and supported my early efforts as a teacher. That is why I began teaching in Paisley—she lived there. The school quickly prospered and, as we grew, Nora proved to be a loyal student and ally: she attended every class, shouldered some of the burden of advertising, and she also took in the class fees, a job which I preferred to avoid for a long time. In addition, we used to meet for a few hours each Sunday to practice push-hands and fencing. She encouraged me when I decided to change teachers, first to Don and then to Wang Lang. I have never forgotten her help during those early years."

"Is that why you put up with her attitude?" I asked, remembering her belligerent tone with me on the phone.

Laoshi shrugged, "Nora wasn't always like that. She has become more insecure and fearful over the years. My guess is that she felt threatened by you, and was afraid that her classes would suffer as a result of competition with you."

"I got that," I acknowledged. "But, the senior students struggle to find anything complimentary to say about her."

Laoshi smiled. "Yes, I know, but that is their problem, not yours. When we find ourselves having difficulties with another person, it would be wiser to search for the reason within ourselves, rather than in them. Some of your fellow students still have work to do in that area.

"You must understand Nora is 'old school.' She was involved in martial arts long before starting taijiquan and belongs to a generation before yours. She sees things in black and white: there is no grey in her thinking—and not much color, either—so she can be abrupt. She lives in a world of profound judgement; either someone measures up to her demanding standards, or else they are 'weak and pathetic.' But this is all a defense. She is a sensitive person, the kind who would lash out before allowing a tear in public. Her real fear is that *she* does not measure up to her own high standards. She hides her vulnerability by deploying scorn and spite as sentinels against the cruel and heartless world she perceives around her. It is the price she pays for judging others with such vigor: she applies the same stringency to herself.

"'Judge not, that ye be not judged,' is not a warning of a vengeful god, but the inevitable consequence of a judgmental attitude being applied to oneself."

"She didn't seem like the type to tear up." I scoffed.

"Mmm... You'd be surprised," smiled Laoshi, "When we were alone and practicing push-hands in the old days, Nora used to tear up every now and then, although she dismissed it as hay fever. Push-hands has a way of bringing stuff up."

"What kind of stuff?" I pursued.

"Oh, Nora never allowed herself to confide in me as to the cause of her tears," said Laoshi, "but I feared that she wanted to be closer to me than I did to her. When I expressed my concerns to Wang Lang and asked for his advice, he told me that I ought to talk to her to avoid a problem arising between us. However, I felt unable to broach the subject, as she always seemed so guarded. The shell she created was very effective. As a result, she was a deeply lonely person, whose fear of being hurt pushed everyone away. I suspect that she longed to open up and embrace who she really was. When the other students complained about her aggressive behavior and advised me that the school would be better off without her, they failed to see that she was coming to class in order to try to quiet her demons. In the end, however, circumstances derailed her efforts, and she moved on."

"How did that happen, Laoshi? What circumstances?" I asked, spurred on by Laoshi's candor. I had long-since recognized Laoshi's ability to delve into the true character of his students and not judge the "masks" we wore to hide ourselves from the world. Laoshi was often the catalyst, which allowed us to see that our defenses were not only unnecessary, but self-destructive. However, on this occasion, I sensed Laoshi's regret at, somehow, having failed Nora and was eager to learn the reason.

"Well... people often seek the validation they cannot provide for themselves in the affection and acceptance of others," continued Laoshi. They need someone to assure them of their inherent value and goodness. In a way, I performed that role for Nora, and she jealously guarded that feeling of being valued.

"For a number of years, we worked to develop the school. I had a mission, and Nora, I imagine, found an outlet for her energies and a feeling of place, value possibly, even ownership. At times, she accompanied me to workshops with Wang Lang and occasionally when I was invited to teach abroad. However, a problem arose when I began seeing a woman called Anna. It was difficult enough for Nora that I was spending less time with her, but when I mentioned my wish that Anna accompany us on a trip to spend some time with Wang Lang, Nora exploded: 'Over my dead body,' she screeched. 'She is not coming with us—period.' Things became heated. It was made clear to me that Nora despised Anna on a number of levels, but I suspect that at the heart of it all was Nora's feeling of being usurped. Continuing her assault on Anna, Nora hissed: 'It's not just me. Everybody in the school hates Anna, including Lachlan. People only put up with her because she's your girlfriend.'"

"That's outrageous!" I exclaimed. "I hope you told her to get lost!" The words were out before I could stop them but, in truth, a part of me relished the chance to have a go at Nora."

"Perhaps I should have," said Laoshi wearily, but then, perhaps, I should also have anticipated that Nora might feel threatened by Anna. What I ended up saying was: 'Nora, you betray yourself! Would you have said such a thing to any of your karate teachers?' It was a rhetorical question. We both knew she would not dare, *Then why do you say such things to me?*'"

Laoshi paused for a moment, sighed heavily. "From that moment on, we were like strangers."

"Where did Lachlan fit into all this?" I pressed quietly, aware that I was treading on delicate territory. "Didn't Nora resent his presence?"

Laoshi nodded gravely. "Hmm… Lachlan was a gifted taijiquan player and as easy-going as he was skilled, a good push-hands player both in class and out, but perhaps, a little naive. He quickly became the most skilled student I had and, *de facto*, senior student of the school. Nora understood that the school had to have capable students, and she accepted him on those terms. They were also both heavy smokers, and the room would be thick with smoke whenever the two of them were together. I'm sure that helped, but Nora was also manipulative, and I suspect Lachlan was not clear about what was going on.

"After my blow-up with Nora, Lachlan continued to meet with her, and I suspect Nora now began using him, in place of me, in seeking her validation. In class, they were often seen together—Nora, with her back to me whispering in Lachlan's ear. It was only then that I understood Wang Lang's half-joking comment; *'Nora has the right air of a conspirator about her.'* In earlier times, it was to me she would whisper during breaks in his workshops, something that did not go unnoticed by Wang Lang."

What was she whispering about? Did you ever find out?"

"I didn't ask, if that is what you mean," replied Laoshi somberly. "But I had a good idea. If she were repeating to Lachlan the same things she used to say to me, she would have been persuading him of his superiority to me and his rightful position as head of the school. She would imply that I was standing in Lachlan's way."

"So… she wanted to be the power behind the throne?" I inquired scathingly, disliking Nora all the more.

"Perhaps," shrugged Laoshi. "Certainly, in the past, and for my ears only, she often briefed against Wang Lang and his students, whom she somehow detested, and continually suggested privately to me that I had progressed beyond Wang Lang in levels of skill."

"What a snake!" I shook my head in disgust.

Laoshi remained silent.

"So… How did it all come to a head?" I asked tentatively.

"Well," recalled Laoshi, "after one of my weekend seminars out in the countryside near Glasgow, Nora and Lachlan approached me for 'a quiet word.' The three of us took a stroll around the wooded grounds of the seminar venue, and Lachlan told me of his decision to leave the school to be 'his own man.' I asked Nora if she felt the same way. Unsurprisingly, she appeared to be of the same mind. Having suspected something of the sort for some time, I did not care to dissuade them from their course, and so our conversation was brief. Since that day, until I telephoned Nora recently, I had not seen or spoken to either of them."

"Er… so how did you resolve the matter of me teaching in Paisley?" I asked. I was beginning to understand something of the past relationship between Laoshi and Nora, but remained curious to hear of their most recent contact.

"I phoned Nora the day after you called me," replied Laoshi. "She reiterated her sense of 'sovereignty' over Paisley. I reminded her that, since she was no longer with our school, she had no say in how and when students became teachers, nor did she have a say in governing the areas they could, or could not, teach. I suggested that her wisest course was to accept the will of the Dao and carry on about her own business. I pointed out that if the Dao wished you, or anyone else, to teach in Paisley, it would happen with or without her blessing."

I never learned from Laoshi how Nora responded to his words, but I surmise that they must have had effect. Fortunately, my class in Paisley blossomed and I taught there unopposed for many years. I did not hear from Nora again, although, from time to time, my posters advertising new classes seemed to mysteriously disappear. I suspected Nora's hand, but, perhaps, I was seeing what I expected to see in random events. Nora, therefore, became a mere footnote in the history of my teaching career.

A few years later, as Laoshi and I were enjoying coffee together after class, he casually remarked, "Do you remember Nora from a few years ago?"

"How could I forget?" I quirked a brow. "Don't tell me, has she been complaining about me again?"

"No... No," replied Laoshi quietly, "she will not complain about you again. She died last month."

"Oh, I'm sorry to hear that," I responded automatically, if less than wholeheartedly. Laoshi gazed directly at me. I imagined he was debating with himself whether to admonish me for my hypocrisy, or lack of compassion. Instead, he added quietly, "It seems she had been ill for a long time with cancer before it finally claimed her. It is not entirely impossible that when she spoke aggressively to you that day, she was already suffering from the early stages of illness; perhaps she reacted more radically than she might have done otherwise."

I remained silent for a while. There was nothing I could say about Nora's passing, which did not sound trite or insincere. But I was troubled. Eventually, I blurted out: "This is what I don't understand, Laoshi. If Nora studied taijiquan all those years, what good did it do her in the end? I mean, I am sorry, but she seemed to remain angry and bitter to the end. Surely, the practice of taijiquan should open people up to reconciling their inner demons?"

"Zheng Manqing would agree with you," nodded Laoshi, "but sometimes fear is so great that its hold on the rational mind needs to be broken before healing can occur. I am not and never will be that kind of teacher. Very few people are, but some try and end doing damage to others—they can 'break' but not heal."

I eyed Laoshi uneasily. What was he talking about? I had no wish to venture into the realm of "breaking" or "healing" my students. It seemed both arrogant and an enormous personal responsibility.

Laoshi was gazing thoughtfully at the milk jug on the table. "You can see this milk," he mused. "To get it from the farm to the table we need a container of some kind, let's say a glass bottle. The milk is the 'heart-mind,' the bottle is the 'rational mind.' The milk uses the bottle to go where it needs to go in order to flow more widely. Do you follow?"

"Er... possibly," I offered, not at all sure that I followed at all.

"Okay. So... it is not that the bottle is 'good' or 'evil,' it is simply is a vessel, which is 'used by' the milk; the bottle contains and protects the milk. However, if the bottle could not be opened and the milk was kept 'prisoner' in the bottle for weeks, it would soon change from something wholesome and healthy into something unpleasant and sour. You might still drink it, but it would certainly be an acquired taste!"

I pulled a face, imagining the taste of sour milk.

Laoshi continued: "My idea here is that the heart-mind needs to move freely and spontaneously in order to remain fresh. Once fear dominates the rational mind, the heart-mind becomes soured and repulsive."

"Er... So are you saying that you need to shatter the bottle of fear to free the heart mind?" I ventured.

"In some cases," Laoshi conceded.

"So, why could you not 'shatter the bottle', Laoshi?" I pressed.

"Because I would not be able to pick up the pieces if it all went wrong. It takes a unique type of compassion and an uncommon degree of wisdom to 'break' a person in order to make them whole again. I do not possess those 'gifts' and I am grateful, as I would not wish to have the responsibility. And, I hope, for your sake," Laoshi added, "you also never venture down that path."

I had no argument with Laoshi there. That kind of "teaching" held no appeal for me.

Chapter 21: Pain in the Dantian

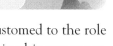

With time and a growing confidence, I became accustomed to the role Laoshi had created for me. No longer was I dutifully keeping his seat warm, awaiting his certain return after a short sabbatical. The position of teacher was fast becoming skin, not mere clothing. My earlier suspicion of Laoshi's motives in pressing me to teach had melted away, only to be replaced by concern that he might actually wish to return.

Laoshi seemed to suffer no limitations as a result of his knee injury. Quite the contrary, in fact, his skills in push-hands and fencing continued to evolve, if anything at a faster pace. I found myself anxious that a rejuvenated Laoshi should not jeopardize my present position. Teaching taijiquan was no longer simply a duty performed for my teacher, now it was my livelihood, as well.

"So, Laoshi," I asked, one evening after push-hands class, hoping to gauge his intentions, "how is your knee these days? I haven't heard you mention it in while."

"Ah, not too bad, I suppose." he replied casually, apparently not inclined to volunteer anything further.

"Yes... right... good. So, it's improved a little bit, then?" I pressed him trying to sound equally casual but failing.

"Perhaps," he said, a frown accompanying the response suggesting that a simple "yes" or "no" would be inadequate. I looked on expectantly. Speaking with Laoshi at times required coaxing to progress beyond a simple shallow statement to reach something more substantial.

"It is certainly not so bad," he continued after a suitable pause, "though it is not completely healed. It becomes painful after an hour or so of practicing form, but push-hands and fencing are less troublesome."

"I'm pleased to hear that, Laoshi," I nodded, before adding cautiously, "Does that mean you might want to start teaching form classes again?"

"Ah-ha," he exclaimed. "So, that's what this is about; you are worried I might take your classes away from you?"

"The thought crossed my mind?" I admitted sheepishly.

"Well, no need to worry on that score," he assured me. "I will not be teaching form anymore. I'll leave that to you and the other seniors."

I was mightily relieved, and sighed aloud, but almost immediately felt a tinge of disappointment. So, that was it: Laoshi's form classes were to be no more. The world seemed a little more arid with the realization.

Fortunately, Laoshi interrupted my somberness. "While it is true that the pain in my knee persuaded me to reduce my teaching commitments, its main value was in stimulating my practice in other ways."

It was a comment typical of Laoshi and echoed the *Daodejing*'s wisdom on the Master's acceptance of whatever circumstances arose:

> *The Master doesn't seek fulfilment.*
> *Not seeking, not expecting*
> *She is present, and can welcome all things.*

The inclination to avoid pain, whether learned or hardwired into our psyche, is almost universal. The "fearlessness to take pain," spoken of by Zheng Manqing, is as rare as the willingness to invest in loss. Laoshi, however, "welcomed" pain as another of life's lessons, albeit an unpleasant and unsolicited assignment.

"In what way did it stimulate you, Laoshi?"

"Well, as I reflect on the matter," replied Laoshi thoughtfully, "I think it is true to say I have benefited in two ways. First, it obliged me to reacquaint myself with a topic I first wondered about nearly twenty years ago, but was unable... no more accurately, unwilling, to engage with: the problem of pain and what we do with it."

"You mean," I interrupted, "because pain is useful in telling us something is wrong but it is unpleasant at the same time." I recalled my own struggles with back pain, my subsequent surgery, and agonizingly slow recuperation.

124

"More than that," Laoshi corrected. "Many years ago, I was engaged to deliver two taijiquan workshops to a support group in the Knightswood area of Glasgow. The community nurse who arranged my visits was youthful and innovative. She was searching for ways to improve the lives of the patients in her 'chronic pain group' by exploring alternatives to the drug routines, which were a daily necessity for her patients. She hoped taijiquan could provide some respite, or, at the very least, moderate the pain sufficiently for a reduction in the dosage of prescribed painkillers. As you know, many painkillers have unpleasant side effects, and non-chemical pain relief would be a valuable addition to conventional treatment.

"I am ashamed to say," sighed Laoshi with a shake of his head, "that in my youthful ignorance, I was adamant that taijiquan would be the solution. I was perhaps a little arrogant, and even before meeting the group, I had persuaded myself that I was about to make a significant difference to their lives. In truth, I felt no genuine empathy—I was motivated instead by my own ego. At the time, I was almost evangelical in my certainty that, while breath remained in the body, taijiquan could fix just about everything.

"When I arrived at the clinic, reality hit home hard. I was presented to a group of people either unable to stand, or, if they could stand, unable to perform even the most rudimentary of movements. I felt uneasy immediately. I felt hypocritical: here was I, in good health, having suffered very little physical pain, about to pontificate on pain relief the taijiquan way. Having been spared the misery of chronic pain, I was only guessing that taijiquan could help. Standing there, as I was introduced to the group, I felt my untested confidence drain away. My conviction that taijiquan was a perfect pain management system had not been forged in the furnace of my own experience, as I had only theory to fall back on. Perhaps sensing my discomfort and being capable of infinitely more empathy than me, the group treated me with generosity and kindness. My feelings of hypocrisy were compounded by a nagging doubt that I was about to disappoint, and I felt it even cruel to raise expectations, which were bound to be dashed by the reality: the reality that I had nothing to give."

Laoshi paused for a while, let out another long sigh, and continued. "I was at a loss and did not know how to proceed. Form was clearly out of the question, and I had not made a study of the chair-bound exercises, which some teachers use with 'special needs' groups. Furthermore, I was not about to use these people as guinea pigs in my attempts to devise an ad hoc series of movements. So, I subjected them to a talk about taijiquan, followed by a demonstration of form. Thereafter, I led the group in a guided meditation, focusing on bringing the qi to the dantian, then leading the qi into the area of greatest pain. My instructions were politely followed, and, at the end of the session, I was equally politely informed that the exercise had made no difference. Who was I to argue? I felt myself a fraud.

"A second session, one week later, was received much as the first, and I was relieved to not be invited to conduct a third. There was only so much I was willing to do for money: offering false hope and untried theories to people in pain was a step too far for me."

I had not heard Laoshi mention this incident before, despite him being an inveterate storyteller. I presumed that his reticence stemmed from a lack of closure over the incident. At some level, he was still troubled by his experience and was unable to come to terms with what may have seemed to him a failing on his part, or on the part of taijiquan.

"This recent problem with my knee," he continued, "reminded me of those workshops all those years ago and gave me the opportunity to practice what I preached."

"You mean by putting the qi into the dantian?" I asked.

"That's right," he confirmed. "I had encouraged the members of the pain group to draw their breath into the dantian, assuring them that the dantian could be experienced as a reality. The next stage was to direct the feeling through the body and bathe the area of discomfort in the warmth of the qi.

"In truth, however," added a rather doleful Laoshi, "for most of my life, though I lauded the benefits of breathing into the belly, I have ignored my own advice. Focusing on the dantian is a cornerstone of our taijiquan, yet for all the years I have practiced and taught, I have not seriously pursued the way of the dantian with any rigor. My attempts were intermittent and half-hearted. My motivation was lacking, and, as a result, I made little headway in concentrating the qi in the dantian. Instead, I focused my energy on the form, push-hands, and fencing."

I was taken aback by Laoshi's revelation. I assumed that he had been assiduously engaged in developing his dantian by focusing his mind and energy in the "field of the elixir." The difficulty of the task hit home: if Laoshi, with his dedication to taijiquan lacked the motivation to invest in the dantian, what hope was there for the rest of us?

"The knee pain I was experiencing," added Laoshi after a brief pause, "inspired me to search afresh for the power that resides in the dantian."

"And have you discovered anything, Laoshi?"

"Perhaps a little," he smiled. "Mostly, I realized that I didn't know what putting the qi in the dantian actually meant."

"Really?" I objected, "Surely, if you feel your belly expand when you breathe in, then you are bringing your qi into the dantian. And, if you are aware of the feeling, then the heart-mind is there as well?"

"I thought much the same until recently," nodded Laoshi, "but these matters are infinitely more subtle than I had first appreciated."

"How so?"

"The first thing I discovered is that we interfere with the breath when we consciously direct it to the dantian, or anywhere else for that matter. To bring awareness to your breathing is to change your breathing. You no longer breathe naturally. To some extent, your breathing has become contrived.

"If you consider the matter seriously, you will realize that you cannot consciously experience natural breathing: we generally have no awareness of breathing at all. The task is paradoxical: breathe naturally, but be aware of the breath. Usually, like most functions in the body, we are only aware of breathing when it is unnatural; when something is wrong. It is akin to Herrigal's difficulty in *Zen and the Art of Archery*: how to shoot an arrow without deciding to release the bowstring. The moment you think 'release,' you have interfered with the process. At a very deep level, *wuwei* is less about 'not forcing' things and more about how to live with total spontaneity, while simultaneously being conscious of the intention to act."

"Hmm… yes," I nodded. "I see what you mean." But, in truth, I did not. Laoshi had drawn us into deep philosophical waters. We were no longer simply discussing pain and techniques for its relief, we were addressing the question of how rational and intuitive thinking are to be integrated.

I felt poorly equipped to follow Laoshi to such depths. I could offer nothing of value in discussing how to be natural on purpose. Instead, I steered us back into the shallows by complaining to Laoshi of my own frustration in bringing together breath and dantian. I revealed how my attempts, hitherto, had brought me dangerously close to hyperventilating, as my lungs became "over-full" with breath. I was forced on these occasions to distract myself from the task until eventually my breathing was restored to normality by the autonomic nervous system, which I was trying to improve upon. Zheng Manqing's instruction to "throttle down" the breathing in meditation seemed depressingly beyond me. Furthermore, if the "long, slow, thin, and quiet" dictum of taijiquan breathing was correct, I was gravely in error, as my breathing was short, choppy, labored and noisy. Aware that something was wrong, I became disillusioned with the practice and returned to the method infrequently, to be met each time with failure.

After explaining the difficulties I had encountered in bringing breath to the dantian, I was comforted by Laoshi's response: "I experienced the same problem. As I inhaled, my body seemed to have an insatiable appetite for air, and I felt myself breathing deeper and quicker to the point of feeling like a massive balloon. Something was certainly amiss. Robert Smith describes Zheng

127

Manqing's ability to refine his breathing to the point that the air could not be felt even with a finger held under the Professor's nose. I, however, could power a wind turbine with the forcefulness of my breath, as I sucked air in through my nose and squeezed it out again. I sounded like a pig snuffling in a trough. Furthermore, Zheng Manqing told his students that even using the diaphragm when breathing was too much when sitting at rest."

"Has your breathing practice improved now?" I asked.

Laoshi nodded, acknowledging that some progress had been made.

"How did you manage it?"

"Hmm... I think reading *Zheng Manqing's Thirteen Treatises* helped a lot. You see, in Chapter Three, the Professor explains that there is a 'pocket' in the dantian, which has to be opened before the qi can be directed there. If the pocket is not open, then the qi is not really deposited in the dantian. These words of the Professor gave me an important clue: the qi pocket in the dantian was only theory for me, so I set about feeling for it as a reality by using my breath more softly. In other words I listened more and did less."

"Usually, a good idea," I agreed.

"Indeed," declared Laoshi before adding, "Very shortly after using my breath to 'look' into my dantian, I fancied that I felt something which could be described as a pocket in my lower abdomen. Prior to this discovery, I had only infrequently felt anything in my dantian at all. This new sensation seemed to inflate with the breath, and crucially, when the breath left my body, as I breathed out, the pocket remained inflated."

"And did your breathing throttle down?"

"To a very great degree," answered Laoshi. "As I focused on filling the pocket in the dantian, I was no longer forcing the breath. It was the dantian itself, which was breathing. I was no longer pushing air into and down my body, rather the dantian was drawing air in from below. The lower abdomen was operating like a bellows: drawing the air in and storing something in the dantian."

"Is that what is meant by 'bellows breathing,'" I interrupted.

"I think not," replied Laoshi, with an emphatic shake of the head. "Do not be confused: there is no forcing in taijiquan breathing. If the breath is not long, slow, thin, and quiet, then we are talking of something else."

"Okay, I get that point Laoshi. But when you began to feel the qi in the dantian, did you then set about moving that feeling to your knee as a means of self-healing?"

"I experimented with the idea following Wang Lang's advice to breathe into the area of injury, and thus direct the qi for healing to occur. Soon after, however, I discarded the practice."

"Why? Was it ineffective?"

"It is not a question of effective or not," explained Laoshi. "It is a question of common sense."

"Common sense, really? In what way is it common sense?"

"Well... think about it. If the qi is so clever that it can heal stubborn health problems, will it not also be clever enough to go to the site of the injury without being directed by me? Ask yourself, when I cut a finger, do I consciously grow new tissue, or do I simply allow the qi to do its work unhindered?"

"That's a fair point, Laoshi," I conceded. "So is it better just to let the body ache as it will?"

Laoshi laughed, "Ah-ha. Now, there's an interesting question, and perhaps a more profitable line of investigation."

"I do my best," I smiled, wondering what was coming next.

"I'm sure you do," smiled Laoshi, like a cat with a mouse. "There was a Zen disciple, who addressed the master saying, 'It's so hot today, how shall we escape the heat?' The master answered, 'By going down to the bottom of the furnace.' The disciple, a little puzzled, then asked, 'But in the furnace how shall we escape the scorching fire?' The master replied, 'In the furnace, you will not be troubled by pain.'"

"Another of those crazy Zen stories," I moaned. "But what does it mean?"

"Well..." said Laoshi. I suppose the story can be interpreted in different ways. One of which is to make the body's pain a subject for meditation. 'Going into the furnace' is bringing awareness into the very heart of the pain, rather than attempting to escape the discomfort. Then the pain either eases or becomes tolerable."

"But, how can that work, Laoshi? Pain is pain after all. You cannot just decide to calmly meditate it away."

Laoshi looked directly at me saying. "Can you not?"

My view of pain was being challenged. Was Laoshi suggesting that pain was a subjective experience to be imagined away?

"Well, I can't," I replied a little grumpily.

"Perhaps you can," said Laoshi enigmatically. "Don, a former teacher of mine, talked about pain in the terms of 'primary awareness' and 'secondary awareness.' Primary awareness, he told us, registers the discomfort of the pain and urges the body to escape. At this point, we can try to escape, or we can make use of our secondary awareness to 'be beside the pain' and embrace rather than reject the sensation. Don argued that we should identify with our self as a witness to the pain, and, in so doing, endure far more than we thought possible. The secret was in not resisting the discomfort."

"In other words," I interrupted dryly, "relax into the pain. But, if I could relax into the pain, surely I would."

"Of course," replied Laoshi. "This is the whole problem: we cannot truly relax. Relaxation is a kind of knack, which we have to relearn."

No doubt my expression betrayed my skepticism, for Laoshi added, "Alright, think of it this way. You know the film, *Lawrence of Arabia*, with Peter O'Toole?"

I nodded.

"Well, in one scene, Lawrence shows a soldier the trick of extinguishing a lighted match with his finger tips. After trying, the soldier complains that extinguishing a lighted match in that manner hurts. Lawrence replies, 'Certainly it hurts.' 'What's the trick then?' demands the soldier. 'The trick, William Potter,' replies Lawrence, 'is not minding that it hurts.' Not minding is the province of secondary awareness—the province of the heart-mind."

I remained unconvinced. "That's a good line from a Hollywood scriptwriter Laoshi, but is that how we are to interpret the Zen furnace story?"

"If you like," shrugged Laoshi. "But you can also think of the dantian as a furnace where you burn negativity. Whatever upsets or bothers you is drawn by the heart-mind into the dantian where it is incinerated. Anger, grief, envy, or any other of the ten thousand faces of fear can be directed to the dantian. Pain can also be directed to the dantian to seek its release."

"Can you do that, Laoshi?"

"Sometimes it works, but not always. I need to spend more time working on the skill to master it, but on those occasions when it does happen, it is tremendously satisfying."

"And when it doesn't?" I asked.

"I take half a paracetemol."

I left Laoshi that day puzzled. I questioned the extent to which Laoshi's words were relevant, either to me as an individual, or taijiquan in general. Over the years, however, as I became more intimate with the unwelcome guest that is pain, I recalled snippets of our conversation, recognizing that Laoshi had provided useful clues for dealing with discomfort in general, and pain in particular.

Laoshi was emphasizing the importance of relaxing the breath while experiencing pain. An ability to breathe naturally and easily amid physical suffering keeps us from becoming lost and allowing the pain to take over.

Furthermore, Laoshi was highlighting the peculiar capacity of the body to tolerate pain through the power of the heart-mind. Trying in vain to escape pain creates an additional distress, often more tormenting than the original source of our misery. The heart-mind is a reservoir of peace and strength of such vast proportions that physical or psychological pain can be absorbed, and, if not eradicated, then eased sufficiently to make life tolerable.

The perception of pain is remarkably complex and is influenced by our cultural beliefs, personal psychology, and experience. Of course, the goal is not to live a totally pain-free life, but to relax until we reach the point where "fearlessness to take pain" becomes a reality.

Chapter 22: Legality

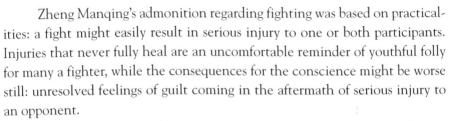

Zheng Manqing's admonition regarding fighting was based on practicalities: a fight might easily result in serious injury to one or both participants. Injuries that never fully heal are an uncomfortable reminder of youthful folly for many a fighter, while the consequences for the conscience might be worse still: unresolved feelings of guilt coming in the aftermath of serious injury to an opponent.

Furthermore, the Professor was acutely aware that, especially in a foreign country, it would be wise to take account of the legal pitfalls when agreeing to "test conclusions." Robert Smith reminds us of a challenge refused by Professor Zheng due to the uncertain legal ramifications in the event of serious injury or death. It would seem that the modern martial artist must take into account the legal position as much as the opponent.

A karateka once told me of a judicial miscarriage, which befell a fellow enthusiast at the hands of the law. A seasoned member of a respectable Glasgow karate club was walking through a fairly rough neighborhood one evening, when he was attacked by a pair of muggers who mistook his lack of physical size for a lack of fighting credentials: not only was the karateka a dan grade of some years standing, he had previously been an amateur boxer. The altercation ended as might have been expected, with both assailants knocked to the ground, pride hurt, but otherwise uninjured.

Perhaps, in another time, small-time gangsters, like the muggers on that evening, might have dusted themselves off and chalked one up to experience, but even in the seedier trades, like street mugging, it would seem you cannot get the qualified staff. These barely competent predators were wiley enough, however, to concoct a sufficiently credible fiction and called the police.

In a less politically correct era, the local constables, familiar with the complainants, might have advised the muggers to sling their hook. Times have changed, and the local police made an arrest—the karateka. Being immersed in the noble arts of boxing and karate may have worked against him and registered in the legal mentality a suspicion of savagery. The brief, hired by the karateka for legal advice, suggested that since his word was opposed by two assailants, he should plead guilty to assault and hope for clemency from the sheriff. Unfortunately, leniency was in short supply that day, and it was the karateka who received a three-month custodial sentence. No doubt his accusers would have claimed criminal injury compensation.

Watching Laoshi demonstrate the martial effectiveness of taijiquan when unleashed as a fighting art, I wondered about his views on martial arts and the law. In between sips of tea, one morning, I told him the story of the karateka, before asking, "Laoshi, do you have any advice on how to stay within the bounds of the law if we ever have to defend ourselves on the street."

His initial reply carried the cutting riposte he reserved for questions lacking depth. "If," he pointed out, "you go into a fight thinking about the legal implications, it is unlikely you will go to jail."

"I see… Is that because a jury will recognize you acted with restraint?" I asked confident of the general thrust of his argument.

"No," he replied with a caustic smile, "it is because you will be in hospital." His demeanor then softened, and he amplified his thinking: "If you want to fight with someone—don't. There is always loss in a fight. Even if you win, you lose something, somewhere. If you have to fight, then fight. But if you fight while considering the legal niceties, you will be divided and not be able to muster your full potential in your service. You either fight or you don't. There is no halfway. If you need to defend your life then, as Zheng Manqing says, 'get mean.'"

He put heavy emphasis on the words "have to."

"*Have to*" he added, "means when not fighting will result in physical injury or death to you or someone you wish to defend. Bear in mind, if you *have to fight*, you are not restricted to waiting to be attacked. You may have to strike first."

Surprised by Laoshi's forthright views, I was eager to hear more. "But… surely a jury will regard the one who attacks first as being the aggressor and therefore guilty?"

"Possibly," shrugged Laoshi, "but you are not fighting the jury. You are out on the street trying to avoid death or serious injury. There may be times when to wait for an assault might prove fatal. That's a high price to pay for the good opinion of a jury, whom you may, or may not, face."

"In that case then, Laoshi, when should we strike first?"

"Hmm… listen," he sighed, "I'm an old man. I have a funny knee. I am not as fast or as strong as I used to be. If outnumbered by armed men, and I feel I must protect my myself or my wife, then I might act first to even the odds. Where the line is drawn depends very much on the feeling I would have in the moment. I trust my heart-mind to guide me to act with integrity."

132

It seems there were no easy answers on this topic, and, much like Zheng Manqing's use of a stick to discipline his children to protect them from the power of his qi, I did not think relying on the special defense of heart-mind would sway a jury in court. I left the conversation with Laoshi not much the wiser.

Weeks passed and the details of our conversation receded from my mind, only to re-surface again in push-hands class. Laoshi was demonstrating a particular application to a group of advanced students. Typically, Laoshi was not inclined to stress the fighting applications of the postures, but, periodically, he would set up an attack-defense scenario to illustrate an important point of principle. In this instance, with Rodrigo in the role of attacker, Laoshi was advocating multiple strikes to an attacker to cause sufficient injury to nullify any further threat. He let loose a flurry of rapid strikes, with fist and fingers, targeting Rodrigo's eyes and throat, with a deluge of touches, light enough to make a point, but without causing injury. Suddenly he paused, perhaps remembering my question on the legality of self-defense, and turning to one of our number said, "Miles, can you perhaps shed some light on the legal view of applying this scenario on the street?"

Miles, an experienced lawyer, worked in the Procurator Fiscal's office in Glasgow determining whether a case of assault had sufficient evidence to merit a prosecution, and then arguing that case in court. Highly intelligent, articulate, and witty, Miles had a well-deserved reputation for not only winning in court, but also winning with panache. Many a street thug was behind bars due to Miles's efforts. I enjoyed listening to Miles's considered observations on taijiquan, martial arts, and life in general.

"Well," replied Miles, a twinkle in his eye, "If someone comes up to you on the street and tries to punch you, but you hit them instead, then you are innocent. If you then hit them again, you are a little less innocent. If you then hit them again, you are a little less innocent still, and if you hit them again… You get the point."

It was an answer worthy of Miles and revealed the plasticity of the law as applied in cases of assault. Right and wrong are seldom the currency in legal argument. More telling and equally chilling, however, was Miles's comment in the café after class: "Don't rely on the law to protect you." It was not comforting advice, and I began to reconsider Laoshi's views on self-defense.

Just when I was confused enough about legalities surrounding martial arts, Laoshi, on the occasion of our next meeting, asked, "Do you remember that chat we had about the law and taijiquan?"

"Yes, Laoshi," I answered hesitantly: where was this going now, I wondered.

"I was thinking about what we discussed and remembered a problem Wang Lang encountered in a push-hands class years ago. Would you like to hear it?"

"Er… yes Laoshi. I would be interested… I think!"

"No problem," smiled Laoshi. "One evening, an experienced student from another school visited Wang Lang's class with the intention of testing his push-hands ability against Wang Lang. The challenger openly stated his intentions. Wang Lang agreed to a 'friendly' round of push-hands. The pair of them lined up, with the challenger's back to the wall in the role of neutralizer, while Wang Lang took the role of pusher. It was soon obvious that the visitor's skills in neutralizing needed some refining. Having hit the wall a few times as a result of Wang Lang's pushes, the visitor strongly resisted the next push, and, forgoing any pretense at yielding, braced against Wang Lang's push with every sinew. Bracing, as you know, is not rooting, and he was pushed as before, but the tension in his body caused by his resistance, magnified the power of Wang Lang's push. The ensuing forceful impact with the wall left the challenger severely winded.

"Taking a few moments to recover, the visitor left with a brief word of thanks. Wang Lang carried on as usual and assumed the matter was at an end. The following day, however, Wang Lang received a phone call from the previous evening's challenger, threatening to sue for injuries sustained at the hands of Wang Lang. He claimed whiplash damage to his spine as a direct result of Wang Lang's push, leaving him in considerable discomfort and unable to work."

"What a moron," I interrupted scathingly. "Who goes to test a teacher, finds themselves wanting, and then goes away crying and threatening someone with the law. Some people are too much. So… what happened next?"

"Nothing," replied Laoshi, "the fellow maybe calmed down or thought better of the whole thing and it was quietly dropped but, you see, it is wrong to assume that the street is the only place you might face legal difficulties."

It was a cautionary tale, and one that came to mind several years later, when Laoshi told me about his former student Archie, then teaching in England. It seems that in a spirited bout of fencing, Archie fell awkwardly and broke his leg very badly; it took almost a year to heal sufficiently for him to resume teaching.

"I bet he was glad it didn't happen to one of his students," I said, perhaps insensitively, "They might have sued him."

Laoshi's reply was informative: "We are martial artists and, as such, we hold ourselves to the highest standards. We should not need the courts to ensure that we live up to our responsibilities. But most of all, we should not mix worlds: when in a fight, fight; when in court, speak your truth; and when in class remain vigilant."

Chapter 23: Triskelion

I still recall attending my first sword form class. I had not had time to equip myself with a practice sword, not even a cheap wooden reproduction from the local martial arts suppliers. Instead, passing a builder's skip on route to class, I spotted a plastic tube of about the right length and thought, "That'll do for now. Buddha provides." The tube was neither straight nor flat, and, being hollow, had all the substance of an empty cigarette packet. Nevertheless, it did suffice, if only for one class, but the procurement of a decent sword engaged my efforts for some time thereafter.

The Scots have a tradition of great swords: the massive two-handed Claymore was a fearsome weapon, wielded by hulking clansmen in times of war; the famous Scottish broadsword, with basket hilt, struck terror into many a government regiment before Culloden, the last battle on British soil. But, in spite of the sword's place in our history, modern Scots know little of our own swords, let alone Chinese swords. As a result, we are at a loss as to what makes a decent sword: the cultural knowledge of generations has evaporated, replaced by the X-box and PlayStation.

Like many taijiquan students, the first sword I bought was a cheap, wooden, unremarkable thing, picked at random from a few on display in a local martial arts store. Too short, poorly balanced, and crudely made, it served well enough, however, for learning the basic choreography of sword form. My teacher at the time made a decent stab at teaching the form, but had no knowledge of fencing at all. Indeed, at the outset, my fellow students and I were completely unaware that fencing was the natural extension of learning sword form. A screening of the now well-known 1970s film of Zheng Manqing in New York changed my whole perspective. The Professor, along with some of the senior New York students, demonstrated form, push-hands, and sword, including both form and fencing. The screening—and it was a screening— using an old projector and draw-down screen, was the finale to an evening workshop conducted by Lawrence Galante in Glasgow's West End and my introduction to the mysteries of taiji fencing. Leaving the course venue, I was desperate to try my hand at fencing, but had to bide my time until I found a teacher whose school curriculum included fencing.

Years later, in studying with Laoshi, I found such a teacher and quickly observed that sword practice, especially fencing, was central to his Dao. Laoshi regularly arrived at class carrying his sword, even when not intending to use the sword that evening. He explained that we should carry our swords as much as possible to "become as familiar with the feel as a soldier with a rifle."

"A good soldier is one with his rifle," explained Laoshi, expanding further on the theme. "Learning to clean and fire a weapon is rudimentary. In the field, the soldier must have his rifle available while eating, sleeping, and even going to the toilet. Simply negotiating daily life with a weapon in hand brings a familiarity beyond basic training."

Not surprisingly, Laoshi also had very definite ideas concerning the protective bag used to house the sword while in transit. He was not impressed with students, who habitually carried their sword in a vinyl case slung on their backs. "Of course, you need to keep the sword in a bag, but vinyl is a poor substitute for cotton. You should be able to feel as though you were carrying the sword in its scabbard. The cotton does not interfere with the feeling, the vinyl does."

Laoshi himself carried his sword in a heavy cotton shinai bag, which folded over at the top and was secured by tying sewn-in cotton tags. He detested the zip in the vinyl bags as much as the vinyl itself. A strap allowed for Laoshi's bag being slung over the shoulder, but Laoshi made use of this feature only when obliged to use both hands on a specific task. He once advised his students that, "You can learn more about handling a sword by opening a locked door, sword in hand, than by doing form. Never stick it under your armpit when you need both hands. Either use the sling or place it against a wall within easy reach."

Laoshi invariably carried his sword as to make it available as an improvised weapon at any time. Approaching the door of the practice hall, he would sling the sword bag only for the shortest time, unlocking the door and turning on the lights, while remaining fully alert. Laoshi thought of doors as useful reminders to maintain the discipline of constant awareness. "You do not know what is on the other side," he would admonish unwary students, "so always be centered as you pass through." The same vigilance was to be applied in getting out of a car or walking in dimly lit streets, especially if using a mobile phone. It was not paranoia that informed his actions, but a commitment to continual awareness, the sword being a perfect medium for this form of mental training. "Being aware, 'in the moment,' as they say, is not so difficult. The difficulty comes in being in the moment ceaselessly, moment, after moment, after moment, after moment."

Laoshi owned many wooden swords, but he favored one above all: a work of art in itself, handmade by Euan, a senior student and skilled craftsman, who was also blessed with a natural affinity for swords. Euan had fashioned

Laoshi's sword from purpleheart wood, following Laoshi's specifications. The result was a stunning-looking sword with a unique deep purple color, measuring 40 inches in overall length, ten inches accounting for the handle and cross guard, the remaining 30 comprising the blade itself, which tapered gently to a rounded point. The black ray skin, wrapped tightly round the handle to aid grip, was turning grey in places from wear. Within the handle, an ingot of rolled lead acted as a counter-weight, balancing the sword according to Laoshi's preference: five inches from where the forefinger gripped the handle when in use.

As a rule, Laoshi did not offer his sword for the casual perusal of his students, but, believing it essential to hold a good quality sword at least once, he made exceptions. When he finally offered his purple sword for my examination, he said, "Meet Triskelion, my sword master. Triskelion is not only elegant, but a great teacher as well." As I took the sword, Laoshi added, "Although my knowledge of sword came from Master Qin and Wang Lang, it is Triskelion who helps me to keep that knowledge alive today."

This was a day of firsts: not only was it the first time I was permitted to hold Triskelion, it was also the first time I had heard Laoshi refer to Master Qin by name. The third of Laoshi's main taijiquan teachers, Master Qin was a man who had made his life study the sword of Zheng Manqing. He was considered an authority on the Professor's sword techniques, supplementing his knowledge by taking master classes with the Professor in those early days in New York. At times, in frustration at my slow progress, I secretly wondered if seeking out Master Qin would lead to a quickening in my own development. Perhaps, ungraciously, I wondered if Laoshi's reticence in talking about Master Qin was precisely to discourage his more adventurous students from forging a direct link to the Master themselves: there are many who would seek out the source if they knew of its existence. Unlike Master Lin in Taiwan, studying directly with Master Qin did not require a letter of introduction. Furthermore, Master Qin had relocated to London several years after the Professor's death, teaching only a few private students.

With Triskelion in hand, I was aware that despite the weight and substantiality of the sword, the balance was so exquisite that it felt as if floating in my hand. I understood then why Lou Kleinsmith was reputed to have named his sword, "Floating in Joy."

That Laoshi would have a name for his sword was not surprising, but the name chosen seemed mysterious and otherworldly.

"Why did you choose the name Triskelion?" I asked, feeling myself succumbing to his sword's mesmeric quality. There was something special in this piece of shaped wood, something more than the materials used and the fashioning of the blade: it had spirit. It almost felt alive.

"Well," explained Laoshi, "the word is originally Greek, but in Scotland, the Triskelion is a Celtic symbol. It is the tri-scale, the triple-spiral. It is the sign of the three-in-one. For me, it reveals the notion that the unifying principle has three parts."

"Right... I see," I nodded, none the wiser, but uncaring, as I was still marveling at the feel of Triskelion in my hands.

Laoshi laughed. Perhaps he was deliberately being obscure, or perhaps, I was not yet ready to hear. "I think we might leave that for another day," he smiled. "Why not take Triskelion for a form and see what reveals itself."

The form felt enchanting, the sword swooping and diving, then seemingly floating in the air. I began to understand Laoshi's meaning, as he encouraged us to search for the essence of each posture in the form. A form without that essential quality was, as he scathingly put it, "waving a stick in the air."

From that day, a new respect for sword form was awakened within me, and I rekindled my efforts to discover the essence of each posture. However, as I realized later, the real lesson from that day was my introduction, albeit briefly, to the three-in-one concept that Laoshi almost casually mentioned in describing Triskelion.

Laoshi had long held the belief that mastery in fencing depended on understanding a single, unifying principle: "the God particle of fencing." Working and reworking through his teachers' instructions, he single-mindedly pursued the goal of discovering that single overarching idea which contained the sum of form and fencing.

Some years later, as I labored in vain to divine that same truth, Laoshi sought to encourage me saying, "Eventually, I stumbled across the unifying principle." The tenor of his voice changed as he recalled the moment of his discovery. He grew more animated and spoke more rapidly as he relived the experience. "It was such a special day: a major satori after twenty years. I immediately experienced a sudden, dramatic improvement in my fencing. My students could do nothing with me. I had combined yin and yang to control their blade, as if holding their sword in my own hand. I advanced on them, directed their swords as I chose and was unconcerned, even as their efforts to escape became increasing forceful.

"As the weeks passed," added Laoshi, developing his theme, "I saw clearly that it is not a single unifying principle after all: it is actually three principles in one. Immediately it was obvious to me: there are three principles because we live in three dimensions simultaneously."

For Laoshi, true skill in fencing depends on acutely sensing the interplay of energy where the swords connect. The precise interplay of yin and yang at that single tiny spot must be perfectly understood. Winning and losing is decided as soon as the yang of the opponent has been felt and gently deflected. It is as the kendo maxim would have it: *Do not win after having struck, but strike after having won*.

Laoshi described the mechanics of the three-in-one principle as follows: "Once we gain control at the point of connection, the battle is over, and only the terms of defeat have to be negotiated." In Laoshi's mind, the principle could best be explained with reference to the game of Go, "It is like a double atari in Go: you threaten two points simultaneously. When they defend one, you attack the other. But in fencing, you can threaten left or right, up or down, front or back: three directions at once. Depending on which point the opponent defends, there will be an opening to exploit. You see?"

Of course, holding Triskelion for the first time, the subtly of fencing at a high level was still something beyond my ken, and I was more interested in the specifications for Laoshi's sword. It was not simply idle curiosity. I keenly felt a desire for my own Triskelion, clearly not the one I held in my hand, but a close facsimile.

The creation of Triskelion had not been a simple matter for Laoshi: the qualities of a good sword, personal preference, and style of fencing all had to be considered.

Triskelion's genesis lay with Wang Lang: "On my first trip to study with Wang Lang," recalled Laoshi, "I had nothing more remarkable than the cheap, wooden effort that was locally available at the time. One or two colleagues favored Long Quan replicas, made from excessively flimsy metal. They were essentially junk, unsuitable for fencing, and furthermore, when imported into Britain, expensive. Wang Lang's assessment of my wooden sword was not encouraging. Although I had attached a lead weight to the handle, hoping to reduce the excessive chop, it was still something of a cumbersome and unresponsive slug."

"Chop, Laoshi, what do you mean by chop?" I interrupted, not being familiar with the term.

"Ah right, okay," replied Laoshi. "Chop means it was like an axe: the sword had a feeling of weight in the tip, fine for a style of fencing which encouraged disconnecting from an opponent's sword and chopping down on wrist or forearm, but unwieldy when used for taiji fencing. You see, different swords have different blends of the four basic qualities: chop, stab, slice, and hammer.

"More of that another time," continued Laoshi, reluctant to be side-tracked. "Now at that time, Wang Lang returned my sword to me, following a cursory inspection with the words, 'You have done as much as you can with this…' He did not care to dignify this oversize skelf with a name. Offering his own sword to me, Wang Lang suggested, 'It should feel more like this.' The sword Wang Lang offered me was heavier, the blade portion flatter and wider than my own. A degree of chop was present, but to a markedly lesser extent. Interestingly, despite the meatier blade, the balance point was closer to the handle than my own sword, a result, Wang Lang assured me, which was achieved without the need for added weights in the handle."

"That's impressive Laoshi. It must have been well-crafted."

"Quite so," confirmed Laoshi. "It was an exceptional piece of work. I was grateful to Wang Lang, who permitted the making of a paper template of his sword, so that on my return home, I could approach a local craftsman in the hope that a sword of equal quality might be made for me. The resulting specimen approximated Wang Lang's sword and was made, like the original, from maple. As with Wang Lang's sword, my new sword was broad from the handle to the tip and without much evidence of tapering. The heavier handle and a substantial pommel slid the balance point closer to the hilt, and, therefore, it was more in keeping with the feel Wang Lang favored.

"I used that sword for close to a decade, the entire time I studied with Wang Lang. With diligent practice, I felt myself awaken to the mysteries of taiji sword but, over time, I grew dissatisfied with the sword itself, as if its personality was gradually grating on me. Something was clearly awry, but I had no sense of what to do. Master Lin did not teach sword when I studied briefly with him in Taiwan, so I had to endure the feeling of discontent with my sword until I sought out Master Qin.

"Master Qin was known to me from one of my many trips to New York while studying with Wang Lang. At the time, I visited as many of the Professor's first generation students as I could. Master Qin had been gracious and kind when I spent a few hours with him all those years before. Reaching out to him after an interval of over a dozen years turned out to be less onerous than I first feared. He remembered me from our initial meeting, and when I expressed an interest in seriously studying sword with him, he invited me to stay at his house in London, where he was then living."

"So you went to London to meet Master Qin after your studies with Wang Lang and Master Lin?"

"Correct," confirmed Laoshi, "as you know, my preference is to only study with one teacher at a time. There is challenge enough in assimilating the teaching of one master, without the confusion of multiple influences.

"Now, let me see, where was I? Ah yes, I remember. Arriving at Master Qin's, I brought the sword fashioned after Wang Lang's model, and with great enthusiasm, presented it to Master Qin for his appraisal. I was taken aback by his lack of comment: he did not seem overly impressed by either the feel or craftsmanship of the sword.

"It later transpired that Master Qin showed very little preference for any particular sword, instead using whatever was to hand at the time. He insisted that, 'when you know the principle, you can use anything. The Professor even used a feather duster.' Tellingly, however, he did later modify his position by conceding that, 'to learn the method, it might be better to have a sword whose qualities lend themselves better to aid understanding. After that you can use anything.'

"It was clear from the start," declared Laoshi, "that Master Qin's taiji sword methodology was subtly but significantly different from Wang Lang's. Just as with push-hands, I was seeing that there was some interpretation at play amongst Zheng Manqing's students.

"Only to be expected, I suppose," added Laoshi. "Each of us is only capable of seeing what we can see. None of the Professor's students had the whole picture: each saw through the lens of previous experience and ability, coupled with their respective reasons for practicing."

"So Laoshi," I interrupted, "are you saying that Zheng Manqing's students fence differently?"

"From my experience," Laoshi nodded, "I would say that is true. There are some differences in approach and emphasis. Some prefer a light contact between the swords, others favor a more meaty connection; some stick religiously to the opponent's sword, others disconnect with abandon; and some make the wrist and arm the primary target, while others seek to cut the body."

"And so," I interrupted once more, "do the qualities inherent in individual swords lend themselves more readily to each of these different approaches?"

"Again, in my opinion, that is so."

"Okay… in that case, Laoshi, would you say there are 'styles' of fencing among Zheng Manqing's students?"

"I think," answered Laoshi thoughtfully, "if there aren't now, there soon will be, provided of course that taiji fencing manages to survive. Sadly, the fencing element is in decline and may disappear within a generation. So might push-hands for that matter."

"How very sad," I groaned. "To think so much of what the Professor taught could be lost."

"Weep not for taijiquan," assured Laoshi. "If it is lost, it will be reinvented in another way—perhaps a better way. The Dao is the Dao after all: it is infinitely resourceful.

"Now, back to Triskelion." Laoshi cleared his throat, ready to resume his account of Triskelion's creation. "After a few days in Master Qin's house, I noticed a wooden sword hanging from a bracket in his living room surrounded by framed photos of Zheng Manqing. This particular sword appeared not to have been used for some time, and being placed among various Professor Zheng memorabilia, it seemed something of a ceremonial piece. My curiosity piqued, I asked Master Qin about its history, and it turned out to be one of the original swords Zheng Manqing had brought from Taiwan, when he moved to New York. No doubt sensing my desperation to examine the sword more closely, Master Qin invited me to make a closer examination. With due care, I took the sword from the wall. It was unlike any sword I had previously handled, although in all fairness, at that time my experience of wooden swords was still limited."

"Can you describe what it felt like," I interrupted Laoshi.

"Oh, most certainly," replied Laoshi. "It felt just as Triskelion does now."

Was there a hint of pride in Laoshi, as he recalled the archetype that gave birth to Triskelion?

"With Master Qin's permission," continued Laoshi. "I photographed, measured, weighed and sketched his sword in order to replicate it when I returned home. The result, after a few initial incarnations, is Triskelion. When Master Qin encouraged me to take it to a local park and 'sense' a form with it, I was enchanted. The sword and the form came together beautifully, and I had a clear sense of the direction Master Qin was nudging me."

As I continued to examine Triskelion, Laoshi excused himself for a moment. He returned carrying a long, black, lacquered box with gold latches and Chinese calligraphy on the lid. After placing the box carefully on the table, he lifted the lid and took out an exquisite looking sword wrapped in blue silk. The sword was about the same length as Triskelion, complete with a black ray skin handle and scabbard. Releasing the blade from the scabbard, Laoshi examined the blade closely before cutting the air a few times and listening as the air parted with a hiss. He returned the sword to the scabbard before handing the sword to me saying, "You know not to touch the blade, right?"

I nodded as I wiped my hands on my sleeves and then took the sword with both hands: I was both nervous and excited. With the handle in my right hand I released the blade from the scabbard as Laoshi had done before. There was the slightest resistance before the blade was freed and revealed itself in all its true glory. In almost perfect condition, the faint hints of restoration work seemed to add to its radiance. The engraved brass fittings seemed to be original, as was the hand guard, shaped as I was later to find out, in "ace of spades" style.

I was astonished to find such a close similarity in feeling between this antique *jian* and Triskelion. There was, however, something extra in the genuine *jian*: a substantiality that I thought could not be equaled by a wooden sword.

"Does this sword have a name?" I asked Laoshi.

"Oh, yes," he answered definitively. "Most certainly."

"And, it is?" I pressed him.

"Not for you to know at this time. It is between the sword and me. Sometimes, as Zheng Manqing reminds us, we would do well to keep our cards close to our chest. I use this sword for form occasionally, usually when I feel troubled. It is like an aid to meditation; it helps me listen to my heart-mind. It is a real sword and must be treated with respect. A moment's loss of awareness, and it will punish me with a nasty cut. Its very sharpness sharpens me when I feel blunt. If Triskelion is my teacher, this sword is my soul."

Laoshi did not invite me to take his "soul" for a form. I recognized my good fortune even to have held so rare a sword. Very few of Laoshi's students even knew of its existence, let alone had the opportunity to examine it so closely. I felt as if the sword resisted my touch and wanted to return to Laoshi, so I returned it to its scabbard and handed it back. Laoshi was almost reverential in wrapping the sword in the blue silk and ensconcing the sword in its varnished box. Watching the ritual of returning the sword to its lodging, I wondered if I would ever see this magnificent weapon again and under what circumstances.

The time did come when I held the sword in my hand once more, but that day came too soon, and when it did, I wished it had never dawned.

Chapter 24: Stick, Adhere, Connect, Follow

The sayings attributed to Zheng Manqing include his comments concerning key concepts in push-hands: "One may pay special attention to four ideas: sticking, adhering, connecting, and following. Then one will be able to easily neutralize."

Despite the Professor lauding these four ideas, Laoshi barely mentioned them at all, let alone pay them special attention. I wondered why. Rather than approach him immediately, I hoped to familiarize myself more fully with these concepts, as understood in the wider taijiquan community, in the hope of being better prepared to discuss the subject with Laoshi when the time arose.

The four concepts referred to by the Professor are frequently mentioned in taijiquan literature but are often left untranslated, appearing in their original Chinese: *zhan* (粘) is said to mean "sticking to;" *nian* (黏) is "adhering;" *lian*

143

(連) conveys a sense of "linking with," or "connecting;" and *sui* (隨) is usually described as "following." Beyond a simple translation, however, there is a degree of latitude in the precise interpretation of these terms. Was this the reason Laoshi avoided the use of these expressions? Was he trying to avoid adding another interpretation to those already prevalent within the taijiquan community?

"Quite so," replied Laoshi, when I eventually aired the subject for discussion. "I use the concepts but not the words. Is not the point to be able to do push-hands rather than be good at talking about it? Of course, I also expect that my understanding of these ideas may not echo exactly the views of those who use the terms habitually. Why get into pointless discussions of who means what."

"Wouldn't it be better," I bemoaned, "if we could all agree on the same meanings in martial arts terminology? Wouldn't that remove much of the confusion and promote better understanding between schools?"

"Probably not," said Laoshi ruefully, before adding, "Did you know that the ancient Chinese had large, bronze, sacrificial cauldrons called *ding*, used to make offerings to the spirits and ancestors?"

"No, Laoshi, I can safely say I didn't know that," I was both amused and intrigued by another of Laoshi's tangential excursions.

"Well, it seems the ruler of one ancient kingdom convinced himself that engraving the laws of the realm on these cauldrons would be beneficial, since his subjects, in the performance of their rituals, would be constantly reminded of the laws they should adhere to. However, when the king consulted the Daoist sages, whose advice he often sought, he found them against his scheme on the grounds that once the law is formalized and written down, the people would become devious and constantly seek to exploit loopholes. In short, they would become litigious.

"Is this not the case with taijiquan as well?" asked Laoshi rhetorically. "Take, for example, that simple but fundamental maxim, 'use no more than four ounces.' Has it not become a matter of conjecture among differing schools? Furthermore, is there not considerable disagreement over the meaning of deceptively simple instructions, such as keep the spine straight?"

Laoshi's case was well made, and to me, unanswerable. An old joke came to mind concerning the number of taijiquan teachers necessary to change a light bulb: thousands apparently, one to change the bulb and the rest to say how they do it slightly differently.

Seeking clarity, I asked Laoshi if he could explain his own understanding of "stick, adhere, connect, and follow," and reveal the phrasing he used in preference to terms in regular use.

"It is not so simple," he cautioned, "but I will try. These terms have a shallow meaning and another which is altogether deeper."

"Intriguing, Laoshi. Go on."

"On a basic level," he began, "these four words could be taken as the stages of receiving a push, successfully neutralizing, then counterattacking. Master Lin meant much the same when he described the sequence as 'yield–turn–return.' The concept is simple enough, even if the precise application is not.

"Yielding is much the same as the ideas suggested in *zhan* and *nian*, usually translated as stick and adhere. We could discuss the differences between stickiness and adhesion but why would we bore ourselves at this time. The difference will become clear later.

"Then," continued Laoshi, "once we have yielded in the initial direction of the push and have adhered to its energy, we use the idea of connecting—*lian*, which is much the same as Master Lin's 'turn.' This phase of the push-hands cycle involves 'catching' the push and harmonizing with it to the extent that we can alter its path away from its intended target. It is like firing flares to lead a missile away from a plane.

"Finally, *sui*, or 'return,' as Master Lin might say, can be understood as following the rerouted push, and, with the addition of our own force, it is returned from where it came."

Laoshi paused for a moment, eyeing me to assess the degree of my comprehension. "Does that make sense?"

"Of course, Laoshi," I nodded. Laoshi had used the 'yield, turn, return' phraseology frequently when discussing neutralizing technique, and, although I still felt inadequate in effectively translating theory into practice, I did at least have a firm grasp of what was expected.

"Splendid," he said, before raising his eyes upward as if seeking inspiration, "now for the tricky bit."

"Marvelous," I thought, "This should be good."

"We can," he resumed, "also think of these four terms as levels of martial understanding, each one progressively more refined than the one before. *Zhan* is almost coarse in its application, whereas *sui* is supremely subtle. Describing these levels in push-hands leads to complications because of its two-game nature, so I suggest we use fencing as the focus of our discussion here. In principle, what is true for fencing is true for push-hands, and vice versa. You could say that fencing is a continuation of push-hands by other means."

Laoshi's lips betrayed a slight smile. He had a fondness for recycling well-known quotations into taijiquan aphorisms. On this occasion the words of von Clausewitz were the victim of his predilection, but I had also heard him singing his version of "Love is All Around," which he called the "qi song:"

> I feel it in my fingers; I feel it in my toes.
> The qi is all around me, and so the feeling grows.
> It's carried on the wind; it's everywhere I go.
> So, if you want to feel it, relax and let it flow.

Allowing a moment to pass, he re-engaged with his theme, this time through the medium of fencing: "When you begin fencing, a heavy emphasis is placed on permitting no force to be present in your blade." He paused momentarily once again before wondering aloud, "Maybe I shouldn't say a heavy emphasis, when we are aiming for lightness, but you understand my meaning. We allow only the lightest of connections between the blades.

"The temptation to use force in fencing is virtually irresistible, so much so that Master Lin taught no fencing at all, lest the temptation to use force contaminate push-hands and lead his students away from the softness he felt was indispensable in learning the art."

Laoshi had previously mentioned Master Lin's view on fencing, a view I found disappointing, if understandable. Fencing, for me, was a key aspect of taijiquan. I wondered how I would fare in a school where fencing was forsaken. Forced to choose between a supremely skillful push-hands master who allowed no fencing, and a less able teacher whose syllabus made room for rigorous fencing, I would be in a quandary. Fortunately, Laoshi's skills in both fencing and push-hands were of the highest order, and I benefited from the best of both worlds: a blessing, which was as rare as it was valued.

"At the outset," continued Laoshi, "in our search for sublime skills in sword, our fencing might be characterized by the phrase 'yin on the outside, yin on the inside.' We permit not the slightest build up of force on our sword with the result that, in the initial stages, we have a truly ineffective system of fencing. This is 'investing in loss' applied to sword. Our sword gets pushed around as we yield, in much the same way as does our body in the initial stages of push-hands.

"Assuming we do not allow frustration to blunt our sensitivity and react with force against force, we might, over time, glimpse the possibility of a second, deeper stage. Still keeping a soft contact, we learn to direct our intention to the point of contact between the swords. It might be said that we put our qi into the sword. We send our feeling into the point of contact with our opponent's blade. This leads to a feeling that we can call adhering."

"So," I interrupted, "we could say that *nian*, that is to say, adhering, is sticking in an active way, while *zhan* is sticking in a passive way."

"That is absolutely as I see it," nodded Laoshi. "The initial stages of training require that we progress from contact in a passive way to contact in an active way, but crucially, without ever forcing against the yang of our opponent's blade. Our opponent, if sensitive, may be able to sense our qi as we develop the skill of active listening, but our contact will offer no forcefulness that can be used against us. Of course, at this stage, a superior fencer will still defeat us with skill, while an inferior fencer will defeat us with force and speed, but progress has been made, rest assured.

"Now," said Laoshi with greater emphasis, arriving at the nub of the matter, "we come to *lian*, connection, or conjoining, indeed, which ever word takes your fancy. My preference is the Japanese word *musubi*.

"We can think of sticking as yin-yin, that is, we aim for a receptiveness both inside and outside the sword. Similarly, we can think of adhering as yin-yang, that is, we present a yin softness to our opponent, who feels no resistance, while we press the yang of our intention or qi against their sword. Following on from these two ideas, we can then think of connection, or *musubi*, as yang-yin, that is to say, yang on the outside but yin on the inside."

"Does that mean we can dispense with the idea of softness in fencing?"

"No, no, no," corrected Laoshi. "Not at all. The outside is full, not hard."

"I don't get that, Laoshi," I protested. "Then, isn't musubi just a clever justification for putting in some force?" I was a little disappointed, not to say dismayed with Laoshi's explanation. I had observed many times a tendency in a school's senior students to berate a beginner for being over forceful, only then to take advantage of the ensuing softness to secure victory by using force themselves. Cajoling a beginner into becoming compliant in order to beat them seemed, not only manipulative, but self-defeating, yet I had witnessed such a dynamic played out many times.

"That can happen," conceded Laoshi. "And it is precisely why we find our way to *musubi* through the yin route. We make a true commitment to softness to ensure that the yang component, so necessary to fencing, is not simply force in disguise. Without the yin, there is no sensitivity. Remember, softness by itself, is essentially worthless. We study softness to arrive at sensitivity. Other martial arts approach *musubi* from the yang side; they risk never finding sensitivity; we risk contaminating our softness as we try to temper it with fullness.

"You will recall hearing that a number of Zheng Manqing's students described his fencing, like his push-hands, as the softest of the soft. Others described facing him with a sword as if being pressed back by a 'ten-ton truck' or 'as a mountain range moving against you.' Due to the inherent contradiction in these statements, I initially dismissed them as perceptual errors in Professor's students. Later, however, their comments made perfect sense, when the principle of *musubi* became clearer."

"But how, Laoshi?" I interrupted shaking my head. "Either Zheng Manqing was completely soft or he was as hard as a ten-ton truck. You cannot reconcile these two extremes, can you?"

"I think so," smiled Laoshi. "Imagine an exquisitely balanced revolving door. Now, if you push on the edge, what will happen?"

"The door will turn, and I will be able to walk through it."

"Correct," agreed Laoshi. "Now, what happens if you push it on the central column—on its axis connected to the floor?"

"Nothing," I replied, "I would not have enough strength to make the central column move."

"Exactly," smiled Laoshi, "it would be like pushing against someone's resistance, but if you use the same amount of pressure at the side, the door will revolve. It is not that we cannot apply pressure to remain consistent with principle, but that the pressure must be on a point that cannot defend itself. This is the understanding inherent in *musubi*.

"It is as they say in the military: advance to contact, then move forward till you experience resistance. Imagine now Zheng Manqing driving through the yin point of his student's sword. If the student is completely yin and offers no effective resistance, it might well feel as if a mountain range is pressing forward. Other than resisting, the student can do nothing but run away. If, on the other hand, the student tries to halt the Professor's progress by resisting with strength, they are simply exchanging one weakness for another, allowing the Professor's full but sensitive connection to control the yang and deflect it with minimum effort."

"Like the oft-quoted bull being led by a ring through its nose."

"Precisely," confirmed Laoshi. "There is no escape. The Professor's students either yielded before him, as they tried to remain soft, or they resisted and found their defense softly deflected to the point of ineffectiveness. Crucially, very little active pressure is required to deflect force, provided there is sensitivity, of course."

"Just the right amount, at the right time, in the right direction: *shizhong*."

"There you have it," nodded Laoshi.

There were times, listening to Laoshi talk about taijiquan, when he could just as easily have been talking about aikido. Similarly, Billy Coyle, my aikido instructor, could just as easily have been talking about taijiquan, when expounding on the principles of aikido. On the concept of *musubi*, Billy wrote: "...any contact with any part of an attacker's body shall be such that the

148

aikidoka can 'feel' any tension and 'read' any intention that the attacker may have. *Musubi* with someone's arm, for instance, will inform the aikidoka if there is any possibility of a counter, or the attacker is truly off balance. Much can be read from true *musubi* contact."

On expressing my observation to Laoshi, he replied, "It does not surprise me. All martial arts have an instant of *musubi* or contact. Indeed, a martial art is, almost by definition, the result of a coming together of two bodies, even in archery—the target with the arrow. Martial arts have this in common, whether grappling or striking arts: the moment of contact. The differences arise from what happens after that moment. Some throw, some strike. What is important is to control that very first instant of contact."

Laoshi was echoing Billy once more: "We must seek to maintain a solid *kokoro kamae* (posture of the mind), as well as a flexible *katatchi kamae* (posture of the body). Equally, we should try to break these in our partner at the instant of musubi."

I began to understand why Laoshi considered musubi, or lian, to be so important. The instant when two fighters connected together was pivotal. Whoever could control the body and mind of the other at that precise time would have a decisive advantage.

"So Laoshi," I asked, "if *zhan* is yin-yin, *nian* is yin-yang and *lian* is yang-yin, then does that mean there is a more advanced principle which is yang-yang? Is that what sui is? Is *sui* yang on the outside and yang on the inside?"

"I believe so," he nodded, the slightest smile on his lips.

"But how can that be? If something is yang both on the inside and out, then surely there must be a hardness or forcefulness present?"

"Interesting idea isn't it: Yang on the inside, yang on the outside, but still not forceful. How can that be?"

I shrugged. "I'm sure I have no idea, Laoshi."

"Perhaps this will help," he suggested. "Imagine that you were placed in a room blindfolded and told to find the door. What would you do?"

"Well…" I replied, "I suppose I would put my hands up and walk forward till I found the wall, and then move along the wall till I found the door."

"Very good. So now imagine that you were put back into that room in exactly the same position, with the same blindfold, and told to find the door a second time, what would you do?"

"I'd just go straight to the door."

"Why?"

"Because I know exactly where the door is. I wouldn't need to find it first: I would know where to go."

Laoshi smiled, apparently pleased that his analogy was bearing fruit.

"The study of *musubi* is like examining the wall to distinguish between solidness and emptiness, between yang and yin. The more familiar you become with solidness, the more you understand where the emptiness lies. A rigorous study of *musubi* leads to the level of sui, where, with a touch, we know all there is to know about the opponent and slide past their defenses to deliver the denouement without delay. They may know we are coming, they may know when we are coming, they may even know how we are coming, but they are powerless to stop us.

"If they simply yield, they will be overwhelmed. If they resist, we slide past them like a gentle breeze on a summer's day. By knowing their strengths, we know their weaknesses."

Laoshi then looked at me pointedly and said, "There can be no escape."

It can be reassuring to remember that those whose attainments we seek to emulate also passed through levels to reach their position of mastery. It is sometimes tempting to imagine that a colossus such as Zheng Manqing emerged from the womb of the Dao fully formed as Master of Five Excellences. We forget that the brilliance of a sunset is the culmination of the day. The Professor leaves clues in his writing as to the obstacles he faced and leaps of understanding that marked his progress.

Laoshi's talk of levels reminded me that taijiquan is never static: we may plateau for a time, but new insights are always only a form or a push away. Of course, as we mark the levels we pass through in our own practice, another question arises regarding masters like the Professor: who had the better Zheng Manqing, the Taiwanese or the Americans? Was the younger, more vigorous and apparently more martial Professor Zheng the better, or was it the more mature Master of Five Excellences who was more well-rounded and easy-going? Is progress always linear? A question for another day, perhaps, but realizing that a new perspective in my practice may be just around the corner revitalizes me, when the plateau I'm on threatens to bore me into submission.

The next form could be the one.

Chapter 25: Competition

To my knowledge, none of Laoshi's senior students ever sought to test themselves by entering taijiquan competitions. The true value of tournament participation, however, was discussed periodically in conversations conducted outside of class. The after-class coffee was the usual setting for this kind of discussion, where the nuance of technique, as well as the "oral tradition" of the school might be assimilated in an informal way. It was where the unwritten rules of the school came to light and where school culture evolved. More junior students also participated in these gathering and absorbed those aspects of the art, which are only communicable by osmosis.

From these informal conversations, I was aware of Laoshi's views on taijiquan competition, whether for form or push-hands, and his verdict was that they were rather pointless.

"'Competitive relaxation?' A bit of an oxymoron, don't you think?'" Laoshi suggested, when coaxed to offer his view by a group of younger students. "Have you ever heard of a 'meditation tournament?'"

"Form competitions do take place, to be sure," acknowledged Laoshi. "It is just that, to me, it is like watching an elephant bouncing on a trampoline—perplexing. You wonder how this could have happened, and what exactly the elephant is getting from it?

"Let's be honest," suggested Laoshi, with all appearance of earnest contention, "watching other people doing form over and over can become mind-numbingly boring. Having people perform the same postures for hours on end, without providing beds for the spectators, is verging on crowd abuse. I can just about understand why someone might want to enter a taijiquan competition, but, as for the officials and judges, what heinous crime condemned them to having to watch the slow suffocation of taijiquan for an entire day?"

If Laoshi's views on competitive push-hands were only slightly less scathing, I suspect this was due to his recognition of the ease with which he himself, not to mention his students, could become prisoner to the competitive urge during push-hands practice. Our need to "win" regularly provoked in all of us recourse to force, eschewing all pretense of sensitivity, as we engaged in full-on, sumo-like battles with each other. At those times, we were, *de facto*, in competitive mode, albeit outside an organized tournament setting. Less scathing though he may have been, Laoshi still believed that the skills he sought to develop in the *peng-lü-ji-an* version of push-hands, the mainstay of his school, were essentially undermined by an overtly competitive approach.

While the senior students, by and large, respected Laoshi's view, some of the younger students began to question Laoshi's objections, especially when it was reported that the one-hundred-year anniversary celebrations of the Professor's birth, held in Taiwan, included a push-hands competition. Perhaps, Laoshi's view was old-fashioned, they suggested, and might not Zheng Manqing himself have been an advocate of competition if competitions had existed when he was alive? After all, had Zheng Manqing not encouraged a competitive attitude among his students? Had he not been a fiercely competitive personality? Wang Lang had even commented on the Professor's penchant for playfully competitive games, even in apparent trivia, such as "fingernail toughness."

The opportunity to discuss the matter arose one evening after class. Danny, a keen junior student, suggested that since so many Zheng Manqing schools were involved in competition, and had participated in the Taiwan celebrations, our school should send a team next time in order to "make a splash." Danny eagerly presented the usual arguments: competition would provide a benchmark for students in assessing their progress; it would also generate greater enthusiasm in regular classes in preparation for the event. Furthermore, Danny proposed, competition would test the extent to which relaxation could be maintained in pressurized situations, and it would foster better relations with like-minded students and schools.

The senior students exchanged wry glances as Danny held forth with increasing exuberance, while a succession of vivid expressions passed across Laoshi's face. He seemed at first to channel horror, then disappointment, followed by a theatrical scowl. I tried not to smile, as I anticipated some entertainment to come.

"Ah... so, you have heard of the one-hundred-year anniversary celebration?" Laoshi opened neutrally enough. Danny nodded vigorously.

"Good, good. No doubt it was a great success, and everybody enjoyed themselves?"

Danny continued nodding in agreement, "Sure, I imagine so."

"Well, as long as everybody enjoyed themselves," Laoshi replied, a twinkle in his eye. "After all, having a good time, that is the chief purpose of taijiquan, is it not? Nothing to do with pursuit of Dao or anything equally mundane?"

Danny quickly glanced around the circle of senior students present, most of whom were doing their best to keep a straight face. Perhaps, picking up on the hint of mischief about, Danny said nothing.

"I heard a different story, mind you," continued Laoshi smoothly. "Yes... I heard that one of the Professor's most senior students, Master Lin, avoided the competition. Apparently, he was to be found in an adjoining room, alone and forlorn, looking at an exhibition of Zheng Manqing's artwork and calligraphy. I wonder if he enjoyed the tournament?" Laoshi gave Danny a searching look, as if Danny might hold the answer.

Danny's gaze flicked rapidly around the room once more, trying to gauge reaction. He offered no reply.

"I can tell you, he *did not*." Laoshi looked pointedly at Danny, whose gaze dropped to the floor. "Furthermore, one of Master Lin's students entered the push-hands tournament and caused not even a ripple, never mind a splash. And, afterwards," Laoshi gazed around the room in seeming outrage, "afterwards, the student added insult to injury by asking Master Lin to explain his dismal competition showing: had it been his yielding, which had let him down? Or, he wondered, the stiffness of his waist? Or, was he investing in loss too much?"

Laoshi's hands flew into the air in mock consternation. "Master Lin informed the unfortunate student, 'You lost the moment you entered the competition.'"

To his credit, Danny was not easily dissuaded. Evidently frustrated by Laoshi's summary dismissal of his argument, he pursued: "But what, exactly, is so bad about competition? Surely, the competitive approach improves our understanding, and... well... people like competitions. Look at the UFC."

Laoshi snorted, "Competition push-hands has more in common with sumo than with MMA! The ideal competition push-hands physique is a huge belly and short legs. At least they keep their clothes on in competitive push-hands," added Laoshi nonchalantly, "so we have to be grateful for small mercies."

"Yeah, okay, but..." Danny did his best to ignore the ripple of laughter around the table. "But, wouldn't competition help us better understand our usual push-hands? Wouldn't we get a chance to try out our abilities in a more realistic situation?"

Now, the senior students had witnessed Laoshi's ways in conversation many times and knew that he relished a bout of verbal swordplay. Thus, while he gave the deliberate impression of being outraged, those who knew Laoshi better saw the suppressed smile, which betrayed his amusement: "Ha!" Laoshi snorted again. "I tell you: competition push-hands aids our push-hands to the same extent that arm-wrestling assists calligraphy. If you are set upon testing your relaxation under pressure, and are keen to try your martial skills for *real*, I suggest you visit The Viking Bar in Maryhill on Friday night, and search for the big guy with muscles the size of tractor tires and 'ACAB' tattooed on his forehead. Inform him that he is being a little too loud and interfering with your quiet evening's lemonade."

Guffaws broke out among the circle of students; even Danny laughed ruefully at the vivid scene conjured by Laoshi.

"Okay, okay! I get it!" Poor Danny was beginning to lose steam. "But, what does ACAB mean?"

"ACAB? It stands for *All Coppers Are Bastards*," replied Laoshi cheerfully. A fresh round of chuckles swept around the table. Danny looked exasperated. Laoshi was giving him the run-around, a practice not unfamiliar to the senior students present. Although Laoshi often professed that there was "no such thing as a stupid question," we all, at one time or another, felt that we had asked the question that proved the exception. Accordingly, there was a degree of sympathy in the room for Danny. This extended to Laoshi:

"Listen…" said Laoshi in a conciliatory tone, relenting from his earlier mischief-making, "the *real* problem with push-hands competition is that it puts the emphasis in the wrong place."

"You mean it puts the emphasis on winning, rather than playing the game? But isn't winning important as well?" You had to hand it to Danny. He was persistent.

"Well… in a crude way, you are correct," acknowledged Laoshi. "But there is a more subtle level." Laoshi glanced around the table to ensure our attention.

"What level?" asked Rodrigo.

"Here's the thing," continued Laoshi. "Competition divides us against ourselves. Our mind becomes obsessed with the end of the process, rather than the whole of the process: our mind becomes tight. We become split and so effectively useless. As Zheng Manqing says: 'Fear makes you stiff. Competition makes you even stiffer. The desire to do your best also gets you stiff.' Follow?"

Danny looked blankly at Laoshi, and he was not the only one. Usually, Laoshi did not dwell overmuch in his criticism of taijiquan competitions, as if the reason for his disdain was entirely obvious. I eagerly awaited Laoshi's expansion on the topic, intrigued by the possibility that he might reveal a deeper insight into the competitive frame of mind. I nodded meaningfully at Danny, a tacit "thank-you" for coaxing Laoshi into fuller explanation.

"Do you know the story in the *Zhuangzi* about the archer shooting for gold?" asked Laoshi. Danny shook his head. Laoshi quoted from memory:

When an archer is shooting for fun
He has all his skill
If he shoots for a brass buckle
He is already nervous.
If he shoots for a prize of gold
He goes blind
Or sees two targets —
He is out of his mind
His skill has not changed,
But the prize divides him.
He cares
He thinks more of winning
Than of shooting —

And the need to win
Drains him of power.

"But, isn't that, well… just nerves he's talking about," queried Danny.

"It is about more than simple nervousness," asserted Laoshi. "Consider, the kyudo master who looses his arrow and proclaims it a perfect shot, despite the arrow sailing over the target. For him, the shot took place at the moment of release, when the arrow 'shot itself.'"

Laoshi, now in full flow continued, "We always want to know what 'good' something is: what is its 'purpose' or 'use.' We are so fixated on the useful purpose of a thing that we are blind to all else. Even worse, we have been conditioned to put a price on everything, so that usefulness has now become synonymous with *value*. But as the *Daodejing* reminds us, often it is the *use-less* that has value: we cannot literally live inside a wall, and yet we talk about buying four walls. Actually, it is the space within these four walls that we live in. In other words, we live in nothingness, but nobody has yet managed to charge for that nothingness."

"Give them time!" quipped one of the students sarcastically.

Laoshi smiled. "Ego is target-orientated. When we are target-orientated, the mind has raced ahead to the target and is waiting for the arrow, not only to arrive, but also to be judged upon its accuracy. Where is relaxation in this? It has disappeared, replaced by anxiety and doubt, and, worst of all, comparison. The difficulty is that when you compete, you compare, and when you compare, you become dissatisfied. Being dissatisfied, you become fearful, and being fearful, you are now double-weighted and, therefore, weakened. You have defeated yourself!" chortled Laoshi.

"Wait, wait! Go slow," entreated Danny, now genuinely interested. "How does being dissatisfied make you fearful?"

"Ah… good question," rejoined Laoshi. "Dissatisfaction feeds our fear that there is something insufficiently available for us to receive our share. When such fear takes hold, we have parted with the Dao and can no longer trust life to give us what we need. When such a mind-set enters, you find yourself obliged to seize what you can, and then to protect what you have managed to grab hold of."

The cogs whirring in Danny's mind were almost audible, as he intently followed Laoshi's exposition. He was less "gung ho," but no less intent upon pursuing answers.

"So… what about fighting for real? Isn't that similar to competition?" he pressed.

"Well now, if it is," considered Laoshi, "then you are not *really* fighting.

Take push-hands, for instance: the rules *insure that it is safe*. You know this. If push-hands tournaments routinely resulted in competitors' serious injuries, or even death, the practice would be outlawed overnight. Fighting *for real* means fighting for your life! This is a different mind-set entirely: as close to 'no-mind' as some of us will ever get. The sheer intensity of the fight for survival breaks the hold of the rational mind. We are free to act spontaneously, pursuing extreme measures, fiercely aware of the moment, alive to the slightest gesture of the adversary before us, who would take our life."

A murmur of understanding rippled around the table.

"Of course, the problem we face," continued Laoshi, "is that just at the point where we need our taijiquan to work for us, for our body to be loose and our mind to be spacious, our taijiquan deserts us! It is even worse if we have become double-weighted by entertaining thoughts of 'winning' and 'losing,' or by favoring a preconceived strategy and expecting things to go as we anticipate."

"Then what should we be thinking about?" asked Danny. I half-expected Laoshi to reply, "Think of nothing." I recalled that I had heard this advice offered, when I had once asked a similar question of another teacher. To be honest, I had not found the advice helpful. Instead, Laoshi answered, "Consider the advice given to Robert Smith by Zheng Manqing for moments such as these: 'Don't over-analyze your opponent. Don't worry about his posture, his hands, which leg is forward, or things like that. And don't even think about your own hands. Instead, keep your mind on your own legs. This way everything will work out fine.'"

"What?! But, that's absurd!" poor Danny couldn't help himself. "'*Just think about your legs and everything will be fine?*' I mean... *really!*"

"You may well think it absurd, but I do not," said Laoshi solemnly. "As students of Zheng Manqing's taijiquan, we are advised to put our heart-mind in our lower body and respond from our *gongfu* that is built up by regular training in push-hands, fencing, and form. Below the navel is where our power resides: here is the foundation of our relaxation, the home of our *qi* the place where the jin energy sprouts. I repeat Zheng Manqing's advice, 'Keep your mind on your own legs. This way everything will work out fine.'"

I could hold back no longer. I was now as keen as Danny to understand this perspective on martial arts training, something I struggled with. "Laoshi," I intervened earnestly. "You are saying that you believe the real value of practicing the method as taught by Zheng Manqing is not in learning 'techniques' for self-defense. Rather, if I understand you correctly, the method shapes our minds and bodies so that we can gradually release our natural energy and intuition: respond appropriately and effectively to the challenges at hand.

156

Is that so?"

"I know it to be so," said Laoshi simply.

"Really, truly? From personal experience?" pressed Danny, genuinely intrigued. "Can you tell us?"

Laoshi seemed momentarily reluctant, appearing to consider his response before replying, "Very well. But I tell you of this incident only to aid understanding. It was the beginning of my true faith in the teaching of Zheng Manqing. Each of you must find your own 'catalyst' to faith in the power of the Professor's method.

"So... I had been practicing taijiquan for over a decade, a diligent student but still at the mercy of my doubts and fears regarding the method. One afternoon, I interrupted my daily walk near Kelvingrove Park for a quiet coffee in one of the trendy new cafés, which were appearing at that time to cater for the aspiring middle classes colonizing the area. The café was busy, but a few seats remained.

"My hopes of a peaceful hour, reading over coffee quickly evaporated, however, when a brash young couple clattered in with stroller and child. When I say 'brash,' I mean that they managed to draw the attention of every other customer in the place, not to mention the staff, as they proceeded to talk at the top of their voices. Engrossed in themselves, the couple paid little heed to their toddler, who, quite naturally being bored, began running up and down the length of the long bench sited against one wall of the café. The elderly gentleman, sitting at the far end of the bench (I recognized him as a regular, who liked to read his newspaper) clearly felt uncomfortable, as he promptly got up and left. All eyes turned to the parents, but they, entirely oblivious, made no move to quiet the child. Remaining unchecked, the child took to running around the tables in the center of the café, while the wait staff did their best not to be run into nor spill trays of hot food and drinks. An elderly couple exchanged glances with me, rolled their eyes in disapproval but said nothing. Another headed for the door, pausing only to avoid a collision with the youngster. Belatedly, the café owner tried to intervene, diplomatically by attempting to engage with the child to bring some calm to the café once more. But he found himself outmatched by a youngster who ran rings around him, literally. The harassed café owner looked helplessly toward the parents, who paid not the slightest heed, and, admitting defeat, he retreated behind the counter.

"Having been silent witness to these café capers for the past fifteen minutes, I decided it was time to leave. However, as I rose from my seat, I happened to catch the eye of the father. He looked to be in his late 20s, sporting an unshaven look, with a large round face and razor-short ginger hair. Since he happened to be looking directly at me, I took the opportunity to suggest to him that he should not let his child run around to the hindrance of others. In an instant, he snapped up to his feet, pointed a finger in my direction and snarled, "You! I'll see you outside!" A pin dropping would have rung out loud in the café.

"Interestingly though, I felt wholly unconcerned. I said nothing, but simply packed up my stuff and sauntered to the door to wait on the pavement outside the café. Now, I don't think for one minute he actually expected me to wait for him. I noted the fleeting expression of perplexity before he bristled up to me as he left the café, once more jabbing a finger in the direction of my face: 'You don't talk to my boy like that! Got it?'

"He was a big man, maybe six-foot three or six-foot four and 250lbs. He was decked out in the T-shirt, tracksuit bottoms and branded running shoes, denoting the expensive uniform of the Glasgow tough-guy. His demeanor shouted: 'See me? I'm pure mental and gallus with it.'

"I found myself noting these details, even while he was busy posturing menacingly in my face. Although I was in a tactically weak position, square-on with my hands in my pockets, I experienced a feeling of calm and was relaxed. Ten years of push-hands practice made this range entirely familiar and not unduly alarming. Ignoring his attempts at intimidation, I replied evenly, 'I wasn't talking to your boy, I was talking to *you*.' Well... he didn't like that too much. In fact, he seemed positively enraged and screamed, 'See you? If you ever talk to my boy like that again, *I'll rip your fucking face off!*'

"I still vividly recall my feelings in that moment. There was not the slightest flicker in my body. As he continued yelling, mere inches from my face, I found myself thinking only: 'I recognize this energy.' I did not feel an internal response to his threats, in spite of his obvious attempts at intimidation. I replied levelly: 'If you want to hit me, go ahead.' I was relaxed and centered, my legs filled with qi.

"He snarled, 'Right! You and me: in the park. Now!'

"'No,' I returned calmly. 'Do it now.'

"There was a pause, and suddenly he seemed unsure. Then he lunged toward me aiming his shoulder at the middle of my chest, hoping to provoke a reaction. I felt myself sink onto my left leg and turn my waist in the manner of ward-off left in the form. I yielded to his attack and guided him to the side. Fully expecting to meet resistance but finding only air, he lurched forward off-balance, my left hand guiding his right elbow.

"A look of genuine surprise registered on his face as he pulled away from my hand. In an alarmed voice he screeched, 'Oi! What you doin'? What you doin'?'

"'Well… *you* did barge into me, mate,'" I pointed out matter-of-factly. "What can I tell you? The guy looked astounded, furious, but astounded.

"At that moment, he seemed to lose confidence and made off toward his car, with his girlfriend holding the child and scurrying to catch up. Having put some distance between us, he turned to face me once more yelling: 'This doesn't end here… you fucking cunt; you fucking bastard; you fucking peado. I'll find out who you are… I'll find out where you live, ya bastard, and I'll come and get you… you fucking… whatever.'"

Laoshi looked around the table as his tale was nearing its end, twinkle in his eye. "You know, I think he kinda ran out of insults after that.

"As I watched my would-be adversary drive away, I took stock of what I was feeling. The words of Sunzi sprang from somewhere in my consciousness: *To subdue the enemy without fighting is the acme of skill.* More importantly, I understood the wonder of the method; I felt neither post-traumatic adrenalin shakes nor any residual hostility to that guy. I realized that it was truly possible to bypass the fight/flight response and remain relaxed in threatening situations. That was the moment that I truly began to believe in the Dao of Zheng Manqing."

Chapter 26: Who You Are

I vividly recall meeting Billy Coyle on a bus one evening before class. He had finished late at work and had barely enough time to return home and collect his gi and weapons en route to the nearby Habonim boys club where he taught his aikido class. Concerned that he might be tired, I suggested that he take the night off. Billy, however, had no such concerns, informing me that he was used to arriving at class after a grueling day.

To pass the time, Billy told me something of his early aikido training in the sixties. At that time, London was the center of expertise for aikido, having been introduced there from Japan. In those early days, competent instruction was a rarity beyond the capital. In order to study with high quality instructors, Billy was compelled to go to great lengths to learn the art, which was to become his life.

Living in Glasgow, it was impractical for Billy to attend regular weekly classes with the aikido masters in London four hundred miles away. Instead, he relied on attendance at weekend courses in London in order to acquire the majority of his advanced training. Employed as a blacksmith throughout the week, he would regularly return home from work on Friday evenings, only to depart again immediately on the night bus to London, and try to catch some sleep en route. In those days, long-distance bus travel was slow and uncomfortable; the journey took all night, and the bus passengers were crammed together on uncomfortable seats.

After arriving in London early on Saturday morning, Billy would make his way to the dojo for a full day of intense aikido training. Short of funds, he habitually slept on the mat overnight before another full day of training on Sunday. The return journey to Glasgow on Sunday evening was a rerun, in the opposite direction, of the same Spartan bus service. After a few hours sleep at home, Billy would rise again at six in order to ready himself for work on Monday morning. Maintaining this onerous and exhausting schedule was the price exacted for the acquisition of skill by this aikido pioneer in Scotland.

Impressed—moved even—by my old teacher's tenacity, it was vexing to me when a prospective taijiquan student demurred from attending class, simply due to their proximity (or lack thereof) to the venue, especially when the actual distance was no more than a couple of miles in the comfort of a car. "Err... do you offer any classes nearer to where I live?" they sometimes inquired indifferently, as if mere personal convenience was their paramount concern. I found myself frequently lamenting the disappearance of simple desire to pursue one's art. How times have changed.

With commercial space in the city renting for high premium, most of Laoshi's Glasgow teaching activity was accommodated in old church halls. One of these, though typically "tired" around the edges, occupied the perfect location in the best part of town to attract potential students: nearby car parking was free, public transport was close at hand, and the bohemian feel of the neighborhood complemented the taijiquan "vibe" nicely.

On the other hand, this particular church's prominent position and accessibility brought problems of its own. Every so often, those in need of financial or pastoral assistance would appear at the hall door, seeking advice or alms from what they presumed to be a church group. Usually, when it was explained that no church members were present, the seekers left with little fuss. Occasionally, however, an altercation would ensue, as the expectations of those with various needs were not met.

One evening, a particularly insistent wayfarer found his way to the door of the church hall, demanding assistance from the minister and God himself if necessary. The student on door duty, embarked on the customary gentle explanation as to the absence of any minister (leaving aside the more complex issue of the absence, or otherwise, of God) only to have the determined "visitor" push past them into the downstairs interior, intent upon seeking the absent minister and threatening menace with a knife to anyone who might thwart him in his quest.

At once alerted to the unstable nature of this particular gentleman, the student immediately raced upstairs to the hall, where the class was proceeding in order to warn Laoshi of the potentially dangerous intruder.

Swiftly apprised of the situation, Laoshi deputized a senior student to takeover the class, while he went to assess the next move. From my position in the hall, I observed through the open doorway that a stranger was making his way upstairs to the upper landing, where Laoshi was waiting to intercept them. Laoshi's manner betrayed no sense of alarm as he registered the loudly muttering, disheveled figure approaching. He merely closed the hall door softly with a reassuring nod to the senior student, indicating that we should continue with the class untroubled. None of us, however, were able to lend the form our full attention. Some were concerned for Laoshi's safety, but we were also itching to witness how Laoshi would deal with the matter, particularly when the whisper had gone around the class like wildfire that the interloper was potentially armed with a knife and threatening violence.

After a few seconds, the hall door was pushed slightly ajar from outside, and Laoshi's voice calmly requested me and another senior student to join him on the landing: "If you two lads would be good enough to step out here for a moment as witnesses..." Laoshi's tone was no less than good-natured, "because, you see, if this gentleman pulls his knife, then I may have to throw him over the banister."

As we two senior students emerged cautiously onto the upstairs landing as requested by Laoshi, I immediately clocked our "visitor" standing at relatively close quarters to Laoshi outside the hall, with his back to the stairway banister. The barrier to his rear was the only thing between him and a drop of some twenty feet onto stone steps. He was in his early twenties, scruffy, with one hand concealed in his jacket pocket, as if holding something out of sight. But he was also silent and standing as if frozen. Laoshi patiently inquired almost kindly: "Now, what was it you were saying about your knife?"

With no reply forthcoming from our would-be assailant, Laoshi continued in the easy tone of one talking to a neighbor on the doorstep.

"Listen, my friend, I know you have problems, but there is no one here who can help you. By forcing your way in, you are putting yourself in the path of trouble; by pulling a knife and stabbing someone, you will put yourself in a great deal more. Is that what you need?"

His former belligerence now vanished, and our intruder explained that he only wanted to see the minister: he had not meant any real harm. After a further brief and quiet exchange with Laoshi, the man agreed to leave. As he began to remove his right hand from his pocket, I tensed, involuntarily, still anticipating the sight of a naked blade. I relaxed, however, as the only thing produced was a grimy, nail-bitten hand, which was extended towards Laoshi who shook hands with the now peaceful fellow. His parting words to Laoshi remain clearly with me; "You know something... you're alright." He then turned to leave, watched hawk-like by we two senior students. Laoshi nodded to us and returned to his class as if nothing of consequence had occurred.

I could barely wait until class was over, and I was alone with Laoshi, in order to ask him about the management of the situation.

Laoshi nodded gravely, "It is always helpful if people do not feel you are against them, so it is better not to instantly demonize people in such circumstances. This is a lesson from push-hands: energy is neither 'good' nor 'bad,' so do not allow your prejudices to add fuel to the potential fire. Fill yourself with qi as you set out to deal with matters and remain neutral, listening for the yin and yang in the situation. If that young man's intention had been to attack, he would have done so the moment I confronted him, however, I perceived that he was more lost soul than dangerous killer."

"But, Laoshi, you threatened to throw him over the banister onto the steps below! Is that not adding fuel to the fire?"

"Ah..." said Laoshi, smiling a little, "You see, I wasn't threatening him. I was demonstrating to him, in a way that he understood, that we were not the meek and gentle church folk, as he might have anticipated, to be easily intimidated. Can you imagine an aggressive vagrant wandering into a boxing club or karate class and announcing that he was going to stab someone? There would be no shortage of volunteers looking for some realistic training! So, you see, in the case of our young interloper, I was simply letting him know who we were."

If Laoshi's assertion seemed curious, I did grasp that our use of a church hall might lead unwitting outsiders to assume we were church members, full of the milk of human kindness and ready to emulate the spirit of the Good Samaritan. Not that we taijiquan players were without these qualities, but we were not there to be taken advantage of either. An experienced taijiquan player recognizes their freedom to choose what, or *what not*, to make their business.

"But why should we have to 'let people know who we are' Laoshi?" I pressed. "I thought we were not about making statements."

Laoshi nodded his agreement but added, "Sometimes it is necessary. It might even save your life. Let me tell you a story. When I was a teenager, I joined the Army Cadet Force. I was serious and conscientious. I did as I was told, learned quickly what was taught, and avoided trouble as best I could. Before long, I was promoted to the rank of lance bombardier. With the rank came trouble. As soon as I acquired my stripe, the problems started. I was younger than the majority, and with less time served, I had overtaken others in rank. As might be expected, jealousy and hostility arose from some quarters. Even my fellow NCOs were not supportive, viewing me as a rival. The prevailing culture favored pulling down those who aspired to excel: teach them their place.

"Things came to a head one Friday evening. We were staying overnight in the drill hall in preparation for a full day of activities on the Saturday. Quite naturally, young lads freed from home and regular routine have their minds set on causing mayhem and mischief! Accordingly, as soon as the lights were turned out, the improvised, unauthorized evening activities began. The initial harmless jokes and horseplay were soon followed by more sinister entertainment, which culminated in a dubious pact between the unranked cadets and some of my fellow NCOs, who handed me over to the cadets in exchange for a boy they collectively despised and wished to punish with a beating. As the 'sacrificial lamb,' I was in line to be subjected to the violent whim of the, by now, feral pack of cadets."

"But, that's shocking, Laoshi" I interjected. "What age were these thugs?" I demanded, outraged on Laoshi's behalf.

"Oh… We ranged from thirteen to eighteen," replied Laoshi somberly. I was fourteen at the time and so among the youngest and smallest."

"What happened?" I asked quietly. I felt my own apprehension at Laoshi's predicament.

Laoshi eyed me silently for a moment before continuing matter of factly: "In the semi-dark of the hall, I was jostled to the floor, my hands were tied behind me, my legs bound together, and a rope was thrown round my neck and drawn tight."

I gazed horrified at Laoshi, as he continued calmly: "In other words, I was 'hog-tied,' trussed up legs attached to the rope round my throat. The tension on the rope squeezes the throat; the only way to relieve the tension is to keep your back and legs arched. But as fatigue creeps in and you are unable to maintain position, you can end up strangling to death. That evening I found myself struggling to stay alive, and though I tried to communicate that I was choking, the collective mayhem was advanced beyond reason. I doubt they even heard me. They did not mean to kill me, but you know, a resulting death remains final, whether intended or not."

"Hell's teeth, Laoshi" I mumbled. "How did you survive?" I could still scarcely believe what I was hearing. Laoshi's experience would have been harrowing for an adult, let alone a young lad.

"Hmm… Well, fortunately for me, the officer in charge, alerted by the noise had entered stealthily to investigate, and discovering my predicament, he dealt with the situation decisively."

"Dare I ask how," I ventured uncomfortably.

"He pulled my attackers off me, delivering a few uppercuts in the process, barked an order for the lights to be turned on and untied me."

Laoshi's tone remained neutral, while I remained outraged.

"I hope those little bastards got what they deserved?"

"No, no. It was left at that," said Laoshi mildly. "You have to understand—this was a different time: 'rough and ready' was the order of the day; being a victim did not gain you sympathy. We were expected to look after ourselves and not rely on either the intercession of the authorities or the forbearance of the violent.

"A week later I was assisting the officer who rescued me in his office. We had not discussed the incident but he suddenly asked me: 'Can you fight?'

"'Well… I suppose so,' I replied cautiously. I was not sure where this was leading.

"'Then why the hell did you not put up a fight when those idiots grabbed you?' he demanded.

"'But, you have told us we are not allowed to fight; what else could I do?'

"The officer looked at me in startled disbelief: it seemed he did not know whether to chastise me for my naivety, or congratulate me on my self-discipline. 'You mean to tell me,' he inquired, astounded, 'that you submitted meekly to those morons because you did not want to break the rules?'

"At my stunned silence and reddening face, he continued more gently. 'Listen, son. You need to learn when to obey the rules, but don't let yourself become a slave to them. Your life may depend on it.'

"He searched my face for understanding before gripping my shoulder in a gesture of gruff solidarity. We never spoke of the matter again, but I learned a valuable lesson."

Now Laoshi searched my face for understanding. "You understand?"

"I think so, Laoshi."

Laoshi nodded, gesturing me to take a seat. He wanted to tell me another story: "Long ago, there lived a Hindu saint who wandered the length and breadth of India in order to serve the people as best he could. He did not stay long in any one place, stopping to rest a while, heal the sick, and talk to the people about God.

"One day he came across a village wracked with poverty and misery. The saint was puzzled as to why the villages did not grow food, when there was so much fertile land on the outskirts of the village. Upon inquiring, he was informed that the problem was a large and ferocious snake that lived in the fields: anyone entering to work the soil was likely to be attacked and killed by the snake. As a result, the villagers feared to work the land, and so the land remained uncultivated.

"The saint decided to seek out the fearsome serpent. His approach did not pass unnoticed by the huge cobra, who drew near and prepared to strike without mercy. But, as you already know," said Laoshi with a knowing wink, "snakes are prohibited from attacking saints. So instead, the snake demanded that the holy man declare his business."

"I guess saints and snakes can also talk to each other," I commented wryly.

"Quite so," smiled Laoshi, then with a shrug continued: "The saint spoke with the snake for quite some time, explaining that it was not the will of God for the villagers to be killed as they went about their business. He reminded the snake that all living things represented God in disguise, each one playing a cosmic game of 'hide and seek', and each pretending to forget they were all aspects of the divine while engaged in an epic earthly drama. The snake was impressed by the words of the saint. He vowed never to kill a human being ever again.

"The saint then returned to the village to tell them of his meeting with the snake, and the snake's promise. He encouraged the villagers to work the land in safety and prosper.

"Now, some years passed before the saint happened to pass through the village once more. He was met with a scene, which gladdened his heart: the people were now prosperous, happy, and full of vitality. Delighted that the snake had honored his promise, the saint thought to visit his serpentine friend. Nearing the field, where the once-terrifying cobra had made its home, he came across some children gripping the serpent by the tail and swinging it around their heads. The snake was in severe distress.

"Chasing the children with angry admonishments, the saint sought to comfort the battered and emaciated old serpent. Recognizing the saint, the disconsolate snake groaned, 'Leave me alone! I wish I'd never set eyes on you! I was happy and content until you came along. Now I live in misery.'

"Shocked by the sorry state of affairs, the saint implored the snake to tell him all that had come to pass in the intervening years. The dejected snake explained that initially nervous about entering the field, the villagers became emboldened as the snake, true to his word, kept his distance, and pursued only rats and mice. At first, they were grateful to the snake and left him little offerings in the course of the day as they tended their crops. As time passed, however, the people quickly forget their gratitude to the snake. The offerings ceased, and the snake found himself increasingly ignored by more confident but less considerate villagers. Indifference soon turned to disdain and the village people, resenting the presence of the snake, pushed him to the very margins of the field, where the pickings were slim. Before long, having lost their fear, and growing haughty over their prosperous lives, the villagers set upon the snake, pulled out his fangs and allowed the children to abuse him as a plaything.

"Upon hearing this sorry tale, the saint shook his head in sorrow and compassion. 'I told you not to kill them, old friend; *I didn't tell you not to hiss!*'

"Now this story," concluded Laoshi, "made a deep impression on me. It was not the end of my difficulties; indeed, I experienced more than one challenging incident throughout my teenage years. But, I grew to understand that we have a choice as we make our way along life's thorny path. We can either allow ourselves be 'bound' and 'abused' by injustice and thuggery, or else we can hiss! And I can tell you from experience that hissing is usually enough. *Sometimes you have to let people know who you are in order to protect the space to be who you are.*"

Listening to Laoshi's words, it occurred to me that "hissing," or being prepared to hiss, was akin to what Laoshi had taught us about "remaining full in our energy." Confronting the potential knifeman at the door, Laoshi's energy remained constant and neutral, neither apologetic nor aggressive, but fully present and prepared for whatever came next.

As I progressed in teaching taijiquan, I increasingly appreciated Laoshi's words on being "who you are." It is less about teaching what we know and more about teaching what we are, as Laoshi would sometimes remind us. Initially, I was perplexed by this apparent show of arrogance: *why should we parade ourselves as an example for our fellow man to follow?* Over time I came to realize that teaching who we are is, fundamentally, about unflinching honesty. By simply modeling relaxation to our students, rather than expounding on the subject in abstraction, we pay our students the compliment of demonstrating authenticity, rather than attempting to impress them with "expertise," genuine or otherwise.

It is tempting for a teacher to hide behind "certification" and "accreditation," not to mention the unverifiable esoterica of the dantian, the qi, and the channels, which is concerned with impressing via "expertise." But, to present oneself as one truly is, without misrepresenting one's skill, experience, or attitude, and even personal flaws, is the action of an authentic individual. It is the greatest encouragement that the teacher can offer their students. It is the gift of sincerity.

It is said that the aspiring martial artist should embark on the Way with a "beginner's mind," i.e., a mind free of opinion and preconception, the better to remain open to the knowledge and wisdom of the teacher. Few of us, however, approach learning in such a virginal state.

Indeed, some would-be students arrive equipped with a deep-rooted resistance, doggedly sieving through the teacher's every phrase in order to challenge and critique at every turn. While Laoshi was at ease in encountering independent thought, the bristling tension, which frequently attended such individuals, sometimes proved bemusing as well as challenging to harmonious student relations.

Of those disposed to actively resist Laoshi, while curiously still attending class faithfully, I encountered none more fervent than Glen, who upon approaching retirement, had taken up taijiquan in a conscious attempt to ameliorate the effects of aging. Glen was a thoughtful, well-mannered, educated gentleman, with "old school" values; he was also possessed, however, of a tendency to express himself in a brusque manner, bordering on haughty. He was a self-proclaimed devotee (not that he would approve of the description) of Realism: a long career in engineering inclined him to distrust any notion that was not easily measured or classified. He had no truck with concepts such as "qi" or "heart-mind," rather he sought a "rational" explanation for all phenomena and cursorily dismissed anything which fell beyond the parameters of "reason." Given the unashamedly esoteric nature of taijiquan, I often wondered why he attended class at all.

Over the customary after-class "cuppa," his favorite sport was to bait his comrade taijiquan players over their "woolly thinking" and lack of logic in adhering to a practice, whose precepts and phenomena might fairly be said to go beyond the limits of "scientific" explanation.

Of course, the obvious riposte would have been to question Glen's own consistent attendance in order to study an art he seemed set upon disparaging. Call it good manners, deference to Glen's advancing years, or simple lack of concern—but no one ever seemed to resent Glen's criticism, least of all Laoshi, to whom everyone looked whenever Glen threw a verbal grenade in to the conversation.

"Surely," he remarked, almost scathingly, to Laoshi one evening, "the physical and mental benefits of taijiquan can be likened to some sort of placebo effect?"

"Are you asking me or telling me?" queried Laoshi with a smile.

"I'm just interested in your opinion," countered Glen sniffily.

"Ah... my opinion," mused Laoshi, good-naturedly. "My question to you Glen is, what have you got against placebo? For it seems to me that placebo is a wonderful phenomenon: if only we could encapsulate it, like in a pill, like a tablet, then all kinds of illness might be cured."

I was about to correct Laoshi on his obvious naivety regarding placebo treatments until given pause by his innocent-looking smile: Laoshi was at play.

Glen looked alternately suspicious and uncomfortable as Laoshi continued. "Perhaps, we do placebo phenomenon a disservice by frequently dismissing it as merely 'the placebo effect.' Is there not still an effect, a positive effect for the most part? The capacity of the mind to cure illness in the body is a genuine wonder to be celebrated, not reduced to an 'effect.' Don't you think?"

"Are you asking me or telling me?" replied Glen snarkily, seeking to disguise his unease in sarcasm.

"Can't I do both?" asked Laoshi mildly.

"How can you possibly do that?" retorted Glen. "You are either asking me or telling me."

"Well... I can do both," laughed Laoshi quietly, "by respecting the demands of your rational mind, while appealing to the urging of your heart-mind."

"Go on then," offered Glen grudgingly.

"So... placebo," obliged Laoshi, "is viewed as a nuisance by the pharmaceutical industry. They go to great lengths to develop effective medicines, yet frequently find themselves thwarted in clinical trials designed to compare the efficacy of the new drug with the body's own capacity to heal itself. How frustrating this is, given the huge investment in time and money to discover that the sugar cube placebo appears at least as effective. It is understandable if their view of placebo is a negative one. Their new product has to outperform placebo in order to reach the open market and make profit for the company."

"I understand the facts of your statement." Glen broke in impatiently. "But what is it you are asking of me?"

"I am asking your rational mind," continued Laoshi smoothly, "to lay aside the irritation that you experience in encountering the mysterious workings of placebo, and celebrate the fact that placebo exists at all! And I am reminding your heart-mind that to experience a sense of wonder at the unknowable only contributes, rather than detracts, from the flavor of our existence. *Mystery is not your enemy.*"

Glen had fallen silent, but another of the students, Tom, now addressed Laoshi: "So... would you say that the experienced benefits of taijiquan are similar to the placebo effect?"

"Would it matter to you greatly if that were so?" asked Laoshi with a grin.

"Er… I'm not sure," admitted Tom, "I need to think about it."

Laoshi nodded understanding: "A friend of mine spent a year of his childhood living in a small village in Pakistan. Entranced by its exotic sights and smells, my friend loved to wander around the bazaar, delighting in the dramatic contrast with the dreary, depressing Glasgow housing scheme, where he had spent his infancy. He was particularly enthralled by the local apothecary, who was respected by all in the village as a man of healing. A displaced twelve-year-old boy, my friend had no duties to perform nor school to attend, so he amused himself as he pleased, and it was not unusual for him to spend all day helping out at the apothecary's shop.

"One evening, an urgent knocking on the door demanded the attention of both the apothecary and my friend. It seems a local woman had taken ill, complaining of terrible abdominal pains, and the apothecary had been sent for immediately. The apothecary quickly donned his white coat and hurriedly packed his ancient satchel with a selection of jars and bottles, before making haste through the streets to attend the woman. Arriving at a modest house on the edge of the village, they were greeted by a large crowd pressing against door and windows, in order to gain the best view. The crowd murmured respectfully as the apothecary arrived on the scene, parting before him to allow access to the woman's house. Taking command, the apothecary immediately ordered all extraneous personnel from the room, leaving only my friend and the woman's anxious family as witnesses to the examination procedure. He produced from his bag a well-used stethoscope and listened closely to the woman's heart and lungs, nodding to himself in silent affirmation. Next, he took her pulse, and then carefully examined her eyes followed, by her tongue, pausing intermittently to stroke his beard as if in deep thought. Finally, the apothecary declared, 'Just as I thought!' With a flourish, he produced a jar of white powder from his old satchel and addressed the woman's anxious family: they must follow his instructions *to the letter!* The powder was to be administered to the patient in strict adherence to the schedule he laid down. The family collectively murmured their fervent thanks to the apothecary and pushed payment upon him.

"Once back in the dust of the apothecary's shop, my friend ventured to ask what ailed the woman so seriously.

"'Ah, it was a simple case of wind.'

"'Wind?' repeated my friend. 'But… you carried out a full examination and seemed to consider your findings at great length. Why go through all that if you knew it was only wind?'

"The apothecary paused and smiled down at my friend standing alongside him. 'Sometimes, you have to put on a show. People expect a performance:

they find it comforting.'"

Glen was immediately on the offensive. "Yes, well, surely that would be unacceptable behavior from a proper medical doctor?"

"You think there is no theater in Western medical practice," countered Laoshi. "The costume of the white coat, the stethoscope draped around the neck, the clipboard with its unpronounceable terminology? Consider, the daily ceremony of the ward round, the medicine-dispensing chariot, the unquestioning acceptance of the omnipotent status of the consultant by the trainee acolytes? Even our hospitals, some of them architecturally magnificent clinical temples, where life and death dramas are played out daily, are these not part of the theater of healing? And do we not participate willingly? Does not the theater and ritual contribute to our sense of well-being?

"Our faith in the knowledge and competence of our doctor is helpful," continued Laoshi. "You could say it allows us to relax and more effectively harness the latent healing properties of our own body and mind to return ourselves to good health.

"On the other hand..." mused Laoshi, who appeared to be thinking aloud, "There can be difficulty in placing too much faith in the wrong quarters. I'm thinking of Tam Gibbs..." Laoshi clarified. "We all know the story."

Tam Gibbs, one of Zheng Manqing's most devoted students, had such faith in the Professor and in traditional Chinese medicine that even after Zheng Manqing died, he would consult Chinatown herbalists in New York in preference to Western-trained medical professionals. On one occasion, the result was a misdiagnosis of appendicitis by a less competent herbalist. By the time Tam found his way to a Western medical facility, it was too late: his appendix burst and he died as a result, robbing the taijiquan world of a player with talent and potential.

Laoshi offered a further example: "You could say that certain faith healers in India do people a great disservice by claiming ability to cure venomous snake bite: their degree of 'success' is not as a result of their superstitious practices, rather it is due to the fact that venomous snakes do not always inject poison when they bite. But widespread belief in the healer's power can deter a genuine victim of a venomous bite from seeking effective treatment with anti-venom."

I thought I was beginning to see the broad shape of Laoshi's commentary. I interjected: "So, Laoshi, you're saying that, on the one hand, our beliefs can have considerable influence on the health of our bodies, but, on the other hand, ... what?... that there is more involved? That there is more complexity at work than an unexamined belief structure?"

Laoshi nodded toward me thoughtfully. "Hmm... something like that. I cannot claim certainty here, thus I am simply sharing with you where I have arrived at, so far, in my own thinking.

"At a very basic level, the value of placebo is the demonstration of our mind and body's ability to effect a degree of self-healing. As for how far-reaching such healing can be, who can say? Perhaps it depends on the individual. Take the case of the Professor. He believed that it was his taijiquan practice, which kept the symptoms of his tuberculosis at bay. And since I have always found Zheng Manqing's person compelling, I am inclined to find his assertion, likewise, compelling."

Laoshi paused and looked from face to face, as if to insure understanding. He continued carefully: "However, it is true to say that other people, who do not practice taijiquan, also have latent tuberculosis, but remain symptom free. What I am saying is that we must guard against our health being hijacked by anything including our belief in taijiquan. The adherence to beginner's mind is a lifelong commitment. Those, who think they know, do not know. It is as the Daodejing says, 'The five colors blind the eye; the five tones deafen the ear; the five flavors dull the taste.' When we think we see, we stop looking; when we think we have found, we stop searching; when we think we understand, we overlook."

There followed a thoughtful silence, with glances exchanged amongst the students present. What was Laoshi saying exactly? Did he believe in the health benefits of taijiquan or not? Did he doubt that it was Zheng Manqing's taijiquan practice that kept his symptoms at bay?

Of course, it was Glen who seized upon the opportunity to interrogate Laoshi directly: "Don't you believe in the benefits of taijiquan practice, then?" he demanded.

With his customary calm, Laoshi demurred to answer directly, but nodded to Glen to acknowledge the question. "Years ago," he continued quietly, "I attended a *zazen* course with a venerable monk from Japan. We would sit in meditation for a time, before he proceeded to talk about Zen. I was struck by his frankness as he recounted his first experience of *zazen*. After his first session on the cushion, he recalled, his legs were in such pain that he could not stand and had to crawl to the bathroom. 'The difference between *zazen* and torture,' the monk remarked wryly, 'is that in *zazen*, you do it to yourself.'

"*You do it to yourself*—that phrase," continued Laoshi, "has remained with me. Now, to be scrupulously fair, what I am going to say next is perhaps not what the monk meant precisely, but it occurs to me that, whether it is *zazen* or taijiquan, or any other spiritual discipline, the discipline does not do it *to you* or *for you*. *You do it for yourself*. The discipline is only a skillful means to release your true potential. Whatever the method, we become engaged in a process of transformation, a conscious empowerment of the heart-mind, both for wisdom and strength. As I recall, Zheng Manqing said that we should remain self-reliant, and I would add, not in thrall to any pills or particular beliefs that we hope will make things all right. It is *we*, our being, which is the ultimate instrument of efficacy, not the pill, nor the meditation, nor even our taijiquan practice."

It was an unexpected and challenging perspective from Laoshi, as evidenced by the uneasy silence of the group, even Glen. Yet, it also proved significant in that it served to remind me that even Laoshi experienced limits upon the absolute knowledge and certainty he could offer to his students. As I progressed in my own teaching, and accompanying limitations, I came to deeply respect Laoshi's unswerving honesty.

But everyone sees things differently: Glen stopped attending classes shortly after that evening's discussion, alleging to fellow students his frustration with Laoshi's insistence on using airy-fairy explanations. I have always suspected that, for all Glen's bluster and challenge toward Laoshi, in the end, he was secretly disappointed that Laoshi could not offer absolute certainty.

When I suggested the same to Laoshi some months later, he nodded sadly: "I have only compassion for Glen. He is looking for a certainty I am unable to provide. A life spent building a fortress of the intellect is not easily abandoned as the prospect of death and infirmity approaches, unbidden, at the gate. To reduce taijiquan to placebo is to try to gain control over ill health by chasing the illusion that sickness will one day be eradicated. It is illusion of thought that everything can be explained and therefore controlled. I cannot control the nature of my own death, nor the manner of my dying: I can only prevent myself from falling into illusion."

Laoshi's mention of the prospect of his own death was not comfortable. It was becoming clear to me that Laoshi was experiencing a change in his own understanding, a change which elicited in me a sense of foreboding: I felt a degree of excitement at my old teacher's continued evolution, but also experienced a pang of concern for his well-being.

Chapter 28: Testing Conclusions

A sincere martial artist appreciates that, sooner or later, they may be required to demonstrate the efficacy of their art in the "real world." As a result, while some are keen to persuade all comers of their combat credentials, others prefer to side step the issue entirely. I heard tell of one taijiquan teacher, who had a unique way of discouraging potential "tough guys," who might want to check out his class. He would rid himself of their interest by leading his students in singing nursery rhymes, while holding hands in a big circle. The teacher's martial capabilities were, therefore, never questioned, and those in earnest search of *martial* taijiquan went elsewhere.

Although those drawn to study taijiquan as a martial art are in the minority, the fact remains that for those few demonstrable effectiveness is the key consideration in choosing their teacher.

In former times, and in cultures more martial than our own, the fighting skills of a teacher were gauged by means of a challenge: a "testing of conclusions," as Robert Smith would say. The late Zheng Manqing, having learned his art in such a culture, accepted a number of challenges and emerged from each encounter able to say that, "his skills never deserted him."

Having transplanted itself into Western consciousness, taijiquan has either flourished, or diminished, depending on your point of view, without recourse to much rigorous "testing of conclusions." In our culture, debate surrounding taijiquan's martial efficacy is largely confined to cyberspace: a forum where claim and counterclaim can be made in relative anonymity and safety.

Nevertheless, I felt it prudent to prepare myself, mentally at least, for the possibility of a dojo-buster appearing at class in order to test my mettle as a fledgling teacher, particularly after Laoshi related a story he had heard from Wang Lang.

Wang Lang had once witnessed a challenge to Zheng Manqing, while the Professor was teaching in New York. A young man wearing the uniform of the United States Marine Corps came to the Shr Jung School with the purpose of "testing conclusions" with the Professor. In the first instance, the young challenger's request for a match with the Professor was politely refused, the Professor citing his advanced years as the impediment. However, the young man, undeterred, pursued the point. Once again, the Professor refused the challenge, but added that he would defend himself if attacked. Taking this as an invitation, the challenger launched a punch at the Professor, who deftly neutralized the attack, depositing the marine's backside on the floor.

Now, Wang Lang surmised that the marine's attack, possibly making allowance for the Professor's senior years, had been less than full-blooded. His second attack was more vigorous, but the result was as before: the Professor avoided the attack and once more acquainted the young man's backside with the floor. Now infuriated, the young marine lost all restraint, hurling himself at the Professor in an aggressive and violent assault. To the relief of all present, Zheng Manqing once more controlled the attack, guiding his assailant to the ground without injury to either party. Chastened, the young man picked himself up from the floor, straightened his tunic and bowed to the Professor. Thus, he departed.

When it came to Laoshi, in all the time I had been his student, I had never heard of him being involved in an argument inside or outside of class, let alone a physical fight. When I sought to confirm this with the senior students, one of the oldest, Jonny, looked at me in amazement saying: "You mean you haven't heard about the guy Laoshi half-killed in a pub fight years ago?" I admitted I had not.

"Oh, this you got to hear!" said Jonny, with relish. "So... Laoshi was having a night out in a Glasgow pub one evening, yeah? He was minding his own business, standing by the bar, when this big drunk guy lurches into him, intentional-like. You know? Anyway, Laoshi politely tells this bum to mind himself. Next thing, the guy takes a swing at Laoshi, who just belts the guy and sends him flying straight through the plate glass window onto the street! The guy was lucky to survive. Amazing, huh? Anyway, just dinnae mess wi' Laoshi. That's all I'm saying."

"Er... yep. Amazing," I could only agree.

"Nah, nah, nah," Jonny amended: "What's really amazing, is that Laoshi didn't even spill a drop o' his pint."

Naturally, I wanted to hear from Laoshi about this incident, especially since I had not heard tell of this altercation before. At the first opportunity, I recounted Jonny's tale. Laoshi listened intently right to the end, without the barest expression, before erupting into gales of laughter so intense that he collapsed helplessly into a chair. His mirth subsiding momentarily, he croaked, "And I didn't even spill a drop, I did it all one handed!" before creasing up anew. Laoshi's laughter was infectious. I couldn't help but join in, even realizing that I had been taken in like a rookie.

"So... a total fabrication on Jonny's part, then?" I sought to confirm once Laoshi had regained a modicum of his customary composure.

Laoshi, with tears of laughter glistening on his face replied: "Well... possibly. I suspect it is an exaggerated version of an altercation I had with a drunken youth on the High Street years ago. To be fair, it was I, who bumped into him as he staggered about pointing out some feature of the Glasgow afternoon streetscape to his equally drunk pal. Annoyed at my own lack of awareness, I blamed him, suggesting that he take more care in his actions. No doubt aggrieved by my accusation of 'reckless pointing in a built-up area,' he came at me."

The smile was still on Laoshi's lips. Clearly, he did not consider the incident serious.

"What happened next, Laoshi?" I pressed.

"Not a lot," responded Laoshi dryly. "The lad threw one of the slowest punches I have ever encountered. It was so slow I could have taken a train to

174

Edinburgh and back before it arrived! Anyway, let's just say that this lad had little enough ability before an afternoon spent pickling his liver robbed him of even that. His skimpy fist orbited toward me and I simply ducked under and found my hands on his rib cage. His balance was so compromised that my push launched him clear across High Street; his momentum carried him straight through the doors of the Tolbooth Bar."

"Seriously?" I inquired.

"Seriously," confirmed Laoshi. "I waited but he did not re-emerge, so I went home feeling foolish and vowing to improve my awareness."

Laoshi eyed me meaningfully: "So, you see, the truth is: I have never thrown a drunk *out* of a bar, but I *have* thrown one *in*!" And with that, Laoshi resumed his mirth, rocking back and forth with laugher. I could only join in.

Who knows if Jonny deliberately fabricated that tale of Laoshi and the drunk, or simply embroidered a half-true tale told to him? Laoshi agreed. The fact is 'you had to have been there,' as they say; otherwise accounts of so-called challenges are frequently riddled by inaccuracy and/or amplified for effect. And who can blame anyone? We all know that the "truth" never got in the way of a good story. My old teacher, Billy Coyle, was once accused of assaulting a young man by a passer-by. However, this "witness" had only happened upon the final act of a drama, which began when Billy went to the aid of an unconscious woman lying in the street. The well-meaning witness informed the police that he had seen Billy down the young man with a vicious blow to the chest. What he had not seen was the improvised blade, which the youth had strapped to his hand! Nor did he see the stab wound suffered by Billy as the youth attacked him, while Billy attempted to aid the prostrate woman. In fact, Billy only resorted to violence when the young man kicked the already unconscious woman in the head. But, of course, the witness made no mention of this, having missed the majority of the preceding action, he entirely misconstrued events.

"You see the difficulty?" said Laoshi.

"Yes," I nodded. "I guess it's easy to miss the bigger picture and jump to conclusions if you are reacting to a fragment of the real thing."

"Exactly," confirmed Laoshi. "It's even more difficult to discern reality when individual recollections are influenced by other agendas: conscious or otherwise. Take the 'match' between Wang Shujin and Chiba Sensei, for example: there are conflicting accounts of what happened there, depending on who tells the story."

"Er... don't think I've heard that one, Laoshi." My brow creased in attempt to recall, since I had met Chiba Sensei and attended a number of his courses. "What was that about?"

"Well…" Laoshi chuckled softly, "an old aikido acquaintance of mine once tried to persuade me of the superiority of his art, as compared to taijiquan. He cited as evidence, a contest between Chiba and Wang, who had traveled to Japan from Taiwan to teach Chinese martial arts. Mutual students of the two masters apparently arranged a 'friendly' challenge, whereupon, according to my old aikido friend, Chiba Sensei broke Wang's wrist. Diplomatically, a draw was quickly declared by the students, however, as the situation was in danger of rapidly turning 'old school' rather than friendly.

"Now, my aikido pal happily construed Wang's broken wrist as proof of his aikido's superiority, but Chiba sensei himself made no such claim. Anyway, sometime later, I read about the same incident as related by Terry Dobson, who was the first American *uchideshi* to study with O Sensei Ueshiba in Japan. Now what you need to know here is that Dobson was not disposed to show Chiba in a favorable light: he reported a dramatically different outcome from that related by my aikido chum. According to Dobson, it was Wang who handed the youthful Chiba a lesson he would not forget. As Dobson tells it, Chiba was 'screaming like a baby' as Wang got the better of the encounter."

Well, I could not help but laugh out loud. Having encountered the genuinely fearsome Chiba Sensei, the notion of him "screaming like a baby" seemed highly unlikely. On the other hand, I also knew of Wang Shujin's reputation as a formidable opponent. "Where do *you* think the truth lies?" I asked Laoshi, hoping for some sensible adjudication.

"Och, with the man on the moon!" laughed Laoshi. "Listen, what difference does it make to you or me? Wang is dead; Chiba has retired and lives six thousand miles away. The point is too many students bask in the reflected glow of their teachers and they are so blinded by that glow that the plain, ordinary truth has no opportunity to be glimpsed."

"Hmm… I guess we all see the truth we want to see," I mused.

"Of course," concurred Laoshi. "And I repeat, ordinary truth is hard to see, since it is usually obscured by our opinions, prejudices, and social conditioning. You know the story of the Emperor's new clothes, right?" said Laoshi with a grin.

"Yeah—a classic bit of spin!" I laughed.

"Exactly!" Laoshi joined my laughter. "Truth was a fashion victim that day! But, you know, you need to be on your guard and properly 'test conclusions' because spin is frequently seductive: the mundane ordinary truth less so. Don't be taken in! It is always possible that some deluded individual might show up at class to test conclusions with you; but the real challenge you face is simply to sift plain fact from fiction."

One of Zheng Manqing's students, himself a celebrated taijiquan teacher, asserted that the quality of a taijiquan school's push-hands might be judged by the number of women actively involved in that particular discipline. He argued that a good school would engage in a type of push-hands which valued softness and sensitivity ahead of sumo-style physicality—and that consequently, more women would be inclined to participate.

As I mentioned before, in the years I studied with Laoshi, there was a general decline in the number of female push-hands students to the point where, in later years, there were seldom any present at all. In contrast, women were strongly represented in form classes, often in greater numbers than men. Sword also continued to attract women, both for form and fencing, but those who opted to try push-hands rarely attended for long. From time to time, I sought to understand why keen female students should become increasingly reluctant to engage fully with push-hands and debated with myself what the optimal gender mix might be.

Laoshi frequently emphasized the virtues of softness and encouraged us to refine our approach to push-hands by continually stressing the importance of "using no more than four ounces of pressure in order to make progress." Over time, however, I observed that Laoshi iterated this instruction less and less, often simply shrugging his shoulders as two over-enthusiastic young men "went at it" with gusto—certainly more than four ounces of gusto.

Perhaps Laoshi's preference for limited interference was understandable. I watched one evening as two experienced students, Bob and Ian, were becoming increasingly extreme in their attempts to dominate each other in their push-hands practice, each responding to increased forcefulness in the other with an escalation of their use of force. Laoshi watched for the better part of fifteen minutes before approaching the pair and remarking quietly; "Aye, you are both showing each other a lot of gongfu there, but neither of you will learn anything by doing so."

Bob spent the rest of the evening sitting at the side of the practice floor looking despondent, while Ian wasted no time in finding another partner and taking up where he left off. I causally sauntered over to Bob, "What ails you Bob?"

"Och, did you not hear?" he moaned. "Laoshi said I am learning nothing."

When the opportunity arose, I also asked a contrastingly upbeat Ian what Laoshi had said to them both. "Oh!" beamed Ian. "He said we both had a lot of gongfu."

Around that time Laoshi was heard to remark, "People might listen, but they seldom hear." Was Laoshi tiring of repeating the four ounces mantra, which so many of us simply did not hear?

When I began offering push-hands classes independently of Laoshi, I was determined to make improvements, believing that a strong endorsement of the "four ounce rule," with the resulting softness and sensitivity, would encourage female students to attend. One young woman, Mandy, showed particular promise, and with a background in Japanese martial arts, I expected that she would become one of the most skillful push-hands players in the school. Her natural affinity with push-hands was obvious from the start, and I had high hopes of her example encouraging other women who might have doubts about participating in push-hands. The gender balance in the class was reasonable, I felt (if still slightly with more men): a very positive omen for the future. But my hopes were soon dashed.

One evening, I arrived early for class to find Mandy waiting for me in a state of agitation. It was clear that she had something on her mind and was seeking a word in private. With a mix of embarrassment and angry forthrightness, she told me that Duncan, one of the long-term students in the school, had touched her inappropriately the previous week during practice. I listened in dismayed silence.

"Do you think it could have been an accident?" I asked eventually, trying to read what Mandy needed from me in this situation and wondering how best to deal with her complaint. Push-hands, by its very nature involves push and counter-push; a hand can occasionally—inadvertently—slip off and land where it ought not to. Usually when this happens, the unintentional nature of the contact is understood by both parties and is either ignored or swiftly followed by an embarrassed apology.

But, Mandy was alleging something more serious. "It was deliberate," she insisted. "I'm sure of it. I've had it happen before in other martial arts clubs, and I won't put up with it."

I was at a loss as to how to proceed. Intentional inappropriate touching in the UK is legally regarded as a sexual assault, carrying a maximum of ten years imprisonment on conviction and inclusion on a register of offenders. I had no doubt that Mandy was sincere in her distress, but I felt extremely reluctant to accuse Duncan without having witnessed the offense myself.

An added complication was that this was not the first complaint I had received about Duncan, although this was the first with a sexual element. Unfortunately, Duncan was easy to dislike, although people initially tended to feel sorry for him: "He just doesn't get it," commented one student referring to Duncan's awkwardness in dealing with other people. Six months later, his

178

original sympathy now turned pathological, the same student exclaimed over Duncan: "Sometimes I could just murder him!"

It was not only Duncan's lack of social skills, which irked his fellow students; being close enough to push with him was an endurance test in itself, due to his poor personal hygiene, as I know from personal experience. I tried to describe to Laoshi the disgust I felt pushing with a sweaty, smelly Duncan, who often came to class directly from his work driving a bus. (In contrast, I recalled an aikido elder lecturing beginners on what was expected of them in terms of cleanliness: a clean gi, a clean, odor-free body—particularly feet, and trimmed fingernails). I mentioned this to Laoshi adding, "I feel as if my hands are contaminated after touching Duncan's smelly T-shirts."

Laoshi seemed unperturbed, "Then wash your hands afterward," he replied mildly. "Can you insist that only clean people should attack you? We must deal with whatever people present; we do not get to choose what that might be."

Though we tolerated Duncan's olfactory offense, Mandy's complaint was of a different order. "Don't practice with him again," I advised, "and I'll keep an eye on what he is doing in the future."

I hoped this would be reassurance enough, but sadly Mandy never returned to class. I could not help but regard Duncan with suspicion—and I did from that time on, not allow him to push with the remaining women. Sadly, possibly without the reassuring presence of Mandy, the other women in the class abandoned push-hands one by one, even though they remained committed to form classes.

I felt I had failed some sort of test as taijiquan teacher. Laoshi had been on an extended holiday, and so I was unable to discuss Mandy's (and my own) concerns with him. When Laoshi returned, I arranged to visit him, looking for reassurance and hoping for advice on how to proceed.

Laoshi listened patiently as I described the unfolding of events and the subsequent departure of women from push-hands class.

"Hmm… Awkward situation, to be sure," mused Laoshi. "Aren't you glad that you are a taijiquan teacher and get to deal with these problems?" he offered with what I assumed to be an ironical grin.

"Not really," I sighed, shaking my head ruefully. "I signed up to teach taijiquan, not to deal with this kind of thing!"

"Comes with the job," said Laoshi softly.

"I know Laoshi, but *what should I do?*" I implored.

"Learn what you can from the situation and move on. It is too late to do anything in this particular case."

A small silence fell between us. Perhaps Laoshi, like me, was bereft of ideas. I couldn't help but feel disappointed. Perhaps he sensed my desperation for some sort of solution and, after some additional moments of thoughtful silence, he continued: "You know, years ago, when taijiquan was taking its first faltering steps in Glasgow, the attitude of the times, although rather different, was just as difficult to deal with. One of the teachers encouraged close physical contact in some of his classes, an approach wholly at odds with the, let's say, more reserved attitudes of the majority of the Glaswegian students. Whenever he was challenged over his unorthodox approach, he sought to imply that anyone who disagreed with his methods must be 'closed off' emotionally; the evident 'defensiveness' of those who challenged him was the very thing, he insisted, that his method aimed to expose and root out.

"The zenith of 'hippiedom' had waned, but its legacy lingered. I suspect some taijiquan teachers saw their role as akin to Aquarian-age evangelists. Skeptical as I was that the New Age was dawning in Glasgow, it amused me to witness brusque, middle-aged Scottish women, sporting sensible shoes and a flinty countenance, giving the gimlet eye to this 'chancer' teacher and his dodgy version of emotional freedom. They had the confidence to give as good as they got—to openly scoff—and were not easily manipulated. On the other hand, the struggle of sincere and earnest but (usually younger) and less self-assured women to adopt this teacher's ideas concerning emotional 'stuckness' was disconcerting to witness. From my present perspective, it feels as if he sowed the seeds of doubt in women's minds for his own not-altogether-wholesome ends: on occasion our warm-up routine culminated in a partner massage exercise, which he called 'whole-body brushing' to clear out 'negative energy.'"

I rolled my eyes. Laoshi smiled fractionally and continued: "Anyway, whole-body brushing entails sweeping your hands down the front and back of a partner's body, touching firmly the first time and gradually lightening the pressure on each subsequent sweep, until you are not touching at all, just brushing the air around the body." Laoshi paused briefly. "You can perhaps, er… see the problem." He caught my eye meaningfully.

I said nothing but my raised eyebrows told Laoshi that I had indeed grasped the problem.

"Yes… well… precisely," nodded Laoshi. "Speaking for myself, and in common with most of the other men, I simply could not bring myself to go through with this exercise as instructed. Most of us simply brushed the air when partnered with one of the women. But, there is always one guy who insists on performing the brushing on the body 'properly.'"

"Was he at it, do you think?"

"Och, who knows for sure," replied Laoshi. "But given that the whole exercise is supposed to be about 'openness' and 'sensitivity,' you might expect people to avoid distressing others. Don't you think?

"These days such behavior could well be regarded as 'sexual assault,' and the police might become involved. Since the authorities now encourage the reporting of any incident of inappropriate touching, Mandy could easily have made a formal complaint against Duncan, in which case how many men would feel comfortable practicing with her thereafter? Whose interests take priority here? As a teacher you are expected to safeguard your more vulnerable students' interests, but precisely how is not always entirely clear."

As I pondered the implications for push-hands in a mixed group of men and women, a chill ran down my spine. I imagined the aftermath of an accusation, the police interviews and subsequent mutual suspicion. Any class would simply break down under the strain and lack of mutual trust. There would be no safe space (in any sense) in which to practice. I questioned why anyone would be inclined to risk pushing hands at all under such circumstances.

"At present," added Laoshi, "I cannot imagine any taijiquan teacher suggesting any exercise of a potentially intimate nature. A good thing, too, but as the pendulum swings away from this kind of excess, we must be careful not to over-correct and end up sanitizing the value out of push-hands."

"So, do you think it is the close up nature of push-hands, which has discouraged women from attending your own classes, Laoshi?"

"I don't believe that is the whole story," he replied. "The greatest obstacle to participation remains the tendency to rely on physical strength in order to 'succeed.' Women are more likely to feel disadvantaged from the start, due to size and strength."

It was sobering, therefore, to confront the reality of taijiquan. In theory, it is the perfect martial art for women: Zheng Manqing believed that women have the natural advantage of softness. In practice, taijiquan, or at least push-hands, one of the pillars of Zheng Manqing's taijiquan, is the one art women are unlikely to pursue. Was this another of the paradoxes of taijiquan?

"How then," I asked with a sigh, "are we to encourage women to participate?"

"All I can offer is Wang Lang's advice given to women in his classes. 'You are not obliged to push-hands with anyone you wish not to.' Otherwise, I am at the end of my knowledge," said Laoshi quietly. "If you ever work it out, let me know."

The expansion of technology has led to a shrinking world. News of our taijiquan comrades overseas is readily available and a visit to other schools and teachers might be less than a day's travel, provided we have the means to make the journey.

Having the means, however, does not necessarily lead us to action. Like the *Daodejing's* ideal villagers, who heard the dogs barking in neighboring villages but were not inclined to go there, Laoshi's students seldom expressed interest in experiencing the taijiquan of neighboring schools, although they were aware of their existence. It was rare for a student to return from travel bearing tales of taijiquan warriors met in foreign parts, or even Edinburgh. As a school, we tended to keep to ourselves.

As a young, aspiring teacher, Laoshi had sought to take the temperature of the taijiquan community by visiting wherever and whoever intrigued him. With growing experience, however, he no longer sought instruction or inspiration elsewhere, following Wang Lang's preference "to tend to his own garden." As a result, whether taking a short vacation at home or abroad, Laoshi rarely sought out the local man for a "comparison of styles." When I asked Laoshi about this he told me: "I understand only a fraction of what my own teachers taught. What sense is there in piling puzzlement on top of existing confusion?" Instead, Laoshi preferred to apply himself to in-depth review of the syllabus already set out by his teachers.

At the same time, however, Laoshi placed no obstacles in the path of the few students who wished to explore the wider taijiquan community. Indeed, Laoshi was often genuinely interested in hearing of their adventures.

One such intrepid was Ruairidh who, having benefited from Laoshi's instruction for a year, departed for Taiwan on an extended trip in order to "discover the secrets of the Orient," as he put it. Ruairidh was tall, with an appropriately regal air, and sported long, flame-red, curly hair, befitting his Gaelic name, which translated as "The Red-Haired King." Anyone who knew Ruairidh before he set out on his quest would not have accused him of lacking in confidence or conviction. On his return, however, his haughty presence was accompanied by the pungent zeal of a convert.

We, his erstwhile taijiquan comrades, were given to understand that Ruairidh's Taiwan excursion had resulted in his satori-like understanding of taijiquan. Now, he boldly informed Laoshi and the rest of us that he was "looking for bodies to push-hands with." He had "no further need of form classes," he declared, since the superior teaching and sophistication of his Taiwanese master had rendered other taijiquan forms redundant.

If Laoshi was offended at this apparent slight, he made no show of feeling, remarking simply, "Interesting. Can you elaborate on these insights gained from your teacher?"

Ruairidh enthusiastically took the floor, clearly savoring the opportunity to enthrall: "I really 'got it' over there! I mean, you know, your form is fine, as it goes," he nodded in Laoshi's direction, "but what the Master could do, was incredible."

"Really?" responded Laoshi mildly, "in what way?" The rest of us exchanged dubious glances.

Ruairidh was quick to tell. "I spent a month studying with Master Han for two hours in the park every morning. Then every afternoon, I returned for two more hours practice within sight of the master's older students, who were performing their own routines. At first, I felt I was wasting my time, however, after a week or so, while doing waving hands in clouds posture, Master Han looked at me, and *I felt him move my arms.* He was standing about ten feet away from me, leading the class, but he was doing a form—*from inside me!* It was an amazing experience. It was if he had entered my being and was moving my body just by the power of his thought."

"Did your teacher say he was moving you around with his mind?" inquired Laoshi casually, his expression remaining entirely neutral.

"Well... no," replied Ruairidh, "but then, he wouldn't, would he? But I knew he was doing it. *I just knew.* Then, later that day, when I was practicing near the older guys, I saw one of them standing watching me as I did my form, and he started moving me around with his mind as well! It was incredible! These guys can move you around any way they want, just by thinking about it."

As can be imagined, heated debate ensued among us, although it was rather one-sided: perhaps Ruairidh's superior demeanor did not endear him to the rest of us, but we all figured that Ruairidh's experience was the result of his imagination or worse, wish fulfillment in the extreme. Ruairidh remained adamant that his experience was genuine, and furthermore, that it surpassed anything he had encountered before. In the end, one of the senior students, grown weary of the pointless discussion, shrugged his shoulders saying: "Well... It's up to him to believe what he wants; if he thinks that's what happened, who are we to tell him he's wrong?"

Inevitably, Ruairidh turned to Laoshi: "What do you think about my experience?"

Laoshi, who had kept his counsel during our debate with Ruairidh, now replied quietly: "Son, you really need to stay off the drugs."

Laoshi's pointed reply brought an immediate halt to the conversation; some students drifted away into the evening, while those who remained quickly found a new topic for discussion. On my way home that evening, I speculated on Laoshi's response. Had he been joking? Or was he simply checking the hubris of a young Turk? None of us were aware of any drug habit on Ruairidh's part, but perhaps Laoshi knew something we did not. In any case, Ruairidh did not return to class in the weeks that followed.

When I asked Laoshi if he had told Ruairidh not to return, he told me: "Not at all. I was happy for him to attend whatever classes he wished."

"So what happened? Why has he not been back at class?" I was curious.

"Ah, well now... Ruairidh thought his attendance should be free of charge," said Laoshi sincerely. "He told me that, since he wouldn't be learning anything from me, he shouldn't be expected to pay. He just needed a few bodies to carry out his... er... 'research' was how he put it."

"What?" I exclaimed. "What a twat! Other students, who only attend push-hands, pay the class fee without quibbling. What a cheek! Maybe he was on the drugs after all!" I fumed.

"Hmm... so about that..." replied Laoshi, grimacing. "I may have misread the lad a little that night."

"What? You mean he is not on drugs?" I felt wrong-footed.

"Hmm, well probably not the illegal kind you are thinking," said Laoshi. "So, listen. Here is what happened. Shortly after his visit to Taiwan, the trip he told you all about, Ruairidh contacted me to tell me he had been diagnosed with a neurological condition. He was undergoing treatment, no doubt involving prescribed drugs, and was attending a support group. Ruairidh had arranged to teach taijiquan at the treatment clinic, which requested that he provide some form of accreditation. So, he wanted me to furnish him with a letter stating that he was competent to teach taijiquan."

"You're kidding, right?" I uttered in exasperation. "The cheeky... You didn't write him a letter I hope?"

"No, of course not," responded Laoshi dryly. "Instead, I suggested he contact Master Han in Taiwan. Since Ruairidh claimed Master Han as his teacher, a letter of assessment was better coming from him. When Ruairidh told me that this would be impossible—I know, I know," admonished Laoshi, catching my expression. "Anyway, I advised him that his best course of action would be to return to classes with me, or indeed another teacher, in order to gain a deeper foundation in his taijiquan practice before he entertained thoughts about teaching."

"Yeah, right. And what did he say to that?" My tone was scathing.

"Well much as you would expect," sighed Laoshi. "Let's just say my suggestion did not gain much traction with him.

"Anyway, I wished him well, and we said goodbye," concluded Laoshi.

"I have not heard from him since. However, I did look up Ruairidh's condition out of curiosity: apparently, the early symptoms can include mild hallucinations. So, who knows, for sure, what happened in Taiwan?"

Chapter 31: Shi Zhong

Zheng Manqing called his school Shizhong (Shr Jung 時中), which, according to a senior student, meant doing the right thing, at the right time, in the right direction. The right thing was not simply confined to the physical practice of taijiquan. The Professor, being strongly influenced by the teachings of Confucius, held right action to include "maintaining the center" in one's character: being emotionally stable and balanced. *Zhong*, meaning "center," is the same character used in "Central Kingdom" in reference to China itself, and presumes we remain "upright," not just in taijiquan postures, but in character, as well.

Wang Lang, one of Laoshi's teachers offered his own succinct translation: "exact timing in the center," which he often abbreviated further to, "exact timing." Wang Lang, too, was at pains to point out, however, that the notion of doing the right thing at the right time should not simply be considered pertinent only to push-hands or fencing. It was rather an attitude of spontaneous awareness, giving rise to appropriate action in any given situation.

To clarify Wang Lang's meaning in respect of appropriate action, Laoshi often related the story of a Zen master, who was invited to a formal dinner in Japan, and, along with other dignitaries, was served by a group of especially cultured and elegantly attired geisha. The Zen master noted that one geisha in particular performed her tasks with an extraordinary level of accomplishment, the depth of which he decided to test. Toward the end of the meal, the master motioned for the geisha to approach. The guests had been sitting on the floor, Japanese style, at low tables facing inward in the arrangement of a hollow square, with one side of the square left open to allow the access for serving the meal.

The master watched, approvingly, at the exquisite charm displayed in every gesture as the geisha approached and knelt before him. Such was her grace and poise that he became convinced that she had received formal Zen training. The master said to her, "I have a gift for you."

The geisha replied with a bow, "I would be honored to receive it."

The master, using metal chopsticks, picked up a piece of hot charcoal from the hibachi grill on the table and offered it to the young woman.

She bowed and wrapping the sleeves of her kimono around her hands, accepted the "gift" of burning charcoal. She then rose, went into the kitchen, disposed of the burning ember before it could burn through to her hands, changed into a new kimono, and returned to the master. Once seated in front of him, she said, "I would like to offer you a gift."

The master nodded saying, "I would be honored to receive it."

The geisha then also took the metal chopsticks, picked up a piece of burning charcoal, and presented it to the master.

In response, the master produced from the folds of his garment, a cigarette and leaning forward to light it on the smoldering coal said, "Thank you. That is exactly what I needed."

A strange story with several possible interpretations, but Laoshi explained that both the master and the geisha acted with *shizhong*, i.e., they acted from spontaneous awareness, equaling each other in an ability to bring forth an appropriate response to an unforeseen happening. Throughout the time I spent with Laoshi, it became increasingly clear to me that he was attempting to cultivate this same ability to respond with spontaneous awareness to whatever life presented. Appropriate action, arising spontaneously, was the consequence of living fully from the heart-mind. Laoshi viewed push-hands and fencing as indispensable tools for developing this state of mind, offering the possibility of responding to the twists of fate with a grace born out of sensitivity and intuition.

"Becoming skilled in *shizhong*," Laoshi once explained in class, "is not something we can practice directly, let alone control, since we cannot cause unforeseen events to manifest themselves at our invitation: we cannot surprise ourselves on purpose in order to train our response to the surprise."

I was reminded of Billy Coyle's conviction that break-falling could not be practiced as an exercise on its own, since a break-fall is a response to a loss of balance. To deliberately put yourself off-balance to practice a break-fall is to be not truly off-balance at all; you are in control the whole time.

"The best we can do," continued Laoshi in his analysis, "is practice our art with *shizhong* in mind and open ourselves to its wonders. As with Zheng Manqing's contention that, in terms of functional ability, a taijiquan player can only truly know the level of their gongfu when called upon to use it; the same is true of *shizhong*. When you truly act with *shizhong*, you will be surprised and delighted by the elegant solutions, which emerge from the heart-mind: the very depth of your being. The wondrous thing is that it can happen anytime. All we have to do is allow it. In other words, relax the tension both in mind and body." Listening to Laoshi, a phrase from *The Monastery of Jade Mountain* came to mind: "You must live as if something wonderful could happen any time."

186

Of course, an example of *shizhong* in action is always superior to a theoretical description. One such example occurred during a summer workshop Laoshi was conducting in northern Spain. Although Laoshi had ceased his regular teaching trips abroad, he agreed to deliver a few classes as part of the Spanish school's anniversary celebrations. I was delighted when Laoshi asked me to accompany him to better demonstrate the aspects of push-hands and fencing, which were occupying his attention at the time.

My fond recollections of the weekend remain with me to this day. The local students were delightful, not just in the caliber of their taijiquan, but also in their hospitality and appreciation of life. My delight at their warm-hearted, generous welcome was only enhanced by the contrast with the few visitors from other schools, who were somewhat sullen and cliquey. Although few in number, this small group of malcontents appeared unconvinced by Laoshi's methods, and kept themselves aloof, not only from Laoshi and me, but also from their own countrymen. Their reason for attending the seminar was unclear to me, but I suspected a challenge might arise at any moment.

Laoshi took the undercurrent of discontent exuding from their midst in his stride. He was clearly sensitive to a subdued feeling of displeasure from some quarters because he sought to assure the assembled students from the outset that he was not advocating his own lineage or approach as superior to others, something he would not normally feel the need to state aloud.

The morning's activities progressed well as we moved from push-hands to fencing. At some point, I noticed Laoshi explaining to a surly Carlos, one of the younger visiting students, how his fencing would benefit from less force in the arm and greater sticking. My own Spanish was certainly lacking, so the precise nuance of the interaction was lost on me, but Laoshi's tone seemed friendly and helpful.

Some minutes passed before Laoshi called for everyone's attention to highlight a couple of general points in relation to fencing. Laoshi stood in the center of the hall as the students arranged themselves in a semicircle to his front. As is usual, there was a little movement in the group as people changed position to improve their view, but I became faintly aware that Carlos seemed to be separating himself from the group to a position more to the rear of Laoshi. As the greater part of my concentration was on deciphering Laoshi's Spanish, I was shocked to register in my peripheral vision Carlos darting forward in an attempt to stab Laoshi in the back. The sword may have been wooden, and serious injury unlikely, but it was still a grotesquely immature and devious action, regardless of any perceived injustice.

Unable to react, I simply watched as Laoshi stepped sideways to avoid the thrust and, simultaneously, swept his sword up sharply to tap Carlos gently on the side of the neck, in a movement reminiscent of phoenix spreads its wings. Laoshi said a few words in Spanish to a clearly shocked Carlos, who then skulked away, while Laoshi turned to resume his instruction to the group as if nothing had happened.

I felt a wry smile form on my lips as I watched Carlos sneaking out of the room, thinking to myself, "Yep! That's my teacher!"

Later that evening, once we were alone, I asked Laoshi about the incident.

"I think you could say," chuckled Laoshi, "that Carlos suffers from daft-wee-boy syndrome."

"But how did you know he was coming at you?" I asked, pleased that Laoshi seemed keen to talk about the incident. "Did you see his reflection in the window or something?"

"No, I didn't see him," replied Laoshi with a slight shake of his head.

"Did you sense his energy then?" I pressed.

"No, I didn't sense him either."

"Then how did you know he was coming?" I asked.

"I didn't *know* he was coming at all," said Laoshi, deliberately emphasizing the "know."

"What? I don't understand that! So... how did you know to move and cut toward his neck with your sword?" I asked, truly perplexed.

"In all truth, I've no idea," shrugged Laoshi. "I stepped because I stepped, and my sword reacted to a movement. It happened. It was nothing to do with me."

I was staggered. Laoshi's reaction was smooth, swift and seamless, yet he was almost distancing himself from an exquisitely executed counterstroke. His downplaying of his skill astounded me even more than the act itself. Had I managed even half as refined an evasion and counterattack, I would not be slow in proclaiming the feat to every willing ear.

Needing to pursue the matter more deeply, I continued with my questions. "Come on, how can you say that, Laoshi? How can you say it had nothing to do with you? Surely, it has something to do with you?"

He looked at me for a moment before conceding, "You are right. I did have something to do with it."

"Now we're getting somewhere," I thought, only to be surprised once again.

"When such things happen," explained Laoshi, "it is the heart-mind which acts; the speed of response is so fast and the counterstrike so immediate, you cannot register it consciously until the moment before impact. The counterattack has begun before you even know. It is only at the very last instant that you have conscious control over the matter. At that point you have the choice."

"The choice?" I repeated. "What choice?"

"The choice of letting your counterstrike connect with its full unrestrained power or of dampening down the force to merely make a point. This is the only part where the 'me' was involved."

"The 'me' being your conscious self," I added for clarity.

"Quite so," he nodded. "The only control 'I,' the ego, had over the matter was in deciding how lethal to make the response. Understanding that Carlos was simply daft, not a real danger, I was able to stop the sword from hitting him hard in the throat. The tap was enough to make the point."

"He deserved worse," I commented. "But what did you say to him after you tapped him."

"I simply said to him 'you shouldn't do that.' My Spanish is weak, but he would have understood that sneaking up on a teacher like that is not a good idea."

"I should think so," I agreed, "because next time you might really clonk him one."

Laoshi laughed. "Have you not yet realized that in the province of the heart-mind, nothing can happen the same way twice. We are not in control of these things. There is no guarantee that I could do the same thing again, while Carlos could never attempt an identical attack again; a second attempt would be artificial—nothing happens the same way twice. The heart-mind would therefore be forced to respond in a different way. As you recall from Heraclites, you cannot step twice into the same river—the river is no longer the same, but neither are you. You experience a happening once, if there is a second time, it is either different or artificial. It is why our Spanish friends do not let a bull enter the bullring twice: it would have learned and be truly dangerous. It is also the perennial problem of how to teach martial arts: attack/defense scenarios may become ritualized and lose authenticity, but all-out fighting, though real, can lead to injury or death before anything is learned."

I paused for a while, allowing Laoshi's words to sink in. It was the beauty and the terror of a life lived in the company of the heart-mind. We are not protected by precedent, because life, with its spontaneous creativity, presents us with countless new possibilities. To live fully in the moment is to free us from the straightjacket of prescribed action and live each moment fully aware —not an easy task. Sitting there with Laoshi, I recalled one of Billy Coyle's anecdotes from his own training under a very severe teacher, Chiba Sensei.

While acting as Chiba Sensei's *uke* (demonstration partner) during a sword seminar, Chiba Sensei's attack was so powerful that Billy's bokken was knocked from his grasp and bounced several yards across the mat. Billy told me that he was in a state of desperation. As a long-term student of Chiba, he knew that no excuse would be tolerated for allowing the sword to fly out of his hand. As Chiba's eyes bore into him with growing intensity, Billy anticipated that Chiba's next move would be a painful blow to "encourage" a better grip of the bokken.

"What could I do?" Billy told me. "The bokken was too close to Chiba Sensei to retrieve without him hitting me."

"So... what did you do?"

"Well," smiled Billy, "I looked to the side at the students standing watching the demonstration and ran straight for one of the teenagers on the end. He was shocked to see me come towards him and so did not move. As I reached him, I grabbed his bokken with my left hand pushed him strongly in the chest with my right. He was so surprised that as he fell back, he let go of his bokken letting me take it and turn to face Chiba Sensei a sword in hand once more."

"What happened next?"

"Chiba Sensei was furious, though not so much with me as I had remedied the situation. He strode over to the lad, glared down on him as he lay on the edge of the mat and growled, 'You should not have given him your sword.'

"Chiba Sensei then returned to the center of the mat and motioned for me to resume the demonstration.

"You see," explained Billy, "the lad was only a beginner and a boy at that. Chiba Sensei would not have given out the same punishment to someone so inexperienced as he would to me. I was expected to know better. I apologized to the boy later and he understood why I did what I did. Mind you, he told me he wouldn't let me have the sword next time. I said, 'Good enough.'"

I told Laoshi the story and noted the appreciative smile on his lips as he imagined the scene. In their own way, both Laoshi and Billy had reacted with *shizhong*: responding in a creative way to the unexpected. The wonder of a life committed to living in the heart-mind.

Chapter 32: Teaching the Teachers

Novice teachers, emerging from the shadow of their mentor, may suffer an attack of anxiety, fretting over whether their skills are up to scratch. The issue for Laoshi's teachers was especially germane, since Laoshi was not accustomed to handing out certificates of competence to those he encouraged to teach.

"What do you need a certificate for?" replied Laoshi, when a fledgling teacher protested his need for an official declaration of competence. "Is the certificate going to teach, or are you?" When pressed, Laoshi would write a letter of approbation in the event of the new instructor having to comply with bureaucratic protocol in hiring halls etc.

Laoshi was scornful of taijiquan accreditation and once showed a student the only certificate he valued: an amusement dreamt up by a student showing a picture of the cartoon character Foghorn Leghorn complete with the following endorsement:

Ah do declare that the bearer of this here certificate is a
bone fide teacher with the 'No Can Do School of Taijiquan.'
Y'hear.

At the top of the certificate was the school motto: "There can be only one, and I'm it."

It was rumored that once, when a prospective student had asked Laoshi if he was in fact qualified, Laoshi proffering the certificate replied, "Well, Foghorn Leghorn seems to think so."

Laoshi was making the point that the authority of a teacher is generally underwritten by someone we don't know, as a judgment on someone we don't know. "Put a Chinese menu in a frame and it becomes a certificate," commented Laoshi to the same student.

"Then, where does your authority to teach come from?" he was asked.

"It comes from who I am. Your judgment comes from who you are. If they are compatible we can work together."

"But, don't we need regulation to make sure the wrong people don't start teaching taijiquan?" argued the student.

"Then who will regulate the regulators?" answered Laoshi.

Perhaps not entirely sympathetic to his point of view at the time, I have become persuaded of his position over the years, agreeing with his assessment that, "a burgeoning bureaucracy exists primarily for the benefit of the bureaucrats; the tail eventually wags the dog." I am, likewise, less critical of Laoshi's response to a researcher for the Scottish Parliament, who sought his views on a similar matter.

"In what way," asked the researcher, "do you think the Scottish government could help people like you to improve the quality of taijiquan instruction in Scotland?"

Laoshi replied, "If you want to make taijiquan better, leave us alone. If you want to sabotage it, then by all means help us."

At the time, I thought Laoshi's reply unnecessarily abrupt and a little ungracious. I would have suggested tax cuts, or perhaps direct funding of teachers, or possibly, the creation of a taijiquan academy. Laoshi took the opposite point of view, fearing that any government involvement would result in the "right means working in the wrong way."

"Any government money invested in taijiquan," he argued, "will result in regulatory bodies, oversight by committees, and political intrigue. Those, whose interest is truly in teaching taijiquan, will want to teach. Then the committee men, the politicians and bureaucrats, will seize the chance to position themselves at the helm of the good ship 'Taijiquan' as they steer it on to the rocks. Like most politics, it would be a case of putting the foxes in charge of the henhouse. Have you not heard the saying: *Those who can, do; those who can't, teach; and those who can't teach, they teach the teachers.* There's some truth in that statement."

For not wholly dissimilar reasons, Laoshi did not require his students to undergo any formal training in "how to teach." Looking around, I noticed the highly successful model adopted by yoga centers offering a two-year teacher-training program. I asked Laoshi why he had not sought to replicate their success.

"Success? What success?" replied Laoshi, that familiar twinkle in his eye, indulging in one of his mildly exaggerated summations on the state of affairs: "The teacher-trainers are successful I'm told, especially if they can charge for catering: the vegetarian lunch dollar is a big dollar, you know. But, can you imagine the result of churning out even half a dozen taijiquan teachers every two years? Where would they teach? Who would they teach, given that taiji-quan remains a minority interest? Lured by the prospect of a career-change into an ethical business, the unwary would trade the rat race for a crumbling dream, their aspirations sunk in a saturated market place. Hall rental would rise and student fees would plummet, leaving emaciated taijiquan teachers eyeing potential students like salivating dogs. Look at the counseling business in Glasgow: too many therapists ministering to each other in order to remain sane because too few suffering souls can afford to pay for therapy."

"But, you wouldn't need to open a course to anybody," I protested, "just a few students from the school who were likely to be good teachers."

"If you know they are likely to be good teachers, why do they need teacher-training?" responded Laoshi provocatively. "You didn't need training in how to teach. When you are good enough, I'll suggest you teach. You learn the rest on the job.

"Furthermore," continued Laoshi, "the quality of your teaching resides less in *what you know* and more in *who you are*. The teacher is revealed through

192

the teaching, warts and all. And often it's the warts that make a teacher truly effective. Perfect teaching does not make perfect learning. The true enemy of this kind of teaching is politically correct reproduction, which does not trust the Dao and has all the allure of a festering bed sore. Micro-managing teachers is death to taijiquan."

Sometime later, I experienced something of what Laoshi was describing. Hoping to supplement my income from teaching taijiquan, I enrolled on a course leading to a qualification in working with adults trying to improve their literacy and numeracy skills.

I cannot conclusively comment on the success of the scheme, since I flunked out early on, through boredom. Despite years in education, our trainer was obliged to read out, verbatim, the course work approved by an Edinburgh civil servant. Meanwhile, we, the trainees, were expected to listen and absorb, while the monotony crushed any hint of spontaneity out of our souls.

Laoshi had a diametrically opposite approach. All through the years of my study with Laoshi, I did not witness his presence as spectator or participant in classes taught by his students. He seldom offered guidance or critique, as a new teacher took the first faltering steps. Although relieved that I was not to be subjected to his intense gaze as I took to the floor in the role of teacher, I also wondered if I was not missing out on the fruit of Laoshi's years of experience.

He answered this charge when I gave it voice by saying, "I cannot teach you how to teach, because teaching taijiquan is about being yourself. Who is the expert in you? You must discover for yourself how best to arrange your class; when to delve deeply into detail, and when to be content with giving the gist; when to speak of the Dao, and when to remain quiet; when to entertain profit at the expense of the Way, and when to push your students. You will gradually acquire patience with yourself and your students, make your own mistakes and remedy the damage caused by inexperience. You will be obliged to manage disruptive or disharmonious elements while in class and, outside of class, you will decide how available you are to your students. You will have to determine the extent to which…"

"That makes perfect sense Laoshi," I interrupted. "But, surely, you could watch me teach and offer some advice or encouragement, just to let me know if I am doing it right."

"Believe me," Laoshi assured me, "you are doing it right."

"How can you *know* that, Laoshi?"

"Because, I know you: I know your heart and I know you are sincere. Everything else will come with time. I would be doing you a disservice with my presence at your class."

"How could that be?" I asked.

"Firstly," he replied. "It would undermine your authority. You would be teaching, but the students would be looking to me to gauge my reaction. Second, the presence of an observer always changes things. You would not teach your way if I were watching; you would be inhibited. How then would I be able to offer advice, as you would not be truly you? If you get it wrong, then what is that, just an opportunity to invest in loss and correct your shortcomings. You invest in loss in push-hands, and so you will also invest in loss as you teach."

Laoshi's words certainly were persuasive and I was on the point of conceding to his view when he added, "Of course, the most important reason to avoid your class is more personal. It would be too difficult for me."

I gave him a questioning look prompting him to reply, "You know I have a mouth the size of the Clyde Tunnel. Have you any idea how much effort it would take for me to shut it for an hour in your class?"

I recognized that within Laoshi's self-mocking humor, there was more than a grain of truth. He was used to the limelight in class and, in common with stage performers, had become accustomed to being the center of attention —at least while in class. His mute participation would be as onerous for him as student as it would for me as teacher, a form of torture where he would be compelled to suppress his sense of theater and remain drably in the wings, essentially a discomfort arising not from jealousy but from the caging of an overabundance of enthusiasm denied scope for expression.

I doubt he had always enjoyed his "stage," but when he was on form, he was absolutely captivating, holding his students in rapt attention, from which there was no thought of escape. To know that teaching taijiquan was as much performance art as instruction, you needed only to experience Laoshi's teaching style a few times. He understood the value of a little drama in holding the attention of students while teaching an art so easily killed by a tedious transmission. "If a successful taijiquan teacher is one with many students," he once remarked, "then that success is not built on skill or teaching ability alone. It often comes down to who can tell the best stories."

Chapter 33: Emoting

Attending an introductory taijiquan class, we might easily suppose that some people are in the wrong place. Seated expectantly beside the young, fit and strong, are those in more advanced years, visibly suffering from debilitating conditions. Side by side, we may find nervous types, warily sizing up all who enter and the longhaired "hippie," causally leaning back on the chair with a studied indifference. A harassed businessman, wearing the strain of the day along with suit and tie, rubs shoulders with the muscle-bound skinhead, wearing T-shirt, denims and boots, while working his jaws non-stop with chewing gum. Scattered among those assembled, in search of martial arts, a gentle exercise, or a philosophy of life, are the therapists, who are curious to discover whether taijiquan complements their view of the world and the services they offer to clients.

Inhabiting the role of teacher successfully requires an ability to relate effectively to the wide range of people who search out taijiquan with apparently contradictory needs and expectations. I was sure that Laoshi's success relied, to a great extent, on his skill in reading the energy presented by each person and pitching his teaching in line with the expectations of as many students as possible. Assessing my own qualities as a novice teacher, I felt a lack of confidence in my capacity to build rapport with the diverse group of people who found their way to taijiquan classes.

It was at this time of uncertainty that an elegantly dressed, well-spoken elderly lady approached me after a few classes saying, "Would I be able to ask you a question?"

"Of course," I said, feigning a nonchalant confidence, as I gathered my teaching paraphernalia into my bag.

"You have mentioned that Master Zheng, is that the right name... Master Zheng?"

I nodded.

"... that Master Zheng said something to the effect that what we seek to relax is our mind."

"Yes," I replied, eyeing the genteel lady warily. Was she setting a trap?

"That is because, is it not, that a tense mind leads to tension in the body? Did I understand you correctly?"

"That's true," I confirmed.

"But, then," her energy changing as if pouncing on prey, "should you not also be addressing the emotional traumas which caused the tensions to arise in the first place. Surely, just doing physical movements will not lead to the release of deeply held traumas from the past. Do we not have to examine those traumas and maybe even revisit them consciously in order to uncover them and rid them of their power over us?"

Seeing me floundering, she took a card from her purse and presented it for my inspection. Along with her name, the card listed her qualifications and the therapies she offered to clients. Her tone had hardened and, while not overtly confrontational, she was implying that something was missing in the classes as I presented them. I was unsure if she was merely making an observation, or if a business pitch was to follow offering my students a chance to remedy my failings in addressing a crucial area of emotional and psychological well-being.

Scanning her card, I felt uneasy but also grateful that I could refer the matter "upstairs" to Laoshi. I tried to sound casually unconcerned by saying, "I'm not sure what Laoshi's policy is on this matter. Can I speak to him and get back to you once I have? This is still his school, you understand, and I would like to be clearer rather than give you an answer off the top of my head."

"Of course, of course," she smiled, "I look forward to meeting Laoshi one day. He sounds like an interesting man."

As she left, I sighed, thinking that one day I would have to answer this type of question myself without hiding behind Laoshi's coat-tails. The prospect did not fill me with joy.

I called Laoshi the following day, asking if he was free for a chat. At his invitation, I arrived that afternoon, shortly after lunch, to find him reading in his living room. I explained the events of the previous evening and the question that had been posed.

"What did you tell her?" he asked reclining on a large sofa, while I sat nearby on a comfortable armchair. Even though the sight of Laoshi slouching on soft furnishings was not new to me, it still seemed discordant for a taijiquan master to not be upright at all times, especially when he would humorously denounce the deadly sofa for its detriment to health.

"I told her I would ask you for the school policy on these matters."

He laughed a little but did not say anything immediately, perhaps considering my response to the elderly lady, so after a moment or two, I continued. "I didn't want to feel like an idiot, Laoshi. The truth is, I sometimes feel uneasy around New Age types, who have 'worked on themselves' and developed sensitivity to spirituality I find lacking in me. I often feel myself shaped from a grosser material when in their presence, and I think I've developed a sense of inferiority around them. I think this woman managed to touch a nerve."

"How good is her ward-off?" asked Laoshi almost casually.

"Well, not very good Laoshi, but so what, she is just learning."

"And you are just the person to help her learn."

Although Laoshi's point was reasonable, I was still disturbed by my inability to respond to her question on a level that would satisfy her.

"Surely, there is something I could say to her other than 'your ward off could do with some work?'"

"That's what a lot of teachers do," said Laoshi.

196

"But…"

"And they are not entirely being evasive."

Laoshi paused momentarily to gauge my reaction. I'm sure my dissatisfaction was evident, but I remained silent. "The point is," sighed Laoshi, "you are teaching what you know, which is based on the principles you have learned. I will not always be here to advise on policy; there may not even be a policy, but there will always be a question that takes you by surprise. You have to be your own authority and answer from your understanding of principle. As your depth of understanding grows, you may even offer radically different answers at different times or to different people. Do not lose faith in principle when facing someone looking at taijiquan from a different point of view. The taijiquan method we use is at least as good as any other method for understanding ourselves: there is nothing lacking in Professor's taijiquan. The lack, if there is one, is in our understanding. Bear in mind, too, those refined individuals who provoke discomfort in you, may well envy your groundedness in the same way you envy their refinement."

"That makes sense," I conceded, "but what about the woman's question. Is it necessary to investigate the cause of trauma that gets locked into the structure of the body?"

"I asked Wang Lang a similar question some years ago," smiled Laoshi. "We had been talking about various healing therapies, and so I asked Wang Lang if he had studied any therapeutic or meditational techniques other than taijiquan. Wang Lang's answer was instructive: 'I'm glad that you mentioned taijiquan as a healing method,' he said before adding, 'For me, taijiquan has no equal. I have studied various methods and am qualified to teach a system of meditation, which I still practice from time to time to allay my fears. All these methods can keep our problems on the ropes, but it is taijiquan that delivers the knockout blow.'

"Wang Lang then added that in respect of the need to cleanse the body of past traumas, 'if you think it is necessary, then maybe you are right. If you don't think it is necessary, you are certainly right.' It was Wang Lang's way of saying that conventional therapy is necessary only if it is your Way. For us, as taijiquan practitioners, it is not necessary at all.

"There are two important points to grasp," continued Laoshi. "Ours is a way of energy and also one of being present. The energy or sense of flow that comes from our movement clears away the blockages. We are not in a traditional counseling arrangement, sitting on a chair opposite our therapist. Nor are we on a physio's table being 'done unto.' We are doing unto ourselves, working the body to loosen the buildup of tension. Think of the word 'emotion.' It comes from the Latin and means literally to 'move out,' or perhaps we could say, 'express.' The very practice is a moving out, or an *express*-ing of what is inside. You could think of the *express*-ing out as a clearing out. Remember, the problem with emotion is not the emotion itself, but the repression we use to escape feelings we find too uncomfortable. Our society has taught us, inadvertently perhaps, to physically tense up our bodies in response to stress in order to stop the discomfort. This tension, if not released, damages the body."

The second point Laoshi addressed as follows: "As taijiquan players, we locate ourselves in the present: what went before has past, it is the wake of a ship. We notice tension in our bodies and simply drop it. The very act of noticing tension begins the process of dissolving blockages. There is no need to forensically examine the source of the tension: just let it go. As the Professor says: just relax."

"But Laoshi, how does that work?" I asked.

"Well..." he replied, "imagine you have been walking around with a ball and chain attached to your ankle for years without realizing its presence. What would you do when you noticed it? Would you leave it attached to your leg and drag it everywhere to discover from whence it came, or you would you just dump it?"

I was gaining a clearer picture of Laoshi's view and also of how the therapeutic value of taijiquan came about. Laoshi did not dismiss the possibility that tension can be locked within the body, but thought that awareness and the physical movements of the form were sufficient to dissolve away that tension. Crucially, for Laoshi, the advantage taijiquan offered as a therapeutic method was its action in the present moment. The need to dredge up the past or visualize a golden future were distractions to being present now.

Laoshi's comments brought to mind his instruction on the most basic posture of taijiquan—attention posture—the starting posture of the form. In effect, little more than standing upright, heels together, toes apart. Laoshi regularly contrasted the required body position in taijiquan's attention posture with the attention posture of a soldier. "A soldier is taught to stand with chest out, stomach in, and head up. The taijiquan player is almost the complete opposite: chest in, belly out, and eyes level. Is there a reason for the difference?" he often asked rhetorically before answering himself. "I believe so. The rigidity of the body, being disciplined into the soldier, is there for a good reason. The military are no fools: their methods have developed carefully over centuries, either by accident or by design. The soldier has to separate mind from body in order to be effective. Tensing up the body especially the area of the belly accomplishes this very well. The emotions of fear and doubt are to be repressed, so that in battle, the soldier, perhaps standing alone in a trench, up to his knees in mud, hands numb with cold, throat parched from fear, awaiting certain death at the hands of the advancing fantasians, will stand, not run. As an old Sergeant-Major once told me, 'The British soldier don't need philosophy son, just good boots and a decent rifle. And we don't even get them.'"

Laoshi sometimes added to his military musings by mentioning his initial surprise at the lack of martial arts training in the British Armed Forces. Other than a few hours of a rough and rudimentary "army-style" aikido prior to deployment in Northern Ireland, martial arts training was entirely absent, if you discount the "milling" in basic training.

"After thinking about the matter for some time," Laoshi confided to me one afternoon near the time of our first meeting, "I realized the military were wiser than I was on this matter. The army doesn't need martial arts. The army needs aggressive intent. Martial arts, paradoxically, do not."

It was an interesting point of view and one that I shared. Ironically, the study of martial arts makes aggressive, and potentially violent, young men less so, not more so. Bizarrely, it could be argued that the closure of large numbers of boxing clubs in the UK may have added to the overall level of violence in society at large.

As so often happened after a conversation I had with Laoshi, I stumbled across supporting evidence for Laoshi's views from an unexpected source. In this case, a passage from a text on narcissism by Dr. Alexander Lowen, a former student of Wilhelm Reich:

> Inhibiting movement through chronic muscular tension has the effect of suppressing feeling. Such tension produces a rigidity in the body, a partial deadness. It is not surprising that soldiers are drilled in standing rigidly at attention. As we have seen, a good soldier must suppress much feeling and become, in effect, a killing machine.

As often happens, the lady who had prompted my question to Laoshi did not return to hear her question answered, but my confidence in taijiquan as a therapeutic vehicle increased nevertheless. The simple, elegant, yet potent movements have both physical and emotional benefits, while simultaneously, the philosophy benefits the mind and the spirit. The only drawback to taiji-quan is, as Zheng Manqing once said, "It is difficult to learn."

As a senior student and Professor Zheng's disciple, Tam Gibbs often accompanied the Professor on trips, acting as both assistant and interpreter. According to Wang Lang, prior to one such outing, Tam arrived at the Professor's apartment early in the morning. Whether Tam was too early or the Professor running late, Wang Lang did not say. However, as he emerged from his room, the Professor delayed his departure momentarily to drop down into the descending single whip posture. Upon rising, Zheng Manqing pronounced, "That'll do." He then left the apartment with Tam in his wake, his morning practice, apparently, completed.

I have heard it said that toward the end of his life, Zheng Manqing had internalized taijiquan to such a degree that he was constantly exercising the qi; in this way, he negated the need for daily form practice. Was Wang Lang's account of Tam Gibb's early arrival—and the Professor's brief squatting single whip—evidence of this level of attainment?

A year or two into my own study, and still very much a novice, I asked Laoshi whether such a level might be reached, and if so, might it be feasible to suspend daily practice, or even dispense with practice entirely? As was his way, Laoshi's initial reply wandered off down some unrelated avenue, but I was growing used to his ways: I had confidence that he was answering the "energy of the question," as Zheng Manqing might say. "When I was not long a student of taijiquan," he began, smiling as he recalled bygone days, "a debate rumbled among us as to why Zheng Manqing appeared to move through his 37-posture form so rapidly in the black and white film shot by Robert Smith in Taiwan. Some argued pragmatically that in the transfer from cine film to video, the Professor's form appeared speeded up, simply as a result of primitive copying methods. Others suggested, with intrigue, that the Professor was reluctant to reveal his secrets and so gave a 'superficial' performance. Still others concluded that the speed of form depended upon the speed of the qi moving in the body at the time. When I finally met Wang Lang, I asked him if he could shed some light on this piece of esoterica; did he have an explanation or theory as to why a form of customary nine or ten minutes duration was demonstrated by the Professor in only six minutes on that occasion? Well, do you know what he told me?"

Laoshi had that twinkle in his eye. I knew the question was rhetorical.

"Wang Lang told me that Zheng Manqing was in a hurry that day, but having agreed to demonstrate the form for Robert Smith's film, he didn't want to disappoint him. The Professor went through the form more rapidly simply because he was short of time! Hmm... all that speculation," chuckled Laoshi.

"Anyway, the point is," continued Laoshi more soberly, "that we can fall prey to conjecture, most of which leads us nowhere in the least bit fruitful."

"So, you don't think Zheng Manqing dispensed with his daily practice then, Laoshi," I prompted. Laoshi gave me one of his enigmatic smiles—the sort that immediately made me think I had missed the point.

"So, now… listen," said Laoshi, not unkindly. "We taijiquan players get too hung up about how much we should practice. Hardly surprising to be fair, since we live in a 'more is better' culture. But this is to miss the point of practice entirely!"

All too aware that I might be missing the point of my own practice, I sought to casually ask: "So… er… what do you think is being missed, Laoshi?"

Laoshi looked at me carefully, as if he could read my thoughts. "Well… to begin with, we miss the point if we start to judge ourselves and wonder if we are practicing enough; we forget that to practice takes inclination and energy, and that inclination and energy are not always ours to command. We allow ourselves to be influenced by daft notions such as, 'you've got to really want it,' as if the degree to which you want something is under your conscious control."

"It isn't?" I asked doubtfully.

"Of course not!" rejoined Laoshi briskly. "You can only 'want' something to the extent that you genuinely, in that moment, want it. You cannot force yourself to want something. Mind you, that doesn't stop some people from taking credit for the extent of their 'wanting,' as if they were responsible for it. This is just as daft as taking credit for having been born with five toes on each foot. Ridiculous!" scoffed Laoshi.

"I know of one teacher," continued Laoshi, "who was so intent on realizing the promise of taijiquan that he practiced for four hours every day and spent another three hours teaching, four evenings a week. Driven by the prospect of future payoff, he maintained this rigor for seven years, until one morning the flame of his enthusiasm simply died. As a result, so, too, did his practice cease entirely. However, since taijiquan, by this time, was his entire profession, he felt obliged to continue to teach, as he had no other source of income.

"Soul destroying, don't you think?" Laoshi eyed me meaningfully.

I made no reply but listening to the sorry tale, I felt chastened and forewarned. So, I did not pursue the point further with Laoshi that day. I suspected that he was cautioning me not to "forsake the near for the far." For the moment, I concluded that I would be better served by not speculating on the nature of Zheng Manqing's ability in summoning the qi.

Twenty years later, however, with a great deal more experience and understanding under my belt, I came to consider the question afresh. Laoshi had casually revealed to me that his morning routine no longer included several rounds of form. Indeed, some mornings he did not practice at all.

"So… Have you reached the level where you do not always need to practice then, Laoshi?" I inquired cautiously. I recalled all too readily my youthful, inexperienced self, struggling with this same question, as well as Laoshi's response at the time. In all those years, he had not led me to think that he had altered his position. But, Laoshi's response, when it came, surprised me: "You remember Zhuangzi's caution about not needing the fish trap once the fish is caught? I meant something of the same when I mentioned the change in my practice."

"Are you suggesting, Laoshi, that you have caught the fish and no longer need the trap?" I inquired, grinning at Laoshi's love of an intriguing metaphor.

"Ah… well, I may have caught a glimpse of its tail!" replied Laoshi, with an answering grin, "but then you have to understand that comment in its proper context. There's room for confusion here." Of course there was, when wasn't there?

"Go on Laoshi, I'm listening." I nodded encouragingly.

"So… The first thing to understand is that, in a certain sense, a fish trap never actually catches the fish. At best, it can only contain the spirit of the fish for a short time, prior to releasing it back into the wild; at worst, the trap only serves to haul the fish out of its natural environment to die of suffocation in an alien world. The fish that ends up on our dinner plate is no longer the free-swimming expression of spirit that is a 'fish.' A fish is a thing that swims in the river and the ocean; it is not a lump of flesh and bone lying inert on a plate. In the same way, a bucket of water drawn from the river is no longer a 'river,' although the water is the same water.

"Do you follow?" Laoshi checked his flow for a moment.

"Er… so far, yes…" I replied. Laoshi nodded. He continued. "You could say that a similar thing happens when we attempt to imprison the true spirit of life in the conceptual mind: the thing we would control and use for our own ends is no longer the Dao: it is merely the corpse prepped for our consumption. The same idea is contained in the story about cutting open the goose to harvest the golden eggs. Excuse the mixed food metaphors." Laoshi laughed. "Are you still following?"

"Yes, sort of…" I nodded. "In any case, we need to eat to live, don't we?" I thought I might as well run with the metaphor.

"Indeed!" responded Laoshi with a smile, "and that is why we have our form, push-hands, and fencing. Unable to capture the spirit of taijiquan directly, we are compelled to learn something of its nature by examining the

202

carcass dredged up by our technique. It would be a mistake to assume that the wonder of the Dao could be 'imprisoned' in a form, no matter how skillful the execution. At some point, we must discover what is 'taijiquan' when it is alive, not when it is served up on the taijiquan practice floor."

"Mmm, okay…" I agreed cautiously. "You have often said that we are searching for the essence of our art through our form practice. But is there some new twist to this idea that you have discovered?" I pursued.

"Now then, this brings us to the second, more critical, point." Laoshi paused insuring my full attention. "You recall that the Professor talked about The Three Fearlessnesses?"

"Sure, Laoshi," I affirmed. "The fearlessness to take pain; fearlessness in the face of ferocity; and fearlessness in taking loss."

"Quite right," nodded Laoshi. "Our *quan*—our method—is, at its root, about living fearlessly. It is about allowing us to live our Dao and harness the natural energies that life puts at our disposal.

"But, now consider the fearlessness of experiencing loss: Of the three, it might well be the most difficult to achieve; yet the fear of loss separates us from the Dao and our *qi*."

"Do you really think it's the most difficult to master, Laoshi?" I frowned thoughtfully.

"Certainly, for me, it is," replied Laoshi.

"How so?" I pressed.

"Because the fear of loss is like the hydra: having cut off the head of one attachment, we find immediately two more in its place. The more we try to rid ourselves of the fear of loss, the more skillfully it disguises itself and multiplies our fear. Even our attachments seem to have attachments," laughed Laoshi ruefully.

I needed to clarify: "When you say 'attachment,' what exactly do you mean, Laoshi?"

"Hmm… good question." Laoshi seemed to be considering his response. "This is where it becomes tricky: an attachment could be anything we have told ourselves we need in order to be happy; this could be money, status, appreciation, love… But, it could also be taijiquan." Laoshi's keen gaze met my own: "But, Laoshi, that's a hell of a statement coming from you. I mean you have devoted your whole life to taijiquan!" I exclaimed.

"Ah… you see how easy it is to become attached?" Laoshi laughed: "Let me ask you, if you had to choose between being happy and continuing your taijiquan practice, which would you choose?"

I was dumbfounded. What sort of a question was that?! I felt myself becoming uncomfortable, I did not even want to consider what life would be like without my daily form, push-hands, fencing—not to mention Laoshi himself. And yet, I knew enough to know that it was not Laoshi's intent to upset me: the upset was in my own mind. It began to dawn on me that my own "attachment" was being gently pointed out to me. Perhaps, Laoshi read my thoughts, as he did not seem to mind my silence. Indeed, he continued quietly: "Wang Lang once said: *if all it took to be happy was to go down to Times Square and press a button, no one would go.* He was right: we want to be happy, but with conditions. It is those same conditions—the good job, the relationship, the respect of our peers, and so forth—that boil the brew that feeds our fear. To truly be at one with the Dao, which is the ultimate aim of our practice, after all, is to live without fear. But in order to have no fear, we need to let go of our attachments. Do you see?" Laoshi searched my face for understanding. "No attachment; no fear."

I nodded soberly as the full measure of realization began to sink in. Reading my expression, Laoshi sought to offer comfort: "Don't be down-hearted, you are in good company. Wang Lang, reaching his 60th birthday and looking back on his 35 years studying taijiquan said, 'I have to *really begin* to study. I cannot just rely on time to do it for me.'"

Undoubtedly, this was one of Laoshi's most challenging lessons: blind attachment to the method of taijiquan could, ironically, become a means to avoid deep study of the art. Laoshi once mischievously referred to what he called floaters: these were students who were happy to remain on the surface of their study. When called upon to truly examine themselves and their practice, however, they either gave up or else moved on to another teacher. Unable to give up their various attachments, they rendered themselves perpetual beginners.

I was not exempt from this difficulty: the self-examination provoked by Laoshi led me to recognize the extent to which my own attachments were self-limiting—not least among them was my view of myself: my identity as "taijiquan teacher." Taijiquan, along with all spiritual disciplines, demands we drop our attachments, including defining ourselves as taijiquan players.

Chapter 35: Meeting the Buddha

Can we ever say with certainty when a thing began? Did I come into being when I took my first gulp of unforgiving air, or was it earlier, at the moment of conception, that the seed of my existence was sown? Perhaps it might even be argued that my life began at the first meeting of my parents.

As with beginnings, so with endings: looking back, it is difficult to mark the precise moment when my time with Laoshi ended. Often, we find ourselves in the "endgame" before we realize it is upon us. If pressed, I would say, that the beginning of the end came one a stormy autumn evening, some twenty-five years after I first met Laoshi.

That evening, Laoshi and I were returning from a trip to a taijiquan school in Edinburgh, where Laoshi had been invited to conduct some seminars over the course of the weekend.

This was a rare occasion, since Laoshi had ceased teaching classes for some time. Laoshi had made an exception, however, in support of a former student's ambitions to establish a martial arts center in Edinburgh. My duties that weekend included assisting in the seminars, as well as acting as Laoshi's chauffeur, a role I relished due to the opportunity for stimulating, wide-ranging conversation, which arose whenever Laoshi and I were alone. Though tired, I felt contented when we arrived back at Laoshi's house late on Sunday evening. Over the course of the weekend, Laoshi had delivered seminars packed with precise instruction, gentle humor, interesting anecdotes (even some I had not heard before) and philosophical insight. Even the traffic chaos we had encountered on departing Edinburgh had been a gift, as Laoshi seemed keen to talk.

"I know it is late," said Laoshi softly, as we arrived at his door, "but would you come in for a cup of tea?"

"Of course, Laoshi," I replied, noting a subtle shift in Laoshi's manner. He seemed tired, but I was happy to delay our goodbyes and my own journey home.

The house was quiet and dark. Eilidh, Laoshi's wife, had already retired to bed. Laoshi asked me to prepare the tea in the kitchen, while he went upstairs to assure Eilidh of our safe return. Ten minutes later, he joined me at the kitchen table for a cup of vanilla-flavored Rooibos tea, a blend he had recently discovered. Holding his teacup in one hand, Laoshi placed a DVD case with a light blue cover on the table with the other hand and slid it toward me saying simply, "I would like you to look at this film sometime soon."

I reached for the DVD case, automatically glancing at the title as I did so: *Giri*. The film was unknown to me, but I did recognize the two actors on the case cover: Terry Ezra and Terry O'Neill. Both were well-respected pioneers of Japanese martial arts in the UK. I had met Terry Ezra at a few aikido courses years before; Terry O'Neill was known to me as a talented British karateka, who had produced a *Fighting Arts* magazine before moving on to a career in television and film.

Laoshi made no further comment upon the DVD or its content, and so we passed some time in idle conversation, until noting the growing fatigue in Laoshi's eyes, I excused myself and departed.

A full two weeks passed before I settled down to watch *Giri*. I had resisted the temptation to watch the film immediately, as I felt it deserved my full attention. Eventually, a quiet evening arrived, and I switched off my phone, plumped up the cushions on the sofa and readied the DVD player. To my surprise, the entire movie did not last long, less than fifteen minutes, in fact. I had presumed it would be a feature-length offering. Even more surprising, indeed disturbing, was the central plot: a modern-day martial arts instructor decides to end his life by *seppuku*, and wishes his senior student to act as *kaishakunin*. The film title now became clear. "*Giri*" is broadly translated as "duty" or "obligation," albeit with a subtlety not easily translated in Western understanding.

In this instance, the "duty" fell to the student (Terry O'Neill) to assist his teacher (Terry Ezra) with his ritual suicide. Now, customarily, this means delivering the final blow to sever the head, when the pain of self-disembowelment becomes too much to bear.

As the final credits rolled, my discomfiture knew no bounds: was he planning on suicide? Was I being sounded out as a potential *kaishakunin*? Preposterous, surely?

I resisted the urge to call Laoshi immediately and demand to know what point he was making. I tried to recall my recent exchanges with him, searching for some clue in speech or behavior to his state of mind that I might have overlooked. Still, I resisted the temptation to call and ask outright what was going on. But, by the time we met, I was burning with curiosity—and anxiety.

"So... er, Laoshi." I decided to plunge right in when I arrived at his house the following day. "I watched that DVD you gave me."

"Ah," replied Laoshi, betraying no hint of anything amiss. "And, what did you make of it?"

"What did I make of it?" I repeated almost indignantly. "I didn't know what to make of it, Laoshi."

Laoshi merely nodded, indicating an entire lack of surprise at my reaction and ushered me to the kitchen table. He took the seat at the table head close to me.

"Laoshi, what exactly are you trying to tell me. You surely don't want me to kill you, do you?"

"Well, yes, in a way, I do," replied Laoshi, holding up his hands to arrest the protestations, which were forming in my open mouth. "I have very little left to teach you, you see. You are almost there."

"No! No, I'm not almost there, Laoshi," I protested. "I'm nowhere near 'there.' How can you say that? I still have a good deal to learn from you!"

A pause more pregnant than any I could remember fell between us. Laoshi's voice, when the words finally came, lacked his customary assuredness: "My obligation to you is nearly over," he said softly. "You are ready to fly, and your heart will be your teacher if you listen to it. But you must be free of me in order to follow your own Dao."

When I remained silent, Laoshi continued. "Listen, it is the greatest wish of a true teacher that his student should grow beyond him. Our time together these years has borne fruit. You were the son I never had." Laoshi had grasped my shoulder momentarily, "But now we must be like brothers, brothers in pursuit of the Dao. You need to follow your own path, and you are ready."

I had lifted my eyes from studying my hands on the table at Laoshi's touch on my shoulder, and I thought I saw a tear in his eye. Although he spoke quietly, there was no mistaking his sincerity and resolve. The proverb about "meeting the Buddha on the road" sprang to mind. This was what Laoshi was asking me to do: to kill him as my teacher and learn to rely on myself. I felt overwhelmed. I could not speak. Thoughts of possibly losing Laoshi had assailed me over the years, and I had dreaded this moment. Now, the moment had arrived, and I felt ill-equipped to strike out completely on my own. Nevertheless, it seemed that I must accept that the time had come. I nodded wordlessly to my old teacher.

"So…" resumed Laoshi, gruffly. "You understand. We have traveled far together; I thank you for making this easier for me. You see… just as you must 'kill the Buddha,' I must 'kill the student.' I must kill a son to make a brother. I feel like Abraham on the mountain, only there will be no divine reprieve. You need to be free of me."

I remained unable to speak. It had not occurred to me that Laoshi might also be dreading this day. As the implications played out in my mind, Laoshi continued, "This will not be easy for either of us. Your decision-making should not be clouded by my wishes on the matter. You must cast me out of your conscience and do only what you feel you must. Your loyalty is not to me, but to your own path—to your Dao."

I knew what Laoshi meant. His influence on my life had been significant. I had grown used to weighing my actions as if Laoshi was sitting on my shoulder. And when I did depart from my/his conscience in any regard, I often felt a little guilty. I would be nervous to meet him, afraid that he might be able to read my thoughts. It was not entirely healthy, I knew, but I had been certain that surrender of the mind was the cost of fully harmonizing with your teacher.

As if I had spoken this last thought aloud, Laoshi continued: "You need to be free of my expectations; what once might have been a support, could soon become a burden. Sometimes, the cure can end up becoming the poison; what was helpful becomes limiting, even damaging!" Laoshi smiled wryly.

"So… why now, Laoshi?" I pressed, curiosity weighing equally with apprehension.

"The time feels right," replied Laoshi simply, "for both of us. A change is approaching, and if we delay there might be unhelpful consequences. We cannot stall a birth for the sake of habit and convenience; if we resist the change, the Dao might rip us apart in a more harsh and unpredictable manner—and I do not want that to happen; I value our relationship."

I knew there was little point in arguing with Laoshi: I could sense that he was completely single-weighted on the matter. He was committed to changing a relationship of some twenty-five years in the making. My mind, therefore, moved toward contemplating the "how" rather than the "why."

"So, Laoshi, how exactly do I go about killing the Buddha?" I was beginning to accept the inevitable.

"It has been said," he mused thoughtfully, "that some teachers in the past engineered a split with a valued student by dramatic and even 'devious' means. They made a spurious accusation to create an emotional distance, or else tricked the student into leaving the school to carry out some mission."

"Hmm… Well, teachers giving their students a hard time does seem to be a theme in martial arts stories!" I laughed grimly.

"Well you know," commented Laoshi, "to deliberately drive away a student for *their own good* requires a heart that is in fact very large because to injure a student in this way is to injure oneself. Don't worry, my heart is not strong enough to take such drastic action; I think you and I can find our way through without doing unnecessary violence to either of our feelings."

As he spoke, it occurred to me that Laoshi's problematic partings from his own teachers might have been the consequence of resistance (on both sides) to his own inevitable change and development as a student: his growing need for self-exploration in his taijiquan practice had possibly exceeded the capacity of his teachers to accommodate him.

Laoshi's voice broke into my thoughts: "I would like you take over the school, lock stock and barrel. I will retire leaving the running of things entirely to you. I will not appear at class; you should feel free to do your own thing. It will be your school."

"But, will I never see you again?"

"Of course, we can meet," Laoshi reassured me. "Just not for practice or formal teaching. We can be like the Immortals in the Bamboo Garden," he smiled. "Laughing and talking together of nothing and speaking of everything.

I might even take up drinking, so we can get quietly drunk together like a couple of old fools." Laoshi winked at me. "This is the land of whisky after all, and I have been remiss in educating myself to its mysteries."

I could not help but smile at Laoshi's reference to the Immortals of the Bamboo Garden: the image of the truly wise passing their time in drinking wine, reciting poetry, and finding joy in one another's company had always amused me. Years before, as an unemployed youth, I had helped a friend (equally youthfully unemployed at the time) to flit lodgings to a very respectable address in Bearsden. Upon offering us a cup of tea after our exertions, the landlady of the house enquired, "And what do you do for a living?" There was no hint of interrogation in her manner, only polite curiosity. But feeling self-conscious over my current lack of employment, I resorted to being a smart-arse, replying, "Me? Oh, I sit in the Bamboo Garden."

"Oh, I see," nodded the old lady sagely. "Unemployed then, but poetically so!"

Looking back, I wished I had engaged this interesting old lady in proper conversation. When my friend, poe-faced, asserted that he too sat in the Bamboo Garden beside me, she laughed heartily. We could still hear her laughing down the hallway as she went to wash up our tea things.

"Ah yes... an interesting lady," chuckled Laoshi on first hearing of the incident. We had rehashed that little anecdote between us many times over the years. "She was a teacher to you, too, didn't you feel?" he had suggested with thoughtful tone.

"You think?" I eyed Laoshi, unsure for a moment. Then the penny dropped. "Oh... right... you never judge a book by its cover, and all that?"

"Precisely!" rejoined Laoshi gravely. "I mean, what were the chances of addressing your smart-arse remark to the one person in Glasgow who didn't assume the Bamboo Garden was a Chinese Restaurant?"

Back in his kitchen, Laoshi sought to reassure me. "Feel free to visit me whenever you wish to talk. There is nothing you *must* speak to me about, but there is nothing you *cannot* speak to me about. The school is now yours."

"Thank you, Laoshi," I said quietly. "Ehrm... Should we have some sort of handing-over ceremony or something?" I asked doubtfully.

"A ceremony? No, not at present," smiled Laoshi. "That kind of ritual is not necessary between men of the Dao, but I still have one more thing to teach: we might like some sort of ritual for that," he added, mysteriously. But before I could pursue further, Laoshi announced, "Right, I'm off to bed now. Stay as long as you want, let yourself out, and next time you see me, you need not call me 'Laoshi.' You are Laoshi now."

And with that, Laoshi strode out of the room and up the stairs muttering, "The Bamboo Garden, ha ha ha!" I sat motionless at the kitchen table, reflecting on what had just happened between my teacher and me. Although I did as he asked and never addressed him as Laoshi again, he would always remain "Laoshi" to me.

Chapter 36: Going Home

The process of passing a martial arts school from teacher to nominated student sometimes involves a buyout, especially when bricks and mortar are involved. Thus, the initial investment in the school's physical venue latterly becomes the pension for the teacher who wishes to retire. In Laoshi's case, however, there were no bricks and mortar to sell. Instead, he bequeathed to me a roster of students and a reputation built over decades, as well as time slots in local halls, which he had rented steadily over the years. No money was asked and none was paid. I would liked to have been in a position to make some kind of financial gesture, but teaching taijiquan for a living is precarious. Laoshi knew this only too well, and approved my habit of saving towards the inevitable lean times.

Laoshi had warned me that there would be a period of adjustment after he announced his retirement to the students.

"Be prepared for a period of transition," he advised when the day came. "Some will choose to leave the school now. In time, some of the senior students will depart to start their own schools; some might also proclaim themselves to be the true inheritors of this, my school. This is how it is. You will gradually build your school according to your own lights. The spirit of a martial arts school is found in the teacher and their students."

"You really think that will happen?" I asked aloud.

"Almost inevitable." Laoshi gave a grave smile. "But it is better for you in the long run. If students cannot stand full-square behind you, then they will likely become an obstacle in your path. Better that they leave and go their own way. In that way, you can be genuinely pleased for them when they form their own schools." Laoshi winked at me, but I was far from reassured by his apparent levity.

"But, some of the seniors have far more years of experience than I do! Won't they be in direct competition with me?"

Laoshi merely smiled enigmatically. "They might feel themselves to be in competition with you, but you need not to be in competition with them."

Mostly, I appreciated Laoshi's philosophical take on things, but sometimes I couldn't help thinking he's picked the wrong guy to have faith in: "What, you mean let the Dao sort it out? Trust in the flow of life? Och, Laoshi,

I wish I could believe that. But I'm not you! I'm full of doubt."

"Ah… you misunderstand me," replied Laoshi mildly. "Here's the thing: you have already conjured in your mind's eye, a notion of what it means to succeed in this venture; you are already concerned with student numbers, competition from others, and so on. And, from a certain worldly perspective, it is entirely reasonable." He smiled before adding. "It took me years to detach myself from that piece of delusion."

At my uncomprehending look, Laoshi leaned toward me, speaking softly but earnestly. *"Listen, no one can stop you from teaching classes if that is what you want to do.* There may be a few students, or there may be hundreds— *what of it?* You might pass an hour in your hall some evenings, teaching no one but the spiders on the wall and mice in the kitchen, *but you will be following your Dao."*

"But I wouldn't make any money?" I didn't know whether to laugh or gnash my teeth in vexation.

"Indeed," agreed Laoshi calmly. "But then you would cut your cloth according to your means. It is always possible that you have to take a job and cut down your teaching commitments, or you might extend them, but you will always survive no matter what: just follow your heart. Believe me when I tell you that you have *heart* in abundance; people will be drawn to you. As the saying goes, 'When the flower blooms, the bees come uninvited.' There is no need to force yourself to have faith in this, you will see it soon enough. The 'competition' you imagine is not the thing you believe it to be: it is an illusion of the rational mind, which perceives only what it is conditioned to perceive. There is no 'competition' in following the Dao, even though sometimes it appears so: this too is a lesson."

Laoshi was to be proved right on both scores. Over the next several months, students arrived and departed, but before long, the school seemed restored to its own balance. It even started to become a viable living. Then, just at that point, my world came crashing down.

The first inkling of things amiss came when Laoshi returned from an extended trip to Australia: he had always wanted to travel in the southern hemisphere. Laoshi had explained that he would be away for an indefinite period, but that I could expect to see him when he returned. Mind you, there was not a hint of a return date. Three months flew by, and my only contact with Laoshi was a post card from Melbourne in Eilidh's hand, indicating that they were enjoying the sunshine and sights Down Under.

I was taken aback, then, when he called me, seemingly out of the blue, to let me know that he had returned and to invite me to visit when I was able. His voice on the phone had a distinct note of weariness. I thought this was unlike Laoshi, but I put it down to the inevitable jet lag, which accompanied long-haul travel.

The following afternoon found me staring at Laoshi's familiar doorstep. But my joyful anticipation at his return was left at the front door the moment Laoshi opened it to let me in: the figure before me was a shadow of the man I had known for the last two decades and more. Certainly, his skin was tanned from months in the sun, but he was visibly physically reduced. His clothes hung from him, and he moved slowly. The exertion of greeting me and making tea seemed to leave him a little breathless.

Both brought up in the West of Scotland, and inhabiting the roles of teacher and student, we were not in the habit of hugging: A small blessing I thought, as I watched Laoshi lower himself carefully onto a chair: it would be like hugging a bag of bones. Laoshi's obvious frailty was shocking to me, but I made no mention of his state. Instead, we chatted about his trip, the school, my taijiquan practice and of the comings and goings of the senior students.

Soon, however, the "catch-up" chatter was exhausted. There was a pause, and we looked at each other for what seemed like an eternity before Laoshi smiled and broke the silence: "So… You are doing well, waiting for me to make the first move. First one to make a 'statement' loses, eh?" Laoshi chuckled.

I laughed awkwardly, immediately grasping his reference: in push-hands, the first one 'to give themselves away' by using excessive force, in theory at least, loses. But my failure to comment on Laoshi's weakened state was not down to skillful sensitivity on my part, but rather shock and sadness.

"As you can see," Laoshi continued, the smile still playing on his lips, "I am dying."

Perhaps, I had anticipated hearing those three small words, but when they arrived they were huge and simply devastating.

"How long have you known?" It was as much as I could command myself to say.

Laoshi nodded quietly: "I was diagnosed nearly a year ago. Lung cancer. The symptoms were not too bad to begin with. But now I feel I am nearing the end." His tone was somber but matter-of-fact.

I was shaken. "But if you have known all this time, why didn't you tell me? Tell anyone?" I felt shocked, possibly even angry. But that was purely selfish.

I scarcely noticed that Laoshi had not answered my question. Too many other questions were forming on my lips.

"Are you in much pain?" I asked more gently. This was not about me:

this was about my old teacher and I could not bear to think of him suffering.

"From time to time," Laoshi admitted with a wry smile. "The pain and I play a little 'push-hands' every day; I try to delay its grip on my body. I hold it at bay as long as I have the inclination, then seek to banish it with the drugs the doctors provide. So… it is not wholly unbearable. The pain appears mainly in my spine. Ha! The Pillar of Heaven is collapsing to be sure! The rest of me is fine, though."

I would have laughed if this had not been so serious. "*Fine?*" I thought. "The man is dying, and he thinks that the rest of him is fine?!"

"But you have had some treatment, yes? … Some chemo or radiation therapy… or something?" I protested.

"The doctors did kindly offer, but I declined treatment," said Laoshi simply.

"*What?*" I was dumbstruck. "You 'declined treatment?' But, that's crazy! You could fight this thing! Lots of people get cancer and survive for years afterwards… why not you?"

Laoshi leaned slowly toward me, reaching out his hand to gently touch my wrist resting on the table. "Listen to me," he said quietly. "I don't choose to fight. My whole teaching has been about not fighting: don't insist, don't resist, yes? I know…" he raised a hand to prevent my protest. "Our society applauds the 'brave battle;' we are supposed to fight death, but you know as well as I do that it is all an illusion. Death is as necessary to life as is living, indeed death is life, only by other means. To resist death, is to resist life. So…" he patted my wrist. "This is my final lesson to you. When our time comes to go, it is better to just go without looking back."

"But, what about Eilidh? What about me? What will we do without you, Laoshi?!" The old form of address just slipped out. Tears were stinging the back of my eyes.

"You will do as you always have done," replied Laoshi softly. "Your happiness is not dependent upon me, nor any other living being. Would you have me stay here so that you feel better? As for Eilidh, well… she truly loves me. She would not have me endure the treatments in order that she should not be left alone." Laoshi glanced at me meaningfully. "Eilidh allows me to be who I am: that is the true gift of love. If living the Way is a series of abandonings, then leaving the physical body is one of the last."

I found myself unable to respond.

"So…" continued Laoshi, a gruff note attempting to disguise the emotion in his voice, "I came to fulfill my destiny. Now it is time to move on. Life is compassionate always, even when it seems not. In truth, I am not dying, my body, my ego is. My spirit is going home. I feel it yearn to return to emptiness and dissolve in the Dao."

He handed me his well-thumbed old copy of the *Zhuangzi*, page open, and reclined slowly in his chair, as I read the passage highlighted:

> The true men of old
> Knew no lust for life
> No dread of death
> Their entrance was without
> Gladness. Their exit, yonder,
> Without resistance
> Easy come easy go
> They did not forget where from,
> Nor ask where to,
> Nor drive grimly forward
> Fighting their way through life.
> They took life as it came, gladly;
> Took Death as it came, without care;
> And went away, yonder
> Yonder!

"Forgive me, Laoshi." I glanced up at my old teacher. "I don't know what to say," I mumbled as I closed the book.

"Ah, no need of forgiveness; no need to say anything, only this... Perhaps you will do me a kind favor."

"Anything."

"Would you come and live here with Eilidh and me for the next few weeks, only until I am ready to go. I would like you to be here when the time comes."

"Of course," I replied immediately, swallowing the great lump in my throat, swiftly replaced by a knot of apprehension in my stomach. Did I really want to be there when the time came? I did not want to let Laoshi down. One part of me only wanted to fulfill his wishes; the other part of me was afraid of what that might mean in practice.

"You must continue with your classes, of course!" Laoshi perhaps mistook my look of apprehension. "But it would ease my passing greatly if you were with me when I bend the bow for the last time."

In her book Gerda Geddes suggests that the last of the thirty-seven postures in Zheng Manqing's form, Bend Bow to Shoot Tiger—symbolizes the final act of the evolved human being, shooting their spirit into the cosmos.

"Oh, classes. Yes, yes... But, I don't want to miss... er... I mean." I

stumbled around not possessing the vocabulary for this situation. "I don't wai.
to be away from you when the time comes."

"Don't worry," Laoshi smiled, reassuring as always. "I'll wait for you."

And so, I spent the next three weeks living with Laoshi and Eilidh.
Bizarrely, it was a wonderful time, full of joy and laughter. We three talked
for hours, and I got to know the remarkable Eilidh who had, until now,
remained in the background of my interaction with Laoshi. Now I began
to appreciate the special nature of the bond between the two of them.
Sometimes when his strength allowed, Laoshi and I did a little push-hands:
his final instruction to me was that "In push-hands as in fencing, seek the
single unifying principle."

Laoshi did show some improvement in his condition during that time,
and I even dared to hope, but one evening when I returned from my final class
of the week, looking forward to the weekend with Laoshi and Eilidh, reality
intervened.

"I think," Eilidh told me quietly, meeting me at my car in the driveway,
"this is it." I merely nodded. Instinctively, we held hands as we walked up the
garden path. It was a cool night and my breath was visible as a painful sigh
dragged out of me. Class had been uplifting, one of my best efforts at teaching,
and I was keen to share my happiness with Laoshi. Now, silently, I removed
my coat and shoes and followed Eilidh upstairs to their bedroom.

Lying propped up on a bank of pillows, Laoshi smiled weakly in greeting,
as I entered the room. I was immediately aware that his breathing came quick
and shallow. He raised his hand, and I came and stood next to him, taking his
hand gently in mine.

"I waited for you," he whispered… "time has come."

Eilidh curled up on the bed beside Laoshi, while I remained standing
on his other side, holding his hand. The soft light from two bedside lamps
seemed to draw me inward, my entire focus on the gasping frame of my old
teacher.

Laoshi's gaze was straight, unseeing… and I felt my throat burn as I
struggled to repress the grief welling up in me. Absurdly, a line from an old
movie came to mind, "The last sound a warrior hears should not be the sound
of you weeping," but I was struggling to hold back my tears. Nevertheless, I
was determined to honor Laoshi's final moments: I maintained my vigil stead-
fastly, even as I watched his breathing grow ever more labored.

His eyes were open wide, no longer seeing Eilidh or me, but as if gazing
into another world. Was there a hint of a smile on his lips? I cannot say for
sure. But as his last breaths wheezed past his throat, his life essence flying
outward, Laoshi briefly squeezed my hand tightly—and then he was gone.

The weeks following Laoshi's death passed in a haze. In the immediate aftermath, I was to be found at Laoshi's house, helping with the funeral arrangements, respectfully sifting through the belongings of a man who had become a second father to me, and reminiscing with Eilidh.

In an age of "having" rather than "being," it was humbling to discover just how little Laoshi had accumulated in the way of possessions during almost seventy years of life. Those few items that he called his own were almost exclusively related to his taijiquan and martial arts practice.

Aware he was approaching death, Laoshi had consulted a solicitor to make a formal will. The tangible assets and savings account were, naturally, left to Eilidh. However, a few bequests were included, one of which was made to me. Laoshi had entrusted his taijiquan paraphernalia to my care, including his significant book collection. Of particular interest to me, however, was Laoshi's collection of swords: while a number of these were basic wooden or metal reproductions donated by students who had stopped practicing, I was also gifted Triskelion, Laoshi's own Purpleheart wooden sword, together with the antique *jian* which he had shown me some years previously.

These precious items were accompanied by a sealed envelope for my eyes only. Inside I discovered a hand-written note from Laoshi, detailing the provenance of the antique sword, together with notes on how to care for a genuine artifact from Ming Dynasty China. Most significantly, however, was Laoshi's revelation of the sword's name, bestowed in an earlier age by an owner long since departed from this world.

It was Laoshi's wish that I might use the sword for my practice, however, my primary duty lay in acting as the sword's custodian. When the time came, I was to bequeath the sword in turn, to a worthy student, along with the gift of the sword's name. Meanwhile, I was to burn the paper bearing the name and reveal it to no one. I followed Laoshi's wishes in this matter, and the sword remains in my care to this day—until it passes from my hands in the fullness of time.

In keeping with Laoshi's wishes, Eilidh and I planned a modest celebration of his life. Nevertheless, Laoshi's funeral attracted significant attendance from students, past and present, as well as many well-wishers. As things turned out then, rather a large audience was gathered to hear Laoshi's favorite operatic farewell. Not that Laoshi had been a keen aficionado of opera. Indeed, he had often joked that he had no idea what Pavarotti (his favorite interpreter) was singing about; "but you cannot deny the moving power of the Dao in that man's voice!"

In this way, one of Laoshi's last mischievous wishes: that "there might not be a dry eye in the house!" was realized. It was just that there were far more non-dry eyes that he might ever have imagined.

I was not the only one with tears rolling freely down my cheeks. As Pavarotti's "Nessun Dorma" brought the simple proceedings to a close, and we all filed out into the light, I imagined Laoshi, accompanied by Zhuangzi, gazing down from the heavens and laughing gently with compassion for the human condition.

During those last weeks of grief, punctuated by the necessity for pragmatism, Eilidh and I were naturally much in each other's company. As a result, we became firm friends—our connection forged initially by our common bond with Laoshi. As I got to know her better, Eilidh's own bond with her husband, my old teacher, became increasingly clear. They had shared a common philosophy of life and enjoyed an on-going conversation, ranging from the mundane to the metaphysical, which had served to draw them ever closer over the years. In spite of her obvious grief, Eilidh's kindness, warmth, and generosity remained present, and her dignity endured, as she offered patient solace to all who sought it, even those with a tenuous connection to Laoshi, who seemed to have need to assert an imagined close or special relationship with her husband. While I experienced an urge to punch one or two of them, Eilidh only smiled her sympathy and maintained a dignified silence. "They don't mean any harm," she told me simply one day, when I was busy being outraged on her behalf. "No need to take offense." I could only admire her forbearance, or rather her essential wisdom. I could learn a lot from this lady, I thought. And as it turned out, it was Eilidh who brought home to me my final lesson as a student of Laoshi.

"I think it's time I moved back home," I mentioned tentatively one evening. "The time I have spent here with you and Laoshi has been…" I paused, searching for words, but failed to find any adequate enough to express the entirety of my feelings. But my overwhelming emotion was one of deep gratitude for the final chapter of my time with Laoshi.

"I understand," replied Eilidh quietly. "My husband was pleased you could be with us during these last weeks. Me too." She squeezed my arm. "But, you have your life to lead."

"I hope I was able to be of some… er… help," I offered weakly.

Eilidh gave me one of her enigmatic smiles and said nothing for a moment.

"Er… Am I missing something?" I inquired, puzzlement and embarrassment jockeying for position.

"Do you feel you are missing something?" Eilidh returned softly, looking me straight in the eye. At that moment, she reminded me strongly of Laoshi.

"You know that you meant a great deal to my husband," continued Eilidh. It was a statement rather than a question, and I felt my throat contract. "He never said so in so many words," explained Eilidh. "But, my strong feeling is that he wanted to show you something: offer you—and me—comfort. He tried to show you how to live during all those years you studied your art together. And, you know, I feel that at the end, he wanted to show you how to die. He wanted you there for *you*, my dear; not for *him*."

I was stunned. But of course, in the end, it made sense.

In the following days, as I reflected on Eilidh's words, Laoshi's final lesson seeped deeply into my psyche. I had never seen anyone die. Both my parents had already departed by the time I was able to respond to the call from the hospital. My last good-byes were made to what remained of them: earthly skin and bone. I had missed the moment when their life-spirit left the body and headed for the stars.

Laoshi's last lesson to me proved to be a gift in an age where we avoid contemplation of death in a misguided attempt to protect ourselves from suffering. In his own approach to death, Laoshi, although physically weakened, behaved much like his usual self. Indeed, he seemed genuinely content and took pleasure in everything even, remarkably, his daily bouts of pain. "Ah… a little push-hands practice," I would hear him say under his breath.

"Well… you know what they say: It's the life in your years that counts, not the years in your life," he told me near the end. "Who would want to go on forever? The elixir of immortality is to be found in contemplation of the eternal now. It does not reside in the desperate scramble to stretch out our days on this earth—at any cost."

Although it cannot be proved, I remain convinced that, with his own death waiting in the wings, Laoshi only delayed his last breath in order that I might witness him leaving this life unconcerned.

As I move inevitably toward the autumn of my own life, I appreciate—daily—my old teacher's final lesson: I have seen that it is possible to meet death with equanimity. As a result, the fear of my own end is diminished. Of course, I cannot be sure that when my time comes, I will depart with the same grace and dignity as did Laoshi, but he would not expect me "to be" anything other than who I am in that moment. In all his teaching, Laoshi simply wanted to show me that it is possible to live—and die—fearlessly.

Ultimately, isn't that the point of the martial way?

And so… Laoshi is no more. Some may argue that Laoshi never was.

Not so. The spirit of Laoshi is as old as mankind and lives on in all martial traditions throughout the world.

When the sincere presence of a teacher has inspired you to make changes in your life, encouraged you to trust your heart-mind, and persuaded you to pursue Principle purely for its own sake, then you have met Laoshi.

When, through the insistence of your teacher, you have gone beyond what you thought was possible, found the strength in yourself to face life with honesty and courage, and discovered faith in yourself and your art, then you have met Laoshi.

When, through the example of your teacher, you reawaken to the great mystery of life, prefer the pleasures of simple things and feel the core of your being at peace, then, you have met Laoshi.

"Laoshi" illustration by Chang Jungshan and Jungshan Inc.
Background mountain illustration used here and
throughout this book © elen/123RF.com

Made in the USA
San Bernardino, CA
26 July 2018